The Architecture
of Modern American
Synagogues,
1950s–1960s

Sara and John H. Lindsey Series in the Arts and Humanities

The Architecture of Modern American Synagogues, 1950s–1960s

Anat Geva

TEXAS A&M UNIVERSITY PRESS   *College Station*

∞ This paper meets the requirements of ANSI/NISO Z39.48–1992
(Permanence of Paper).
Binding materials have been chosen for durability.
Printed in China through Martin Book Management

Library of Congress Cataloging-in-Publication Data

Names: Geva, Anat, 1947– author.
Title: Pushing the envelope : modern American synagogues, 1950s–1960s /
  Anat Geva.
Other titles: The architecture of modern American synagogues, 1950s–1960s
  | Sara and John Lindsey series in the arts and humanities.
Description: First edition. | College Station : Texas A&M University Press,
  [2023] | Series: Sara and John Lindsey series in the arts and humanities
  | Includes bibliographical references and index.
Identifiers: LCCN 2022042590 | ISBN 9781648431357 (cloth) | ISBN
  9781648431364 (ebook)
Subjects: LCSH: Synagogue architecture—United States. | Judaism and
  architecture—United States. | Synagogues—United States—History—20th
  century.
Classification: LCC NA4690 .G48 2023 | DDC
  726/.309730904—dc23/eng/20220920
LC record available at https://lccn.loc.gov/2022042590

Cover: Courtesy of Congregation Shaarey Zedek Synagogue Archives, Southfield, Michigan.
Designed by Percival Goodman with Albert Kahn: The steel frame system of the sanctuary.
From Bethlehem Steel Company article (1962).

To my parents Charlotta (Lotka) and George (Yezik) Mintz,
who taught me how to be an international citizen without forgetting my Jewish roots;

and to my husband Nehemia Geva,
who helps me to implement everything they taught me.

Contents

Acknowledgments

It was exciting to write this book about my studies of American Jewry's sacred architecture. This architecture expresses my people's way of life, their faith, their strength and resilience, and the realization of the American value of freedom of religion. My excitement was fueled by my visits to synagogues and archives around the country, diving into the literature, documents, and drawings about them, and analyzing the architecture of buildings that were not given the appropriate attention in the study of modern architecture and pertinent publications.

Many contributed and supported this journey, each in their own ways. I'd like to take this opportunity to acknowledge and thank all. First, my eternal thanks to my parents, to whom I dedicate the book, who taught me the Jewish way of life. Enormous thanks to my husband Nehemia, who is part of the book's dedication for his endless support of my career. Moreover, I thank him for being the book's first reviewer, for our invaluable discussions, his encouragement, critiques, and love. I also thank him for traveling with me to most of the synagogues to document, survey, and photograph them. With gratitude to my children, their spouses, and my grandchildren for their encouragement and for serving as my light.

Many thanks to all the synagogues' staff and rabbis who welcomed me to their synagogues, opened the doors to their buildings, toured with me, shared with me their archival materials, and exposed me to other sources such as archives and architectural firms related to their synagogues. Their hospitality was overwhelming and inspiring. Without this support, I would not be able to write the book. Also, thanks to Mrs. Virginia Orlina for her additional photographs of the Chicago Loop Synagogue.

I thank the College of Architecture at Texas A&M University and its former executive dean Professor Dawn Jourdan, and the Department of Architecture and its former head Professor Bob Warden, who supported me with time and funds. Thanks to the university's Glasscock Center for Humanities Research for awarding me the Glasscock Faculty Research Fellowship, which enabled me to write the first proposal for this book. I thank my copy editor, Sabra Helton, and the two external reviewers of the manuscript. Their constructive comments and corrections strengthen the book. Finally, many thanks to Texas A&M University Press and Editor in Chief Thomas Lemmons for publishing the book.

The Architecture
of Modern American
Synagogues,
1950s–1960s

1 Introduction

Let us arise and build.

(*Nehemiah 2:18*)

My mother Charlotta (Lotka) Mintz (1920–2002) was a Holocaust survivor who jumped off a train headed to Auschwitz. She survived the war but lost her family and her faith in God. Still, she felt that Judaism was more than just a religion. She saw it as a way of life. This reinforced her belief in the Zionist ideal of creating a new, modern, secular Jew, and of the establishment of the State of Israel. Like many other Jews who survived the Holocaust, she immigrated to Israel. Zionism had become the answer to the post–World War II political question of whether Jews could be seen as their own people with their own state. These ideals underlined my upbringing in Israel and my way of life. Though my generation, the second generation of Holocaust survivors, grew up under the shadow of the war, we tried to establish our own proud identity based on our faith in the Jewish way of life and the statehood of Israel. Thus, when I became an architect in Israel, it was natural for me to focus on the impact of post–World War II immigration on architectural movements in Israel, and later in the United States. This personal background, and my own emigration from Israel to the United States, bolstered my curiosity to study post–World War II American synagogues and to investigate their designs as architectural expressions of modern American Jewry.

There are many ways to approach the study of these buildings as an expression of Judaism in post–World War II architecture.[1] The objective of this book is to present an analysis that illustrates the design, building technology, and preservation of mid twentieth century modern American synagogues (1950s–60s). Architectural analysis is used to decipher and understand the language and concepts of design and construction. It includes observational and empirical analyses of the design concepts and their solutions that established and deepen often new perspectives investigating the elements of the building.[2] Details of architectural analysis relate to the basic elements of design: building and site relation; the relation of spaces to geometry, size, form, and circulation; materials and systems; environmental conditions and their impacts on design (e.g., light and shadows, thermal comfort, acoustics); and the relation of architecture and art specifically within the sacred context. The analysis reveals architectural problem-solving via design and its expression in the building.[3] Moreover, some claim that architectural analysis also illustrates the "transcend poetry" of architecture and its interpretation in a building.[4] In this book, the analysis reflects the relation of Judaism (faith) to form, ambiance, and the details of sacred architecture. In addition, this approach illustrates the mutual relation of form/ambiance and building technology (as illustrated in the following chapters).[5]

I present this specific approach in order to show-case how modern American synagogues pushed the envelope in architecture and building technology. Moreover, as architecture can be perceived as an identification of place,[6] the next chapter provides a brief introduction of the period's contextual frame-work and its influence on synagogue design.

The designs of these buildings departed from traditional design concepts and embraced modern-ism of the early 1950s in their functional forms. Later, these modern designs evolved into a more expressionistic style that abstracted faith symbols. All synagogues presented in this book reflected their congregations' search for their Jewish identity, their physical fulfillment of the American value of free-dom of religion, their move to the suburbs, and the architects' utility of innovative building technology, which impacted a new aesthetic.

These synagogues were built as part of America's post–World War II construction boom of houses of worship and reflected the nation's religious mind-set. The horrific events of the Holocaust and the tragic aftermath of the detonation of atomic bombs over Japan influenced postwar moral and ethical codes in general worldwide, and in the United States in particular.[7] Religions reexamined their roles in establishing moral values and encouraged congre-gations to construct new houses of worship in new suburbs. These buildings would express the post-war increase in the prominence of religion. Indeed, indicators of reconceptualization in the design and construction of these houses of worship expressed the beginning of a new era of American modernism.

The resilience of the Jewish survivors of the Holo-caust and the establishment of the State of Israel in 1948 were major influences on a new search for Jewish identity in America and Israel at that time. Like a phoenix, the survivors grew from the Holo-caust's ashes and built a new life based on a new image of modern Jewish society. Part of this new life was the construction of their synagogues as insti-tutional monuments, which expressed resilience, redemption, and the pride of the Jewish people. The designs of these buildings were not about forget-ting the Holocaust, or detaching from the event, or rejecting it, or running away from the pain as

Gavriel Rosenfeld suggests in his book *Building after Auschwitz*.[8] They were a demonstration of the triumph over evil. Building these synagogues reflected the same strength of redemption that was at the core of establishing the State of Israel.

Often the survivors who immigrated to the United States joined American congregations that were already established by previous Jewish immigrants of the nineteenth and early twentieth centuries. Historian Oscar Handlin observed that the new immigrants did not differ much from the American Jews who had previously migrated to the United States, joining local congregations or establishing new congregations.[9] The existing con-gregations were exposed to the Holocaust through news, stories, or letters, and notes from lost rela-tives. Still, there was a feeling of solidarity among American Jews that made every Jew at that time a Holocaust survivor.[10] As such, some congrega-tions built their synagogues as modern monuments of remembrance, believing that "visual practices

Figure 1.1. Fifth Avenue Synagogue in New York City (1959), designed by Percival Goodman

are a powerful means of shaping memory and acts of commemoration."[11] Examples include Percival Goodman's Congregation B'nai Israel, Millburn, in New Jersey (1950), which is detailed in chapter 5, and Fifth Avenue Synagogue, in New York City, New York (1959), as described later in this chapter. Though Percival Goodman was an American Jew without a direct connection to the Holocaust, he tried to express in his early synagogue designs the link between suffering and survival using modern architecture. His design of the Fifth Avenue Synagogue was based on a motif of teardrops representing sorrow and anguish, and memory (figure 1.1). The building is a modern adaptation of a residential low high-rise into a synagogue with a new façade built as a concrete envelope with stained glass openings. Though the symbol of a teardrop is associated with sorrow, the artist who designed the windows, Robert Pinart (1927–2017), was inspired by the biblical motif of olive leaves, which symbolize strength and peace.[12] The interior, especially the sanctuary, is filled with light filtered through the stained-glass colors, expressing hope and the presence of the divine (figure 1.2).

Architects Percival Goodman and Eric Mendelsohn demonstrated the relationship between the new modern synagogue and the Holocaust as a connection between the past of the war and the future aspiration for Jews in a postwar America.[13] Other congregations, such as North Shore Congregation Israel in Glencoe, Illinois, kept items, such as the Torah Curtain rescued from the Kristallnacht that occurred in Germany, exhibiting it in their Memorial Hall adjacent to the sanctuary. Meanwhile, many congregations and their commissioned architects used modernism to exhibit pride in their institutions and left the Holocaust's memory and the constant fighting against contemporary anti-Semitism to be taught in the synagogues' educational programs.[14] Analyzing those modern synagogues reveals that all were built with self-confidence and exhibit the hybridity of Jewish life with modern American life.

The American Jewish congregations and their leaders faced the longtime dilemma of Jewish communities in exile: how to build their synagogues

Figure 1.2. Fifth Avenue Synagogue in New York City (1959): The sanctuary

to express the idea of belonging. This belonging expressed two identities. On the one hand was the desire to integrate into American society, especially into suburbia. On the other hand, congregations desired to maintain the traditional Jewish way of life and the historic concept of the "chosen people."[15] In his book *The Chosen People in America*, Arnold Eisen analyzes the American Jewish search for identity as part of fashioning a new self-definition of Jewish chosenness.[16] He calls this phenomenon "the ambivalent American Jew,"[17] in which this trend "[binds] them to God, to their fellow-men, and to each other."[18] This dilemma was not new but was more pronounced in the United States during the 1950s post-Holocaust period, which professor Raphael Marc calls "the belonging era."[19] The urge for belonging also resulted in Jewish congregations commissioning prominent American modernist architects to design their synagogues. Still, architect Philip Nobel's conclusion in his article published in the *New York Times*[20] is that the American synagogue building was and still is in search of a meaningful form that remains unresolved today. However, one thing was clear—the focus of the synagogues was not just on their religious function but more so on creating a space for experiencing Jewish life through educational and social activities. This aim became an integral part of the synagogue complex.[21]

Though there was an expectation from Jewish architects to "authentically interpret Judaism"[22] in their design of synagogues, most commissioned architects were not necessarily Jewish. They all saw these projects as an opportunity to design sacred places that introduced fundamental universal architectural components, creating the sacred[23] and bridging modernism with Judaism. Those architects saw the faith's requirements as part of the synagogue's functional program. For example, architect Philip Johnson noted that once the architect solved the multiple functional needs of the congregation, the design could focus on the building's beauty.[24] The modernist architectural concept of "form follows function"[25] that was fundamental to Johnson's designs was implemented in sacred architecture by others such as Frank Lloyd Wright to become "form follows faith."[26] Faith dictated the form of the house of worship mainly in its interior space. In the mid- to late 1950s and the 1960s, the design concept of form follows faith expanded to more expressionistic aesthetics[27] that transformed the synagogues into spiritual monuments (e.g., the "synagogue cathedral") and established the synagogue as a recognized institution. Modern expression was possible due to the lack of specific style and design guidelines for the exterior of a synagogue. Synagogues are defined as houses of gathering and thus houses for people rather than houses of God. For Jews, the only buildings that served as God's dwelling were the Jerusalem Temples, which were destroyed in 587 BC and AD 70 (see chapter 3). These temples became the collective memory of Jews all over the world and served as sources of inspiration for synagogue design. Still, to avoid persecution, most synagogues in exile adopted the local style of houses of worship in their surroundings and focused only on the interior design as dictated by

Judaism. The interior's shape was and still is determined by the rituals of the service, and is defined by the axial relationship between the synagogue's main elements of the Ark where the Torah[28] is housed and the bimah (platform) where the Torah is read (see chapter 3).

During the post–World War II era, both Jewish and Christian congregations moved to the suburbs. This move was part of the process to start a new way of life and led to building new houses of worship from scratch. Architect Percival Goodman and his brother, author and sociologist Paul Goodman, estimated that approximately 1,800 synagogues were built during this time all over the nation.[29] Most of these buildings showcased the exploration of new design concepts of modern forms drawn out of the use of new materials and systems such as concrete, steel, and glass. I claim that the 2017 article on the contemporary architecture of today by architect María Francisca González[30] could have been written in the 1950s and 1960s about synagogue design. González explains how advanced building and construction technologies open the door to new architectural explorations of form. This was also the case in the development of mid-twentieth-century modern American synagogues that utilized innovations in building technology and construction to showcase new architectural designs.

Despite these developments, modern synagogues were not studied as adequately as other institutions in America.[31] Still, in the last decade, we can see that scholarly interest in modern sacred architecture is growing[32] as part of the investigation of a fascinating experimental period in ecclesiastical architecture (mid-twentieth century). However, this category of scholarship has only begun to explore this type of design and has not necessarily focused on synagogue design. Those who explored modern synagogues present chronological descriptive and visual data as catalogs of American synagogues.[33] Other publications theoretically discuss phenomenology, social, and religious studies with limited architectural analysis,[34] or focus on one specific architect or one specific synagogue.[35] In this unique book, I expand the existing scholarly work by adding a new dimension with a critical and analytical inquiry into the architectural design of those synagogues and their preservation issues beyond brick and mortar.

This is an architectural book that analyzes the designs and the context of carefully selected American modern synagogues (1950s–60s). The selection is based on two criteria: (a) All were designed by prominent architects of the era who were heavily involved in promoting the nation's modern architecture movement and influenced the design of sacred architecture in America. Some, like Frank Lloyd Wright, Philip Johnson, and Pietro Belluschi, affected the design of American modern houses of worship with their church and synagogue designs; others such as Eric Mendelsohn, Percival Goodman, Sidney Eisenshtat, and Minoru Yamasaki focused mainly on the design of synagogues in America. (b) The selected synagogues were built during the 1950s–60s and to this day continue to serve congregations as houses of worship.

As such, this book does not include synagogue designs that were never materialized, like Philadelphia's Mikveh Israel Synagogue by Louis Kahn or Temple B'nai Jeshurun in Short Hills, New Jersey, by Marcel Breuer. It also does not include the design of additions such as Paul Rudolph's addition to Beth El Synagogue in New London, Connecticut. Neither does it include synagogues that were adapted to different functions, such as Eric Mendelsohn's 1950 B'nai Amoona Synagogue in St. Louis, Missouri, which became the Center of Contemporary Arts.

I gathered data on many synagogues that fulfill the above selection criteria. In this book several post–World War II American synagogues are highlighted, while others are mentioned throughout the book as examples of specific topics. This compilation is a representative, rather than an exhaustive, collection of synagogues built by congregations from the main Jewish denominations in America: Orthodox, Conservative, and Reform (see chapters 4 and 5). The selected buildings of worship were chosen carefully to highlight mid-twentieth century American synagogues based on data collected in my field trips to those buildings; archival studies in national and local archives (e.g., the Jewish Museum in New York, the Avery Library's Drawings and Archives of Columbia University in New York, the Cleveland Jewish

Archives in Western Reserve Historical Society, Cleveland, Ohio, El Paso Public Library, Texas, and the archives of each synagogue); visits with various local architectural firms that worked on specific synagogues (e.g., architects at Albert Khan Associates in Detroit, Michigan; In*Situ Architecture in El Paso, Texas); and an extensive literature search that started with Samuel Gruber's book *American Synagogues: A Century of Architecture and Jewish Community* as my inspiration.[36]

My book is organized into seven major chapters, starting with this introduction and ending with concluding remarks. As mentioned before, the analyses presented in this volume are based on an analytical investigation of the design and building technology of these synagogues within their specific American contexts. The architectural examination of each synagogue points out the special contributions of each building to the study of modern American synagogues (1950s–60s). It highlights modern designs that departed from historicism while keeping Jewish roots. Each chapter builds on the previous one, and all are presented in a cohesive dialogue that adds to previous work on American synagogues.

Chapter 1 is this introduction. Chapter 2, entitled "A Contextual Framework," depicts the major contextual characteristics of the era and shows their influences on the design of the modern American synagogue. It illustrates how the juxtaposition of three major elements of the era affected the synagogue's architecture. These characteristics include (a) the post-Holocaust Jewish search for identity, (b) the impact of the move of American Jewry to the suburbs, and (c) the experimentation with modernism in American architecture and its impact on the design of those synagogues.

Chapter 3, entitled "Synagogue Design Concepts," focuses on the architectural design concepts[37] of a synagogue. The chapter defines *synagogue* as a building type, as well as its role as a gathering place and as a symbol of a congregation. It highlights topics such as the universal elements that make a building sacred (e.g., sacred path and plan, sacred verticality, ambiance), and novel building technologies such as new materials (concrete steel and glass) and systems (light, acoustics, thermal comfort). This chapter also introduces the specificity of synagogue design, such as the building's functional modern program, the exterior design concepts that are free from faith constraints, the synagogue's interior design concepts that increase the relationship between architecture and Judaism, and the introduction of abstracted modern art as an expression of biblical symbols beyond the common functional art known as Judaica.

Chapter 4, "Modern American Synagogue Design: Key Developments," analyzes three main developments of the 1950s and 1960s that influenced synagogue architecture: Eric Mendelsohn's Park Synagogue in Cleveland, Ohio (1953); Frank Lloyd Wright's Beth Sholom Synagogue in Elkins Park, Pennsylvania (1956); and Minoru Yamasaki's North Shore Congregation Israel Synagogue in Glencoe, Illinois (1964). First, the chapter introduces Mendelsohn's Park Synagogue in Cleveland, Ohio, as the key example of modernism and an expression of the departure from historicism and the change in synagogues' programmatic functions. Mendelsohn not only reinforced the use of modern architecture and its departure from traditional synagogue design, but he also highlighted the functional program of the synagogue as a changing task for the architect. Scholars believe that his design of Park Synagogue represents the fullest expression of his vision and influenced the future of American synagogue design.

The second key point was the embrace of American values and landscapes in the design of synagogue complexes. Frank Lloyd Wright attempted to design "The American Synagogue" when building Beth Sholom Synagogue in Elkins Park, Pennsylvania. In this design, Wright combined universal sacred architectural elements, local Native American art, and Jewish symbols. Like his church designs, his synagogue departed from traditional European houses of worship and expressed the American landscape and its values of democracy and freedom.[38] Still, his design did not forsake traditional symbols of the faith. Rather, he called for the abstraction of these symbols using metaphors related to faith traditions and myth, folding them into an American values system. As such, he designed the pyramidal

shape of the synagogue as an homage to Mount Sinai, where the Ten Commandments were given to the people of Israel, and also as a reminder of the Native American tipi.

The third key development was modernizing the monumental concept of the "cathedral synagogues."[39] This is illustrated in Minoru Yamasaki's North Shore Congregation Israel Synagogue in Glencoe, Illinois. His design evolved from Mendelsohn's and Wright's synagogue designs. It was a monumental concept reflecting Jewish self-confidence in synagogues as institutions. In Yamasaki's point of view, man must believe in himself in order to believe in God.[40] Therefore, he attempted to design a space of delight and reflection, in addition to having a more modern emphasis on function, economy, and order. His expressionistic design concept showcased 1960s Jewish life in America.

Chapter 5, "Pushing the Envelope: Architectural Illustrations," includes five case studies that reflect the key developments depicted in the previous chapter and identify each one's special contributions to the design of the modern American synagogue. These examples illustrate the continuity and development of synagogue design from 1950 to 1967. They include an analysis of Philip Johnson's 1956 Conservative Kneses Tifereth Israel Synagogue in Port Chester, New York, as a case of form follows function, and two synagogues by Percival Goodman: the 1950 Conservative Congregation B'nai Israel in Millburn, New Jersey, and the 1962 Conservative Congregation Shaarey Zedek in Southfield, Michigan (designed with Albert Khan as the local architect of record). These two synagogues are the major milestones of Goodman's career in synagogue design[41] and reflect his developments in modernrnism. They also exemplify the inclusion of abstracted art in synagogues and the solution for the synagogues' flexible design requirements. Additional case studies include Pietro Belluschi's 1964–68 Reform Temple B'nai Jeshurun in Short Hills, New Jersey (designed with Grunzen & Partners), which highlights the concept of the synagogue cathedral; and Sidney Eisenshtat's 1962 Reform Temple Mount Sinai in El Paso, Texas, which introduced sustainable design long before this notion became popular.

Two levels of architectural analysis are the focus of chapter 5: (a) the architectural expression of the factors influencing the synagogues' design (e.g., the search for Jewish identity in America, the move to the suburbs, and the American modern architecture movement); and (b) the specifics of their architectural and construction elements that were innovative at the time and influenced the design of the modern American synagogue. In addition, the chapter introduces topics such as the exploration of nontraditional design forms; innovations in building technology and construction systems. It presents examples of modern abstracted art inclusion and its relationship to Jewish symbols and to a synagogue's architecture; and the notion of sustainable design.

The synagogues described represent the major denominations of the Jewish faith: Orthodox, Conservative, and Reform. Though only two architects were Jewish (Goodman and Eisenshtat), their designs were similar to those of the other architects. All of the designs focused on creating a modern sacred monument that showcased the suburban Jewish congregation's way of life.

Other examples, such as Loebl Schlossman & Hackl's 1957 Orthodox Chicago Loop Synagogue in Chicago, Illinois; Percival Goodman's 1959 Fifth Avenue Synagogue in New York City, New York; Walter Gropius's 1960 Reform Temple Oheb Shalom in Baltimore, Maryland (with architect Sheldon I. Leavitt); and William N. Breger's 1967 Orthodox TriBeCa Synagogue in New York City, New York, are mentioned in relation to specific topics throughout the book.

Chapter 6, "Adaptations and Changes," introduces a unique perspective of studying the challenges these synagogues have coped with over time. The chapter does not describe the typical brick-and-mortar and maintenance preservation. Rather, it considers the changes in users' needs and comfort, changes in architectural fashion, and the desire to continue and preserve the Jewish life following Psalm 86:2, "Preserve my life, for I am holy."

Scholars of preservation of the recent past investigated modern materials and systems[42] and demonstrated that concrete, for example, represents modernity.[43] It should be noted that congregations proudly maintain the materiality of their houses of worship with an attempt to preserve the buildings' modernist design. However, the attempt to preserve these synagogues caused the congregations to be confronted with additional challenges beyond maintenance. This chapter investigates the need to adapt in four interrelated domains: (a) changes in demographics and service attendance, (b) modifications in liturgy and rituals, (c) compliance to new building codes, and (d) energy conservation due to the rising cost of utilities.

Chapter 7, the final chapter of the book, consists of some concluding remarks. They summarize the findings of the architectural analyses of the modern American synagogues along Vitruvius's design concepts from the first century BC: *firmitas*, *utilitas*, and *venustas*, meaning strength, utility, and delight/beauty.

2 A Contextual Framework

**And let them make Me a sanctuary,
that I may dwell among them.**

(Exodus 25:8–9)

This chapter introduces the book's contextual framework that depicts the major characteristics of the era and illustrates their influences on the design of modern American synagogues (figure 2.1). It shows the synagogue's architectural expression at the intersection of three major background contexts: religious/cultural. location. and design concepts. This intersection illustrates the complexity of synagogue design for all denominations (Orthodox, Conservatism, Reform). It reflects the congregation's identity, the suburban landscape, and modern architecture. Moreover, this contextual framework highlights the synagogue as a house of the people (i.e., a house of assembly) and not a holy building.

   The element of *Jewish identity* denotes the post-Holocaust Jewish search for an identity that would express the ideal of a modern, free Jew. In Israel, this search was devoted to building a new modern nation, while in America it was reflected in the design of new modern synagogues during the 1950s and 1960s. These buildings served as vehicles to showcase congregations' resilience, confidence, and strength. The synagogues exhibited the image of an American institution at the core of the community life, which some rabbis, such as Rabbi David de Sola Pool, saw as the most promising part of

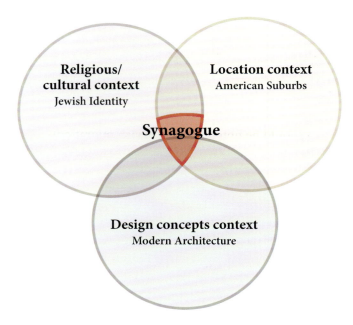

Figure 2.1. The book's contextual model

American Jewish life.[1] In addition, the new synagogues reflected the congregations' realization of the American value of freedom of religion. The latter resulted not only from the legal implications of the US First Amendment but also expressed the American cultural pluralism of the time. It claimed that minority groups in the United States have the right and the duty to retain and develop their culture and thus also their religion.[2] This value not only strengthened the congregations but also enhanced American democracy.[3] In the 1960s, the nation's approval of organized religion as fulfilling its mandate for social justice no longer considered American Jewry as a minority group. Judaism became a prominent leading religious and cultural group, and synagogues—like churches—acted to unfold the American dream.[4]

The second contextual element of the model is the location of Jewish congregations—that is, *the American suburbs* (see details later in this chapter). The move to the suburbs that developed around cities in post–World War II America changed the urban landscape and affected organized religion in the United States, including Jewish institutions such as synagogues.[5] These synagogues, like their church counterparts, became symbols of suburbia itself and eased the congregations' sense of rootlessness.[6] The new houses of worship were expected to provide a fresh solution that would grow out of contemporary life and culture.[7] Furthermore, these buildings expressed and still are the congregations' pride in their Jewish life and heritage.

It should be noted that the Jewish migration to the suburbs was not necessarily part of post-Holocaust Jewish immigration to the United States. Rather, it was part of the American "suburban migration." This "movement" had been triggered by a configuration of several factors: the greater mobility of the population; the growing American middle class; the shortage of housing in large cities; the large wave of African Americans migrating into the city, which increased racial tensions in urban housing; and government-sponsored affordable mortgage programs.[8] Following World War II, the federal government provided the opportunity for GIs to purchase homes through special loan programs and move out of the crowded cities. Low-cost houses were affordable due to the availability of building materials after the war and mass-produced homes. The availability of newer and faster means of transportation, as well as new infrastructure and inexpensive automobiles, made it simple to commute from the suburbs to the city.[9] In addition, there are claims that these federal initiatives were part of the government's efforts to decentralize the American population in response to the Cold War threat of nuclear warfare.[10]

Due to US restrictive immigration laws in the 1940s and 1950s, it was extremely difficult for Jews during the war, and later for Holocaust survivors, to find refuge in the United States.[11] The postwar American immigration policy was to direct displaced refugees back to their homeland. Unfortunately, this policy did not consider those people like Jews, who did not have a homeland to return to. Furthermore, Congress limited the entry and aid to European refugees, including Holocaust survivors.[12] As such, only 400,000 displaced people, among them roughly 24 percent Jewish Holocaust survivors, were admitted to the United States between 1945 and 1952.[13] In 1945, following a directive order by President Truman, 16,000 more Jews were permitted in.[14] In addition, the United States did not sign the 1951 United Nations Refugee Convention until 1967, which removed the previous limitations.[15] Most of the Jews who managed to immigrate during that time stayed in big cities, but many joined the move to the suburbs to live the "American dream." The new locations provided an opportunity for place-making and experimentation with new design concepts in building synagogues.

The third contextual element of the modern American synagogue's design is *modern architecture*. Prominent architects of the era followed architect Eric Mendelsohn's manifest "In the Spirit of our Age" (1947),[16] which called for the departure from traditional synagogue design. They ventured into modernism and bridged it with Judaism in their design of the American synagogue. The new synagogues reflected the congregations' desire to belong to a new era of American modernism that reflected new aesthetics and innovation in building technology.

Before detailing the three contextual phenomena as portrayed in figure 2.1, it should be summarized that the model encompasses the spiritual and physical influences on American Jewry as expressed in their house of worship—the synagogue. The interrelationship among the three contexts serves as the framework for my attempt to decipher the design and construction of mid-twentieth-century modern American synagogues.

Jewish Identity and the American Modern Synagogue

A critical concept to account for the development of the American modern synagogue is its relation to social identity theory.[17] According to Henry Tajfel, social identity is "that part of an individual's self-concept which derives from his [her] knowledge of his [her] membership in a social group (groups) together with the value and emotional significance attached to that membership."[18] However, it should be noted that a given individual's social identity may express more than one social group. In our case, the concept of Jewish identity does not allow for a simple categorization and a clear definition.[19] Some claim that Judaism is a Platonic idea with "a spiritual orientation, which is a possibility for all mankind."[20] Thus, Judaism "is neither a race nor people, even less recognized creed,"[21] while others consider Judaism as a religious civilization.[22]

The complexity of Jewish identity stems from historical factors that are still at the core of the search for identity. There are various Jewish origins (i.e., Ashkenazi and Sephardic Jews[23]) and different denominations (i.e., Orthodox, Conservative, Reform, Reconstructionism). In addition, Jews are scattered all over the world. Still, all are gathered in varying degrees around the core of the Jewish faith—the Torah—the Holy Scrolls. Some remain faithful to the Jewish Laws and principles and strongly believe that Jews are the chosen people, while others became more universalists and expect modern Jews to be part of the society they live in.[24] In addition, following the traumatic effects of the Holocaust, they all struggled to relate their identity as part of an ethnic and religious group of people. In order to overcome this struggle, most supported and still support the establishment of the Jewish nation and its state, Israel. This fulfills a historic dream of generations who lived in exile for more than two thousand years.

Historian Michael Meyer,[25] in his book about Jewish identity,[26] identifies three major forces that influenced and still impact the search for Jewish identity in the modern world: enlightenment, anti-Semitism, and Zion. He claims that enlightenment is "the powerful enticements of reason," which implies a rational person and his relation to universalism.[27] Enlightenment drew Jews to discover the world beyond the boundaries of Judaism. The second element is anti-Semitism, which in his point of view is "the ambiguous effects of exclusion and persecution."[28] On one hand, it strengthens Jewish ties as a community, and on the other, it weakens them. The third is Zion, "the centripetal force of Jewish peoplehood,"[29] which is the historical Hebrew title of the land of Israel. It represents the longing to establish a Jewish nationhood and return to Israel. Meyer claims that this unfulfilled dream of Zion kept Jews loyal to their faith.[30]

The following paragraphs detail each of these points as related to post–World War II American Jewry's search for identity and the impact on their synagogue designs. The concept of enlightenment can be seen in the realization of the American value of freedom of religion, which increased the salience of religion in America during the 1950s. It resulted in building thousands of Christian and Jewish houses of worship around the nation as part of cultural pluralism,[31] and in the establishment of an interfaith prayer room in the nation's capital in 1954, by converting a seventeen-square-foot conference room near the rotunda for this cause.[32] More so, President Eisenhower's call for the American people to embrace their faith and to belong to a congregation was part of this trend. Sociologist of religion Will Herberg mentions in his book *Protestant-Catholic-Jew* (1955) that belonging to one of the three major religions (i.e., Protestant, Catholic, Jewish) is an alternative way of being an American.[33] Thus religion became a way of belonging more than a way of connecting to God and following specific rituals.[34]

American Jewish congregations moved to the suburbs and identified with the gentiles' world, which surrounded them beyond the boundaries of their faith. This phenomenon catered to congregations' desire to belong to the world beyond the boundaries of strict Judaism. This desire can be traced to the eighteenth-century Jewish Enlightenment (Haskalah) movement in Europe. It was established by Jewish philosophers with an aim to broaden Jews' intellectual and social horizons and enable them to become part of Western society.[35] They attempted to combine the traditional Jewish way of religious life with the study of general knowledge, local languages, Hebrew instead of the Jewish dialect of Yiddish, and western European culture.[36] This type of ideal was often hard to realize, as they had to bridge between the "law of man" that preached to live strictly by the Jewish Law of the Halacha and the "law of God" that opened up Judaism to other studies and cultures.[37]

The major criticism of the Haskalah movement was that it threatened Judaism with potential assimilation among the gentiles. American congregations faced the same conflict between the internal continuity of Jewish traditions and the outside free world. The phenomenon of a gradual "Americanization" of religious practices and houses of worship designs was seen in other religions in America and was not specific only to Judaism. Some scholars attribute this phenomenon to secular objects that provide a magical dimension to life replacing religion.[38] This scholarship was part of a trend that was described by the Canadian Philosopher Charles Taylor in his book *A Secular Age*.[39] He studied Christianity in the Western world, believing that the secular world still preserves the transcendent realm and various aspects of religiosity but is not devoted to God as the center of life. This concept stands "in direct contrast to the condition that obtained in 1500" when God was the dominant force in all areas of social and political life.[40]

Less American citizens became affiliated with a specific house of God. However, they still considered themselves Christians or Jews. In 2018, reporter Mike Stunson indicated, "For the first time in eight decades, fewer than 50% of Americans say they belong to a church, [a] synagogue or [a] mosque amid an ongoing steep decline in religious attendance, according to a new bi-annual Gallup poll."[41] In addition, according to Rabbi Michael Knopf, the essence of membership drove worshipers away from synagogues and had to be revisited.[42] Although both Christian and Jewish religions maintained their traditional rituals, there was a trend toward Americanization, such as conducting sermons in English,

holding weekly services, and an increasing role of the laity in managing the church's or synagogue's affairs and activities.[43] Still, American Jews felt secure enough to manifest Judaism and showcase the rise of Jews as proud people building their lives around their synagogues, similar to their Christian neighbors.[44]

Anti-Semitism, the second force that influenced the search for Jewish identity, was extremely influential during the post-Holocaust era. The anti-Semitic event of horrific hate and racism that resulted in the genocide of the Jewish people, killing six million of them, intensified the Jewish search for identity. As mentioned before, some Jews began to doubt if God exists and if they were really the chosen people, while others became more orthodox, believing that despite all the horror, they were supposed to maintain the Jewish faith and culture.

Some studies on Jewish identity claim that anti-Semitism acts ambiguously. It serves as a collective memory that determines Jewishness, as it keeps Jews within a specific circle, or pushes them back to it.[45] However, sometimes anti-Semitism adds reasons for abandoning Jewishness and questioning the value(s) of Jewish identity.[46] The Orthodox Jews believe anti-Semitism is part of God's plan to test his chosen people. In turn, this belief strengthens their identity, while anti-Semitism weakened modern Jews since they were more attuned to the ambiguity of their identity. Architect and art historian Rachel Wischnitzer-Bernstein links American Jewish modernism with the search for "something new, expressive of the aspirations of a more self-conscious Jewishness, at home in America."[47] As such, modern synagogues in America expressed a "new urge to Jewish self-affirmation"[48] but still reflected the historic dilemma of "Jewish minority" versus "belonging in America."

Most important, American Jewish congregations and the Holocaust survivors who eventually joined them wanted to build a new modern Jewish life that would symbolize redemption over evil. This desire was also reflected in their synagogue architecture, which served as a vehicle to express the congregations' modern life and the American spirit. The new synagogues became established institutions in

America, built with pride and self-confidence as part of Jewish strength and the nation's religious landscape.

Modern architecture was easily adopted in synagogue design, as modernism preached to depart from the past, focus on a better life, and choose optimism over despair. Architectural historian Carol Herselle Krinsky claims that the simplicity of modern architecture "accorded well" with Judaism as it encompassed the aesthetics and ethical values of the faith.[49] The embrace of modernism in building postwar synagogues in America was manifested, for example, by the Reform movement that saw the modern synagogue as an expression of a new Judaism in a new age and place.[50] Conservative Judaism, which aimed to conserve the faith, saw the modern synagogue as a confirmation of Judaism being an "evolving religious civilization."[51] It was different from the recurring motif in the American Jewish experience.[52] Previous generations built their synagogues to resemble their ethnic-religious origin, providing continuity not only of familiar rituals but also spaces that created outlets for ethnic solidarity.[53] Thus the design of the synagogue in a historic style or in eclectic collections of traditional styles catered to each of the Jewish ethnic groups. However, during the post-Holocaust era, Jews wanted to detach themselves from these memories and start a new life in America. The move to the suburbs created the opportunity to build new modern houses of worship and reflect modern new American life.

Zion, the third force in Meyer's study of post–World War II Jewish identity, culminated with the establishment of the State of Israel in 1948. It recognized Jews as a people with a nation, at least in the political sense. Becoming a peoplehood with a nation increased their Jewish self-confidence and enabled Jews to get out of the Holocaust ashes and build their new identity based on the ideal of a new modern Jewish society. This ideal followed the visions of Jewish leaders such as Theodor Herzl (1860–1904) and Ahad Ha'am (1856–1927), who saw the new Jewish society based on Western European culture. While Herzl, founder of the political Zionism, focused on the establishment of an independent, secular, and democratic Jewish homeland/

state,[54] Ahad Ha'am, founder of the cultural Zionism, introduced his concepts of a Western, independent, secular modern Jewish society.[55] Zion was a multifaceted representation of peoplehood. On one hand, it focused on a place of historic yearning and religious connotation; on the other, it believed in a secular movement that preached to return to *Erez Israel* (the Land of Israel), settle in it, and create a Western, modern Jewish society. A different concept was introduced by Simon Dubnov (1860–1941), the main opponent to the political Zionism. He claimed that Jews' spiritual and cultural strength required only the landscape of Jewish memory and not necessarily the physical land of Israel.[56] Thus all forms of Zion played major roles in establishing Jewish identity both in Israel and in the diaspora (including America) during that time.[57]

American Jewry attempted to establish the "new Zion" in America. Some rabbis in America "invoked the principal tropes of American rhetoric to argue the identity of American ideals with their own."[58] They claimed that American democracy and its political system are compatible with Judaism concepts. They also saw American religious pluralism as the principle of democracy that shapes America.[59] This political affiliation created a religious affiliation for various groups, including Jews. Still, Zionism and the creation of the State of Israel became the only solution for the Jewish question of identity as it transcended the effects of enlightenment and anti-Semitism.[60]

As previously described, three forces impacted the American Jewry's search for identity during post–World War II: enlightenment as expressed in the American values of freedom and democracy, the Holocaust as the horrific anti-Semitic event, and the establishment of the State of Israel as the result of the Zion movement. These factors forced Jews to rethink and reevaluate their Jewish identity. Scholarly examination of this evaluation shows the complexity of defining Jewish identity throughout history and today.

This complexity was and still is the basis of Jewish debates regarding the self-definition of Jewish identity.[61] Therefore, in building their synagogues, American Jews faced the difficult challenge of how to build institutions to represent their identity. The building should belong to the new era/land, yet it should also bridge modernism with Judaism and let the design shape the building's Jewish character.[62] Often, American Jews solved this dilemma by interpreting the idea of Jewish chosenness.[63] This concept became central in both laity and professional discussions of defining Jewish identity by its relation to God, to fellow men, and to each other.[64] It raised the question of what it means to be a Jew in America, a question that directly influences the synagogue's design. Some wonder if Jewish architects by virtue of their background can better solve this dilemma.[65] Jewish architect Peter Eisenman (1937–) declined this notion, saying that there is no such thing as Jewish architecture or "Jewish identity in architecture."[66] It is interesting to note that the different approaches were already discussed in history by rabbis who stated that if a synagogue was only a holy building, then Jews would be the only ones to build it. However, synagogues are not considered holy buildings, but rather people buildings,[67] and as such many non-Jewish architects designed synagogues around the nation (see the following chapters for examples). Building the synagogue reflected, and still reflects, the challenge of finding the balance between Jewish integration into American society versus highlighting the essential differences from that society. In other words, building "on the old foundation a new structure, [while] keeping with modern style of religious architecture."[68]

The modern architecture movement served the American Jewish dilemma well. It is characterized as new aesthetics inspired by the machine, departing from historicism, heritage cultures, and regional considerations, and utilizing innovations in building technology. The freedom of the synagogue's exterior from faith constraints and traditions (see chapter 3) enabled architects to experiment with new modern aesthetics. Modern aesthetics expressed and utilized innovations in building materials (e.g., concrete, steel, glass), systems (e.g., structure, light, acoustics, thermal), and construction methods, and influenced the building's form. This mutual relation of building technology, form, and its ambiance is illustrated

in the conceptual model as developed in my book *Frank Lloyd Wright's Sacred Architecture*,[69] and is adapted to this book in the next chapter on synagogue design concepts.

Moving to the Suburbs of the 1950s–1960s and the American Modern Synagogue

Books such as *The Suburban Church*, *Temples for a Modern God*, and *Jews in Suburbia*[70] explain the phenomenon of the suburbs and their development from "dormitory" housing areas adjacent to large cities into independent communities that focus on home and family. These books also mention the statistics of the thousands of people moving into the suburbs in the 1950s.[71] Most of the population were middle-class young families with children who were tempted to move to the post–World War II suburbs. As mentioned before, the GI Bill of Rights offered government mortgage programs, and the availability of low-cost housing enabled veterans to purchase their dream homes, fulfilling the American dream.[72] In addition, the development of infrastructure and transportation made the commute to the city easier, and the demographic changes in city neighborhoods made the move to the suburbs more attractive. The suburban way of life across America anticipated an open, modern, and coherent social environment. Jews believed that "the suburbs would offer a better environment for Judaism to thrive."[73]

Though suburbia was supposed to serve as a symbol of the American melting-pot society, people tended to identify themselves as part of one of three religions: Protestantism, Catholicism, and Judaism.[74] Still, the vision of the suburbs was based on the status symbol of the Christian migration that was called the "white flight."[75] Most "white Protestants" refused to accept mixed neighborhoods,[76] often demonstrating anti-Semitism toward Jews and not welcoming African Americans either.[77] The US Housing Act of 1949 permitted segregation by subsidizing mass-production home builders to create suburbs on the condition that the houses be sold only to white Christians.[78] In his book *Making the Second Ghetto* (1983), Arnold Hirsch reports a study of Chicago from 1940–60 that illustrates the "insidious nature of city leaders' schemes to isolate Black citizens."[79] Indeed, local governments encouraged discrimination by issuing unconstitutional racial ordinances, followed by real estate agencies and bankers.[80] In his book *Jews in Suburbia* (1973), Albert Gordon provides statistical data on refusals to sell or rent homes/apartments to Jews by using different claims. He shows that only 43.33 percent did not discriminate.[81] For example, suburbs in and around Chicago were almost completely closed or partly closed to Jewish residents.[82] As with black churches, synagogues were not always welcomed as part of neighborhood developments.[83] It was believed that having this house of worship in the neighborhood would lower its real estate values. Indeed, the congregation of Park Synagogue in Cleveland, Ohio, for example, could not easily acquire the permit to build their synagogue in Cleveland Heights, Ohio.[84]

In the 1950s, when some of the restrictive housing barriers to Jews were lifted, the move of Jews to the suburbs became more popular. Jewish families followed the white Christians and saw the suburbs as the opportunity to fulfill their American dream.[85] They sold their properties in the city and moved away from their old neighborhoods, which were changing due to the increased populations of African Americans, Puerto Ricans, and Mexicans in those areas.[86] "Racial changes within cities speeded the White exodus to the suburbs"[87]and was justified by the white residents who claimed that the security and peace of their city's neighborhoods were compromised. "Suburban life is assumed to be free from tensions, hustle, crowding and crime of the city."[88] Still, Jews often found themselves segregated in their suburban neighborhoods as non-Jews moved out to different neighborhoods or suburbs to be surrounded by Christians.[89]

The move of the Jews to the suburbs became easier when the Rabbinical Assembly of the United Synagogue of America allowed traveling on the Sabbath to attend services.[90] Indeed, *The American Jewish Yearbook* reported that in 1954, "the movement of the Jewish population to suburban areas continued to gain momentum." This movement was also supported financially by different Jewish organizations such as the Union of American Hebrew Congregations and by various national synagogue groups (Orthodox, Conservatives, Reforms).[91] Eventually, the synagogues represented American Jewry that had risen to "a prominent position among the leading religious and cultural groups of the nation."[92]

As religion became an essential part of American society of the period, American suburbs were a perfect location to design and construct houses of worship from scratch and express the congregations' pride in their modern new identity.[93] Synagogues, like churches, became part of the suburban landscape.[94]

The suburban synagogues represented not just the function of religion but also included education programs (e.g., daycares, schools), social fellowships, sports activities, and friendship. These buildings became complexes that included three major wings: the house of prayer (the prayer wing), where religious services were conducted; the house of study (the educational wing), which focused on Jewish schooling; and the house of assembly (the social wing), where the congregation met for cultural, social, family, and sports activities.[95] The synagogue became a central institution of the Jewish community and served as a house of gathering for all ages,[96] expressing Jewish faith and way of life.

One of the first architects to introduce this type of complex and add a fourth wing for the synagogue's administration was Eric Mendelsohn in the design of his synagogues (see Park Synagogue in Cleveland, Ohio, as an example, in chapter 3). Most of the congregations and their rabbis welcomed these centers as they saw in them "the opportunity to know [their] own rich heritage and to live [their] life as an American Jew."[97] This also changed the status and role of rabbis, who now served as preacher, educator, youth leader, and counselor.[98] Indeed, the new approach in building sacred spaces in the suburbs, including synagogues, was to emphasize the assembled community and its needs of the day.[99] Still, criticism was drawn by some rabbis, like Rabbi Eugene Borowitz, who saw these complexes as diminishing the prayer function: "No one wishes to lose Jews for Judaism, but the time has come when the synagogue must be saved for the religious Jew."[100]

Mid-Twentieth-Century Modern Architecture and the American Synagogue

In 1932, architect Philip Johnson (1906–2005) and architectural historian Henry-Russell Hitchcock (1903–87) organized and curated the *International Style Exhibition* at the Museum of Modern Art (MOMA) in New York City. They published the exhibition catalog entitled *Modern Architecture: The International Exhibition*,[101] with the collaboration of art historian and director of the MOMA Alfred H. Barr Jr. and historian Lewis Mumford. Their catalog introduced the exhibited architects, the design concepts of the International Style, as well as issues in modern housing. That exhibition brought forward the style which had emerged in Europe circa 1922 and became the cradle of modernism. It introduced the work of European architects such as Ludwig Mies Van de Rohe, Walter Gropius, and Le Corbusier and projects by American architects, such as Frank Lloyd Wright[102] and Richard J. Neutra. The exhibition made the American public aware of modernism. It "marked the first time the 'international style' became institutionalized and officially recognized."[103] The term international style became part of the architectural vocabulary of modern architecture and design.[104] The exhibition introduced the major design concepts of the style that were linked with the "machine age," industrialization, and emphasized functionality, standardization of elements, avoidance of ornaments/decorations, and volume prominence over mass.[105]

The architectural applications of these principles were expressed in simple, straightforward, bold, "clean" new forms. This design was influenced by new building technology (materials, structure, systems). Functional designs called for flexible forms,[106] which were in line with American architect Louis Sullivan's design concept from 1896:

"form follows function."[107] Geometry was liberated from symmetry, which was frequently required by tradition. New materials and systems were utilized to create new aesthetics. Designs with slender steel posts and beams, reinforced concrete, aluminum, and glass have made possible structures of skeleton-like strength and lightness.[108] These principles served as the main motifs of modern architecture.

Many studies were published on modern architecture in America. Some illustrated this movement in books on the chronology of the history of architecture;[109] some focused on the history and development of the modern movement in America;[110] while others looked at specific modern architects or buildings.[111] All these studies attempted to decipher modernism design concepts, theory, and technology. Their common thread shows the departure of modernism from historicism in design and from regional considerations, and the use of innovation in building technology. Other studies relate modernism to the architectural concept as mentioned previously of "form follows function." This design concept became the basis for a rational approach to architecture,[112] which refers to a building designed along a logical, mathematically ordered design. It created a machine aesthetic that emphasized horizontality, suppressed all ornaments, and radically departed from historicism.[113] The functional approach as the central theme of modern architecture was questioned by architectural critic Douglas Haskell (1899–1979) already in 1932.[114] He attempted to analyze functionalism "both semantically and philosophically," distinguishing true functionalism from the cosmetic variety.[115] He also examined the abstractions of designs by modernist architects such as Le Corbusier and Jacob Oud, and showed the influence of cubism and neoplasticism. He claimed that the designs of architects Frank Lloyd Wright, Louis Sullivan, and Raymond Hood (exhibited in the exhibition in MOMA) initiated the "organic impulse."[116]

As mentioned before, during the late 1950s and 1960s, architects developed this concept into more expressionist forms of modernism to represent the American democratic society and to enhance the expression of freedom and individuality.[117] New materials, such as concrete with its plasticity character, frequently defined the building's form and aesthetic characteristics.[118] Modern design examples can be seen in the designs of dramatic roofs of houses of worship of the 1950s–60s. In his book *Temples for a Modern God: Religious Architecture in Postwar America* (2013), Jay Price remarks that "theologian James White suggested that [modern] religious architecture became 'a study in comparative roofs,' finding that the high and dramatic roofs of churches of that period are almost a trademark of the era."[119] While White addresses only churches, the same phenomenon is also evident in synagogues of that era (see examples in the following chapters). The rationale for this argument about the daring and dramatic roofs is based on three levels of inquiry: (a) the congregations' search for a newer identity as expressed in the new aesthetics (as congregations and their leaders saw in these roofs not only a representation of the post–World War II generation but also a statement of power soaring to reach God); (b) the changes in liturgical programs, which allowed the acceptance of new forms; and (c) the exploration of new possibilities in building technology to create dramatic forms. Architects and engineers experimented with structural systems that worked well with the plasticity of materials in order to reach the height and form of their sculptural roofs. They tested hyperbolic paraboloids, catenary and parabolic arches, and thin-shell concrete in the roofs' designs.[120] The new materials and technologies of the modern age were catalysts for embracing those forms that identified each building as an individual celebration of material and humanity.

Indeed, scholars called the modern era one of the most experimental in ecclesiastical architecture in history.[121] Modernism even appealed to the conservatives, who seemed to have embraced the style to express the time they lived in.[122] Architect Ludwig Mies van der Rohe believed that "a sublime dematerialization of light, glass, and gleaming metal" enhances spirituality.[123] This notion was also expressed by the Bishop of Brentwood, who looked at concrete as "God's gift to religion."[124] Thus modernism of the sacred was inspired by innovations in building technology that justified experimentation

with new materials and systems in the design of houses of worship, which were predominantly associated with history and traditions.[125]

In 1958, the American Institute of Architects (AIA) produced a film titled *A Place to Worship* that introduced current trends in religious architecture across the United States.[126] It starts with a modernist credo that in each time of history, worship buildings were built in the spirit of that period. Therefore, "mere imitation of past periods is out of place. . . . A religion which is firmly anchored in the life of our day is best expressed by the architecture of the day."[127] As a result, more midcentury architects were inspired to reject traditional styles in designing houses of worship and to express the modern era of American technology-driven culture. Architect Eric Mendelsohn's article from 1947, "Creating a Modern Synagogue Style: In the Spirit of our Age,"[128] and his synagogue designs manifested the departure from historicism and called for synagogues to exemplify the era's style and innovations while acting as an inspiring place that lifted the spirit of the worshiper.[129] However, due to the nature of houses of worship, the hybridity of modernist concepts with faith traditions can be traced in these buildings.[130] Hybridity supports the need for tradition since modern designs of churches, for example, are mired in the ordinary rather than in the extraordinary, diminishing "the individual worship experience."[131]

It should be noted that one of the theological schools of thought, the theological aesthetic, which perceived the sacred through the sensation, feeling, and imagination of beauty,[132] influenced the "functional" design of modern sacred architecture. When describing his synagogue design (1954), architect Philip Johnson detailed "a space where awe and reverence are the prime considerations, an inspiring challenge to the artist,"[133] while Mies van der Rohe claimed that "the building art is in reality always the spatial expression of spiritual decisions."[134] To summarize those references to modern architecture and the sacred is beyond the scope of this book, which aims to decipher and add a new dimension to how modernism influenced the design of mid-twentieth-century American synagogues.

Summary

Most of the prominent modern architects of the era undertook the design of at least one synagogue.[135] They were not necessarily Jews, but no matter the faith of the architects, all of them respected the spirit of the Jewish faith and its programmatic requirements. Their designs followed architect and art historian Rachel Wischnitzer-Bernstein's and architect Eric Mendelsohn's calls to create alternative designs to synagogues' historical styles.[136] The new synagogues had to cater to the congregations' desires to depart from European traditional synagogue designs[137] and from early American design traditions, which imitated various compilations of historical styles.[138] Those congregations encouraged the architects to embrace modernism and to push the envelope in their synagogue designs. They saw in modern architecture clean lines, a balance of masses, the utility of new materials, and the expression of belonging to the new era in America. Richard Meier, in his book *Recent American Synagogue Architecture* (1963), declared that "the best synagogues are the purest architecture, the most straightforward expression of what the synagogue should be."[139] Indeed, architects experimented with new architectural aesthetics and innovative building technology, investigating the aspect of what constitutes a sacred space. They included faith, functional, and spiritual requirements, and used modern abstracted architectural forms and art to express the new era. Their attempts were showcased in an exhibition at the Jewish Museum in New York City in 1963 with seventeen examples of modern synagogue designs. The exhibition attempted to illustrate the fundamental architectural questions of what a synagogue is and how it can reflect the modern world.[140] It also intended to raise the attention of the public to these institutions that reflected modern architecture while enhancing the spirit of the Jewish congregation.[141] Some of the exhibited examples expressed a rational approach to synagogue designs, which followed strictly faith requirements and functional demands, and often forgot to express a sense of "cultural and religious meaning of Judaism."[142] The feeling that these buildings "do not feel like a synagogue"[143] was the main criticism of a few rabbis who saw the rational functional design approach as deterring congregants from attending services.

During the 1960s, Jews experimented with new forms of religiosity,[144] and the focus of their synagogues' designs transformed to express more spirituality, community, and traditional values, while at the same time accommodating the synagogue's function and modernism. The main concept was to continue and exhibit the American value of freedom of religion.[145] As shown in figure 2.1, this development in design was part of the congregation's establishment of their identity and self-consciousness, as well as part of their confidence in living the American dream in the suburbs.

3 Synagogue Design Concepts

My House shall be called a house of prayer for all people. (*Isaiah 56:7*)

This chapter outlines the main design concepts of a synagogue and presents them in two main sections. The first looks at the general aspects of designing a sacred building and their relations to modern American synagogues. This section addresses the universal design concepts of houses of worship and the impact of specific faith requirements on their design. The second section addresses the design concepts pertinent to the Jewish faith. It introduces the religious functionality of the synagogue, as well as the spiritual experience the sanctuary creates where the familiar becomes significant and sacred.[1] Thus, it analyzes the architecture of the synagogue's interior, which is the focal point of the structure. Here, topics include the axes between the Ark and the bimah, their orientation, and their influence on the seating arrangements; flexible design of the sanctuary; light and openings; and the inclusion of abstract art. These major design principles apply to synagogues of all denominations (e.g., Orthodox, Conservatism, Reform) and, yet their various heritages (e.g., Ashkenazi and Sephardic). It should be noted that this book does not include the history and developments of each denomination. It focuses on the architecture of the synagogues and how, in all cases, the aim of designing the sanctuary is to "express in a physical structure the spirit of the Jewish congregation."[2] In other words, the design strives to increase the relationship between architecture, art, and Judaism in an attempt to enrich spirituality.

Introduction

The term *synagogue* is derived from *synage* in Greek, which means "to bring together;" in Hebrew it is called *Beth Knesset*, which is literally a house of gathering/assembly. Indeed, a synagogue is defined as a house of people and does not include or imply architectural/building terms. The emphasis of the term is on a quorum of ten men gathering for prayers (called *minyan*) and not necessarily on the built features.[3] Thus the act of gathering and praying, not based on any spatial or geometrical model, defines the synagogue. This notion can be found in Protestant theology, which also believes in the church as the people and not as a building.[4] Yet, in both religions, the house of worship plays "a crucial role in congregational self-definition and community recognition" in addition to creating the spiritual realm for the worshipers.[5] Though synagogues are built for men, in Genesis 28:17, the gathering space for praying is termed in Hebrew as *Beth Elokim*, which means a house of God. This interpretation served as the design concept for the Jerusalem Temple, but not necessarily for synagogues.

Synagogues often are also called temples. But in this case, the application of the term "temple" implies a gathering place that serves as a temporal replacement for the Holy Temple in Jerusalem as a means of keeping alive its memory.[6] A certain view considered that "the one temple in Jerusalem sank into the dust, in order that countless temples might arise to thy honor and glory."[7] Yet, there are fundamental differences between the Holy Temple and the synagogue. First, the Temple is mentioned in the scriptures, while synagogues are not, even though they were built before the destruction of the Second Temple.[8] Second, the Temple as the deity dwelling on Earth served the whole people of Israel,[9] while the synagogue serves a certain local community. The synagogue is built by men who believe that God stands among the congregation and appears everywhere.[10] Third, the synagogue's aim is to serve as a functional structure for human gathering and experiencing spirituality. However, the building is not necessarily a holy place where the divine spirit dwells.

As mentioned in the previous chapter, since the synagogue is not considered a holy building, gentiles (non-Jews) are allowed to design and build it.[11] Examples include the non-Jewish architects Frank Lloyd Wright and Minoru Yamasaki, who designed Beth Sholom Synagogue in Elkins Park, Pennsylvania, and North Shore Congregation Israel in Glencoe, Illinois, respectively. Analysis of these cases shows that the architects diligently studied the congregations' programmatic and spiritual needs. This impressed the rabbis and the buildings' committees, who believed that the architects' designs enhanced the spiritual experiences in the synagogue and impacted how the services are conducted in the sanctuary.[12]

The focus of the synagogue is on people, and as such, there are no specific architectural guidelines for its design. There are general references to particular rituals and services and to the design of the Jerusalem Temples. For example, the interpretations of the design of the First Jerusalem Temple are based on the description in the scriptures (1 Kings 6–7)[13] of how King Solomon built it during his fourth year of ruling Israel. Though there are almost no specific images or evidence of how exactly the two Temples were constructed and how they looked, some scholars attempted to create a guide of how they were

built.[14] It is believed that both the Tabernacle and the Temples "were designed on the model of the 'heavenly dwelling'" that was invisible to human eyes.[15] Thus, in a way, both the Tabernacle and the Temples became the real representation of the invisible. It is stated that the instructions given by God on how to build the Tabernacle were used in building the First Temple and continued to influence the rebuilding of the Second Temple. The instructions appear in the book of Exodus 8–9, starting with "And they are to make a sanctuary for Me, so that I may dwell among them. You must make the Tabernacle and design all its furniture according to the pattern I will show you." Following the scriptures, the Tabernacle was built as a tent: "How goodly are thy tents, O Jacob, and thy Tabernacles, O Israel."[16] Therefore, the tent motif became very popular in modern designs of synagogues. This motif also symbolizes the forty years the people of Israel wandered the desert. An appropriate example is the ceiling of Congregation Kneses Tifereth Synagogue, designed by Philip Johnson in Port Chester, New York (see chapter 5). The image of Mount Sinai is another ancient motif that became a symbol in modern synagogues. Mount Sinai plays a crucial role in biblical literature as a mythical place of no return, a place linked to the people's collective memory.[17] It is the mount of God's revelation (Exodus 19–24)—the mount where the Ten Commandments were given. This is expressed in Frank Lloyd Wright's Beth Sholom Synagogue's pyramidal building in Elkins Park, Pennsylvania (see chapter 4).

While the description of the Tabernacle is detailed in the book of Exodus, and the description of building the First Temple appears in the book of 1 Kings, the Second Temple can be found in the book of Ezra and Nehemiah. Apparently, the latter construction was based on the people's collective memory of the First Temple and the vision of the prophet Ezekiel.[18] This collective memory of the two Jerusalem Temples (the first was destroyed by the Babylonians in 586 BCE; the second was destroyed by the Romans in 70 CE) is embedded in Jewish history. It inspired and still affects the design of synagogues in the Holy Land and in the diaspora. The Rambam (Maimonides) suggests that the construction of a synagogue should keep the Temple's memory but not imitate its image.[19] It should be noted that the incorporation of the Temple's memory also includes the memory of its destruction. As such, it is expected that the latter be symbolically expressed in synagogue design by incorporating an unplastered piece of wall in the sanctuary. I found this symbol visible in the Congregation B'nai Israel Synagogue in Millburn, New Jersey, designed by architect Percival Goodman in 1950.

The collective memory of place is also translated into the rhythm of time. Similar to its celebration in the High Temples, time became part of the rituals associated with the synagogue.[20] Time defines the gathering of people for specific prayers. The cycle of the day is important for prayers of the morning (*Shacharit*) versus prayers of the evening (*Mincha*), so are the cycle of the week (Shabbat versus weekdays), and the cycle of the seasons (holidays).[21] Time is so essential that often it is considered more significant than space (see the next chapter). In building a synagogue, architects need to cater to these time cycles with a flexible design of the sanctuary to accommodate different numbers of worshipers. This constitutes a functional part of the faith. Modernist architect Philip Johnson saw the demand for a flexible sanctuary as the main challenge in the design of a synagogue.[22] He stated that only after the architect overcomes this "obstacle" can the rest of the programmatic and spiritual design be addressed.[23] The notion of spirituality and time was mentioned by modernist architect Eero Saarinen, who claimed that the design of a sacred building (not necessarily a synagogue) "would be a structure without time or place, and therefore of all times and places."[24] More specifically, while the synagogue should reflect time, its design should be both of current time and the timeless, thereby serving as the "focal point of the community's aspirations."[25]

The Halacha (Jewish Law) refers only to the interior functions of the synagogue and not to its architectural image. Ezekiel (11:16) saw the interior as a "little sanctuary" (in Hebrew *mikdash me-at*) that serves the Lord, thus referring to the representation of the invisible.[26] The earthly shrine imitates the heavenly dwelling,[27] and the inspiration of the design relies on religious and scholarly interpretations of the Temple's architectural images.[28] Moreover, the design should first adhere to the functional purpose of a gathering place, and then to its spirituality.[29] The lack of specific guidelines for building a synagogue, and the fear of persecution, pushed the Jews in diaspora to focus on the synagogue's interior, where they could gather and express their religious identity. To avoid identification of the synagogue from the exterior, synagogues' façades used architectural styles similar to churches or mosques in the area where congregations lived.[30] Often, congregations just used a simple dwelling as their gathering place, as seen in the Venice Jewish Quarter. Even in prosperous periods of acceptance of Jews, congregations built their houses of worship with glory but using fashionable architectural styles of the gentiles' houses of worship—for example, the seventeenth-century Sephardic synagogue in Amsterdam (Esnoga), built in Baroque architectural style, or the nineteenth-century Great Synagogue in Florence (Tempio Maggior), built as a cathedral synagogue in a Moorish Revival style. Still, restrictions posited by rulers and governments limited the design of synagogues' exteriors to avoid competition with churches or mosques. Examples include the limitation of synagogues' height to be lower than any church in the sixteenth century; or the nineteenth-century Grand Choral Synagogue, in Saint Petersburg, Russia (1893),[31] which was built more modest than its original design due to the ruling restrictions (e.g., height, faith symbols, etc.). It was built in a mixture of Byzantine and Moorish styles that resembles the styles of the Russian Orthodox churches in the surrounding area. In the modern era in the United States, when Jews realized the American value of freedom of religion, they allowed themselves to include Jewish symbols on the exterior of their synagogues. Since there were no specific guidelines for the exterior design, the congregations and architects could use Jewish symbols at their discretion. Some used Jewish symbols such as the Ten Commandments tablets or the Star of David as the basis for the design of the whole building (e.g., architects Walter Grupius; Pietro Belluschi); others added abstract art to the exterior to symbolize the Jewish faith and enhance the image of the synagogue (e.g., Percival Goodman; Loebl, Schlossman & Bennett).

The development of the Jewish house of worship in history, from the Tabernacle to the Holy Temples, to synagogues, reveals that there is no traditional architectural "Jewish style."[32] This freedom from faith dictation on the exterior design of the synagogue, the realization of freedom of religion in America during the 1950s, and the search for a new American Jewish identity were the foundation for congregations' departure from historicism, traditional European design of synagogues, and the eclectic design of synagogues in America. Prior to World War II, synagogues' styles in America were based on Greek, Byzantine, Moorish, and Renaissance Revival architecture and a combination of eclectic European traditional styles.[33] Scholars such as Lance J. Sussman and Samuel Gruber claim that the last prewar American great synagogue was Temple Emanu-El of New York City (1929–30), built in Italian Romanesque style.[34]

To help construct the new American suburban synagogue, in 1946 the Union of American Hebrew Congregations (UAHC)[35] published a modest guide for congregations moving to the suburbs and sponsored two conferences on synagogue architecture.[36] In 1948, the UAHC organized an Architects' Advisory Panel that traveled around the country and consulted with congregational building committees.[37] Eventually, this group published a series of guidelines for new synagogue construction.[38] In 1954, architect Peter Blake compiled and edited a reference book for synagogue design and construction that included a synagogue building checklist in order to "lay the foundation for a great renaissance in the architecture of synagogues."[39] His book consists of the historic background of synagogues, design approaches to modern synagogue construction, and technical issues of lighting, thermal comfort, and acoustics. Those guidelines called for a departure from historicism and a turn to modern architecture. Rabbi Alexander S. Kline's explanation of the failure of synagogues' historical styles served as the basis for adopting modernism. Kline claimed that the effort to create a Jewish architectural style

and the inability of these styles to convey the Jewish spirit have resulted in an eclectic architecture.[40] Thus, it was easy to adopt modernism with its simplicity, straight lines, and functionality, which expressed the modern spirit of Judaism and its straightforward religious teaching.[41]

American architects saw these projects as opportunities to design a sacred place inspired by universal and Jewish elements that enhance spirituality, while bridging the sacred with abstract faith symbols and particular religious functions. Though the concept of the sacred may be vague and elusive for operational definitions, it seems commonly accepted that there is a need to employ tangibles to "capture" spiritual entities.[42] Thus, the religious building is a juxtaposition of physical (tangible) and spiritual (intangible) realms that represents the multifaceted spiritual experiences of the worshiper.[43] The following analysis shows those universal elements of designing houses of worship as related to synagogue design. In addition, this chapter illustrates the synagogues' architectural concepts that bridge modernism with Judaism.

Design Concepts of Sacred Architecture and the Modern American Synagogues

Often the question of what makes a building sacred is answered by the nature of the activities conducted in that structure (e.g., individual and communal praying, meditation, formal religious holiday/festival services, and family milestone events). French sociologist David Émile Durkheim (1858–1917) believed that humans "need to have an enchantment in their lives that mystifies fundamental social relationships."[44] This need is also expressed in spiritual spheres of humanity "where man/woman seeks meaning to the complexity of life that can transcend daily reality."[45] While the concept of sacred seems elusive, literature shows that architectural features may enhance the sacredness of the building and the worshipers' spiritual experiences.

To decipher those features that make sacred architecture, I have developed a conceptual model that illustrates the relationships of faith, form, and building technology. The model that appears in my book *Frank Lloyd Wright's Sacred Architecture: Faith, Form, and Building Technology* elaborates on how these three components relate to determine the sacred form and its specific ambiance.[46] Faith unilaterally influences the form of the house of worship and its ambiance, while building technology (materials, systems, construction) has a bidirectional relation with form.[47] Form often dictates the selection of building technology, while at other times, building technology influences the form and its ambiance through the use of materials such as concrete, steel, and glass, and systems such as light, sound, and thermal comfort. These multirelations within a context of time and location determine the three-dimensional design and construction of the house of God.

Applying this model to the design of synagogues calls for some adaptation to cater to the specificity of Judaism. Figure 3.1 illustrates the relations among Judaism (faith), the synagogue's form (exterior, interior/ambiance), and building technology (constructions/structure, materials, and systems). Similar to my previous model, faith (Judaism) unilaterally influences the form of the synagogue. However, due to the lack of design guidelines on how to build the exterior image of the synagogue, the model shows a dashed arrow between faith (Judaism) and the synagogue's exterior, while a full arrow expresses the design guidelines of the interior that are directly influenced by faith. It should be noted that figure 3.1 represents a "dichotomous" model that illustrates Judaism as not having specific requirements for the exterior design. While other religions include specific dictations and guidelines for the design of their exterior houses of worship (e.g., until the modern era, Catholics required the design of their church to be longitudinal in the form of the Roman long cross; Muslims preferred mosques to have a central plan covered by a dome over the main sanctuary), synagogues did not include such specific design guidelines for their exterior. It was only in America and Israel where Jews felt free to use symbols on the synagogues'

Figure 3.1. The book's conceptual model: The relationships of faith (Judaism), form, and building technology

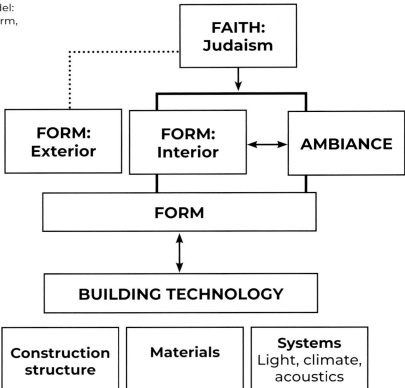

exteriors. As such, the "graphic" representation of the dichotomous conceptual model is a simplifying heuristic to highlight a particular dynamic.

The bidirectional influence between form and building technology includes materials and construction/structure that impacts the exterior and interior; as well as the systems that are directly related to the sanctuary's interior and enhance the spiritual experience in the sanctuary. The bidirectional arrow portrays the mutual relation between form and building technology. As mentioned before, usually the form dictates the use of specific building technologies; however, at times, the availability of building technology is the main factor in the design of certain forms.[48] In the case of modern American synagogues, building technology expresses the innovations of the era. In addition to innovative structural systems, new systems of light (e.g., electrical fixtures), thermal comfort (e.g., heating, ventilation, and air conditioning [HVAC]), and acoustics are also included. Thus, new building technologies pushed the envelope of the modern aesthetics of synagogues as well as many of the churches of the time.[49]

As illustrated in figure 3.1, faith has no impact on the synagogue's exterior design.[50] Yet the synagogue's interior design accommodates the classical proposition that "form follows faith." This can be considered a specific interpretation of the famous modern design concept "form follows function."[51] As described in the contextual model in chapter 2 (figure 2.1), the concept of "form follows function" was practically oriented and tended to be influenced by the machine and modernism. This motif did not necessarily consider the important psychological and spiritual elements of creating a sacred ambiance. This was the basis of the criticism by some leader rabbis who believed that the simplicity of modern materials and minimal decoration deterred members of the congregations from participating in the synagogue's religious services more often.[52] However, manifests and synagogue designs by architects such as Eric Mendelsohn emphasized the modernity principle of "form follows function" but also talked about maintaining the cultural spiritual aspect of "form follows faith" that enhances sacredness.[53] It

should be acknowledged that congregations that welcomed modernism in the 1950s and 1960s claimed later in the 1970s and 1980s that the buildings appeared cold and formal in comparison to postmodern new houses of worship.[54] A good example of this change in orientation is the 1979 addition of a small chapel to Minuro Yamasaki's 1964 modern synagogue of North Shore Congregation Israel in Glencoe, Illinois. The chapel was designed by Chicago architects Hammond Beeby & Babka as a postmodern prayer hall embracing traditional European styles. North Shore Congregation Israel's Rabbi Herbert Bronstein stated that people want a sense of sanctity, not just religiosity.[55]

The combination of functionality and spirituality in the design of a synagogue is introduced in the following subsections and unfolds into two levels: (a) the universal commonalities across faith that make a space sacred and (b) the particular faith (Judaism) requirements and symbolism that influence the design.

Universal Commonalities across Faith and Modern American Synagogues

Across faith, religious perception of the cosmos and the fundamental elements that built it is driven by the search for the divine presence. It refers to God's creation and its spiritual forces that shimmer the cosmos.[56] Throughout history, human perception of the creation has evolved upon myth, rituals, religion, and science. In turn, these pushed sacred architecture to replicate the universe and its order. Sacred architecture is perceived as the intersection between heaven and earth, and a place of cosmological myth.[57] Following this notion, modern architect Eric Mendelsohn claimed that in his synagogue designs he expresses the unknown and "the symbol of man's finite life within the infinite cosmos."[58] This was accomplished by emphasizing the building's dramatic image (e.g., light and shadow, color, texture, geometry, and materials).

The infinite cosmos was introduced already in Genesis 1, where the mighty Creator created the universe out of nothing—an idea that became a major source of myth and mystery for popular religions and a main theme of investigation and interpretations of elite discussions in theology, philosophy, and science.[59] Linguist anthropologist Claude Lévi-Strauss claims that architectural relation to the creation of the cosmos and its elements is used to enhance the sacredness of the house of worship.[60] Such is the perception in Jewish belief that the foundation stone of the universe was located in front of the Ark in the Jerusalem Temples and served as the base of the world's creation.[61] In modernity, the creation story is still relevant. Some, like architect Frank Lloyd Wright, asserted that the closest thing we can see of God's creation is nature, and therefore, sacred architecture should express it.[62] Architects Roberto Chiotti and Michael Nicholas-Schmidt claim that in understanding nature and the meaning of materials, the designer has an opportunity to introduce the sacred through the relationship between his creation and the Creator's.[63]

The study of the book of Genesis also shows that the creation's description depicts the four universal elements of earth, air, fire, and water that built the cosmos. Discussions concerning the order in which the various elements were created are typical of the teachings of the creation as recorded since ancient times to today.[64] Earth and air (heaven) are mentioned already in the first verse of Genesis, "In the beginning God created the heaven and the earth." The element of fire is represented by light, which immediately follows earth and air: "And God said: 'Let there be light.' And there was light. And God saw the light, that it was good; and God divided the light from the darkness" (Genesis 1:3–4). Light is mentioned again in verses 14, 16, and 17 as an important factor of the universe. It is represented by the sun, the moon, and the stars. The fourth element, water, appears in verse 2 where "the Spirit of God was hovering over the face of the waters." Then in verses 7 and 9: "And God said: 'Let the waters under the heaven be gathered together unto one place, and let the dry land appear.' And it was so."

Scholars have interpreted each element, studying its symbolism in sacred geometry and its architectural archetypal forms.[65] I attempt to associate the four elements with materiality, such as architectural forms, the building's construction and finish

materials, and systems that define the sacred ambiance. Specifically, I accept the notion that earth represents stability and permanence and is expressed not only through materials but can also be translated into central plans of the design, such as using a square, which is called a *noble form*. Ancient sacred architecture perceived the square as a symbol of earth, as it symbolized the earthly realm. Frank Lloyd Wright used the square in his Unity Temple, Oak Park, Illinois (1906), as a steady form that demonstrates the "mutual relations between firm, construction materials and technology."[66] Though most modern synagogues were designed in rectangular forms, they were constructed of masonry, which represents earth and stability. Masonry such as stone also represents the layers of earth; brick is produced using earth; and concrete and cement are made of sand, aggregates, and volcanic ashes (earth), in combination with water and air.

Air represents the sky and heaven and is translated into a circle, domes, skylights, and openings. The circle, its geometrical derivation, and its combination with a square symbolize the universe and the sacred realm. The circle expresses the divine, infinite, and eternal. These architectural features emphasize the sacred vertical axis, which is a prominent aspect of all houses of worship and represents the human yearning to be closer to the divine. Often, verticality helps to bring light (fire) into the sanctuary, which captures the divine presence. See, for example, the domical structure of Park Synagogue in Cleveland, Ohio, by Eric Mendelsohn. Mendelsohn tried to make the dome "float" above the walls by introducing horizontal transparent glass windows below the dome and above the walls as a symbol of sky and heaven (see chapter 4).

Fire is an integral part of the production of most construction materials and of buildings' systems (e.g., HVAC, lighting). In addition, fire in the form of light is an essential element in creating the sacred ambiance, with the introduction of natural light and light fixtures. Light, in addition to its functional tasks of providing safety and enabling reading, creates the dramatic atmosphere in the sanctuary.[67] Architect Louis Kahn emphasized natural light as the beautifying element of the building since "a space can never reach its place in architecture without natural light . . . [it] gives mood by space, by the nuances of light during the day and the seasons of the year as it enters and modifies the space."[68] Light and darkness symbolize day and night in nature, the poetic and actual in the sacred building.[69] Various lighting designs can reinforce light as one of the most dramatic elements in sacred architecture. For example, in Frank Lloyd Wright's Beth Sholom Synagogue, a double-layer translucent roof creates a beacon of light. During the day it spreads even soft light into the sanctuary, while during the night, light beams out of the building to the community around the synagogue.[70]

The element of fire (light) is also used in faith symbols. For example, in Judaism, the menorah, a sacred candelabrum with seven branches, was placed in the Jerusalem Temple. It became a feature in every synagogue to commemorate the Holy Temple and its destruction. An additional feature in the synagogue

is the Ner Tamid fixture (the eternal light), which serves as the spiritual light in Judaism (see details later in this chapter).

Water "precedes every form and sustain[s] every creation."[71] It is a symbol of purity, and like air, carries sounds and establishes the thresholds between the sacred and the outside world. In Judaism, the mikveh, a water pool/bath used for ritual immersion and purity, is often part of the synagogue complex or is located in a separate building (such as in Park Synagogue in Cleveland, Ohio). Water also is part of the production of construction and finished materials (i.e., it is used in making bricks, concrete, and cement), and is associated with acoustics since it can carry the waves of sound or destruct the noise by creating its own sound of moving water.

Figure 3.2 illustrates the TriBeCa Synagogue sanctuary in Manhattan, New York, designed in 1967 by architect William Breger, a student of Walter Gropius. This example shows the four universal elements

Figure 3.2. TriBeCa Synagogue in Manhattan, New York (1967), designed by William Breger: The sanctuary

as expressed in a combination of concrete ceiling/ roof, brick and wooden walls, steel and glass skylight, and wooden furniture. The masonry materials, steel, and glass represent the materiality of the four elements, while, above the bimah, the skylight that was created in between the thin-shell concrete ceilings/ roofs[72] lights the Ark and creates the spiritual ambiance within the synagogue. In addition, the concrete and brick express earth, which by the Kabbalah is interpreted as feminine since it nourishes "the seed giving rise to progeny—the harvest, that represents the activity of both men and women."[73] Looking at the interior of this synagogue, we notice the design of curved, soft lines (figure 3.2), which can be also interpreted as a feminine line of design. More so, the word *Schechinah* (God's spirit) is described as a Goddess in the *Zohar*[74] (1:246a) and other Jewish studies. *Schechinah* in Hebrew is also associated with the *Mishkan* (God's dwelling) and indicates the divine presence, which is written in the Hebrew scriptures (Exodus 25:8) and rabbinic literature as a feminine word. Understanding this word/concept may shed light on how this Orthodox congregation accepted this modern and feminine unique design. They embraced the presence of God's spirit within their synagogue.[75]

In addition to the perception that the four elements construct the universe, it is believed that the cosmos's horizontal and vertical axes define its structure. These axes are the basis for the geometry of the sacred place and influence the sacred architectural form and construction. Thus the universe's geometry, order, and symbolism of shapes can be translated into elements of sacred architecture.[76] The horizontal axis represents the line of earth. The vertical links the underground, earth, and heaven, and creates the axis of the world (the axis mundi) that brings God's creation into the sacred building.[77]

Indeed, in modern American houses of worship, including synagogues, verticality is expressed through the design of special roofs that use modern materials such as concrete, glass, and steel. Domes, vaults, hyperbolic parabolic shapes, thin-shell concrete, glass and plastic, are some examples. As mentioned in the previous chapter, modern religious architecture became a study in dramatic

roofs. Architects and engineers experimented with structural systems that worked well with the plasticity of materials in order to reach the height and form of their dramatic and often sculptural roofs. They experimented with new materials, structural systems, and technologies of the modern time to celebrate materiality and humanity (see examples in chapters 4 and 5, such as Frank Lloyd Wright's Beth Sholom Synagogue in Elkins Park, Pennsylvania; Perceval Goodman's Shaarey Zedek Synagogue in Southfield, Michigan; and Sidney Eisenshtat's Temple Sinai in El Paso, Texas).

Sacred verticality is mentioned already in Genesis 28:10–22 with the story of Jacob's dream in Bethel.[78] He saw a ladder (stairway) reaching from the earth to heaven, and the angels of God were ascending and descending on it. Then, he heard the Lord's voice. This energy of the upward movement reaching to heaven and downward reaching the earth became a symbol of the axis mundi (the axis of the world) that creates a spiritual experience with a climax of God's voice.

This axis may represent the verticality of the location of the house of worship or the morphology of the building itself. For example, the Jerusalem Temple was located on Mount Zion—the highest place in the city of Jerusalem. It served as the axis mundi of the city, which is perceived as the center of the Holy Land, which in turn is the center of the universe.[79] In ancient times, Mount Zion, as with other mountains, was an integral part of the biblical cosmos and its sacred geography.[80] Ascending toward the Jerusalem Temple prepared the worshiper to leave day-by-day experiences and be ready to enter the Temple to get closer to the divine. This journey combines the sacred path (the horizontal axis) with verticality (the axis mundi). The mount's height points to divinity and provides security.[81] Mountains are also perceived as the link between heaven, earth, and the underworld. Robert Cohn claims that the sacredness of Mount Zion is in its erased boundary between heaven and earth.[82] On one hand, God sits on the top of the mountain; yet, at the same time, God resides in the Temple. King Solomon, in his dedication speech of the First Temple, said, "The heaven and the highest heaven cannot contain thee; how much less this house which I have built" (1 Kings 8:27).

The notion of height as part of the definition of the Temple's location later directed the preferred sites for synagogues. However, restrictions by governments and city ordinances in the diaspora denied Jews from using the higher sites in the city/area. These limitations called for a reinterpretation of the meaning of height.[83] The focus of the height dimension shifted from the location of the synagogue to the height of the building. Domes and high ceilings expressed the axis mundi of the building and the congregations' yearning to be closer to heaven. Still, it should be noted that this was difficult to accomplish during periods of additional restrictions that did not allow the synagogues to exceed the heights of local houses of worship.

To reach the axis mundi of the synagogue, Jewish Kabbalah[84] expresses spatial hierarchy and sequence as bringing "the worshiper through a clearly defined threshold into the inner sanctum separated from the profane."[85] This notion is actually a description of the sacred path that expresses a journey as a pilgrimage from the mundane to the transcending spiritual realm that reveals the vertical axis of the space.[86] This transition is enhanced by setting apart the house of worship. The attempt to separate the house of worship from the mundane is an additional aspect of sacred architecture that appears across religions. The idea of separation already appears in the Old Testament: "I am set apart and you must set apart like me" (Leviticus 11:46); and "Take the sandals from your feet, for the place on which you stand is holy ground" (Exodus 3:5; Joshua 5:15). It also is expressed in different definitions of separation in various ancient languages. The Hebrew word *k-d-sh* for "holy" is used to refer to the separate holy sacred, while the world *sacer* in Latin defines the areas set apart and pertinent to God, and the Latin word *templum* means to cut out.[87]

This journey from outside to enter the sacred continues inside the Temple's complex as the worshipers move through a hierarchy of spaces before reaching the holiest of the holy. This inner path characterizes most houses of worship, including synagogues. The journey into the synagogue starts through a courtyard located in the front or on the side of the building. This courtyard is one of the thresholds before entering the sanctuary. The Maharal of Prague, a rabbi from the sixteenth century, mentioned this journey when he explained the need for two entrances to the synagogue's complex.[88] One entrance separates the worshiper from the street (the mundane); the other serves as the entrance to the holy, where the worshiper seeks to be closer to the divine. Thus the journey is characterized by a series of thresholds creating hierarchical layers of spaces.

The courtyard feature evolved from the Tabernacle to the Holy Temples and then to synagogues. In the Temple, the courtyard was used to perform sacrifices, and to announce punishments and lost items.[89] As such, it became a public courtyard similar to the Babylonian city square where Ezra read the Torah to the people of Israel (Ezra 8:1–5). In the synagogue, the courtyard becomes the first threshold—a space that prepares the worshiper to leave the mundane and enter the sacred. Often, it includes sinks for washing hands as a symbol of purification. It also serves as a place for services in the summer, as an extension place for holiday prayers, as well as a space for celebrations of festivals and family events, or as an outer lobby to enter the building. In America, many modern synagogues include courtyards as the first threshold, serving as the entrance to the synagogue (see chapter 5). In those synagogues, the journey into the sanctuary is through a foyer or a corridor leading to the sanctuary. Often, an inner courtyard connects the various parts of the synagogues, extends the interior space, and enables light and air to penetrate the interior (see chapters 4 and 5).

The notion of the sacred as another world is summarized by Mircea Eliade as a representation of the other reality "which does not belong to this world."[90] In this sense, the modern design of synagogues focused on creating the "other world" inside the building not only using the religious requirements and symbols but also introducing the play of light and shadows and abstracted art to emphasize the sacred. These help create majestic sacred interiors (see the various examples in the following chapters).

In summary, the design of these monuments as sacred architecture was based on the utility of universal commonalities across faith that characterize a space sacred. These commonalities are related to the creation of the cosmos, the elements that build it (e.g., earth, air, fire, water), the axes of the world, and the meanings of materials. They impact the geometry of the building and its form, and maintain the building as a transcended realm separated from the mundane.

The other part of the inquiry of what makes a building sacred relates to a faith's particular requirements, as expressed in its specific rituals and traditions. For example, the procession requirement by the Catholic Church is associated with the symbol of the longitudinal cross, which became the footprint of the church's floor plan. Other specific requirements can be found across faiths: the building's orientation (toward the sun or a specific holy city), its seating arrangements (mainly the separation of men and women), lighting requirements, and particular iconography and symbols. The following section describes the specific Jewish requirements for synagogue design.

Judaism's Particular Requirements and Modern American Synagogues

Some claim that during the post–World War II era in America, architects attempted to relate the synagogue's exterior façade to the interiors, suggesting the bimah's interior location on the exterior.[91] A good example is Temple Oheb Shalom in Baltimore, Maryland (1957), designed by Walter Gropius and architects Leavitt Associates. The synagogue expresses the interior location of the original bimah on the main façade, with a curved concrete wall decorated with an abstracted metal depiction of the Ten Commandments tablets. The Decalogue became the motif of the building itself, which is built as four large vaults from brick and concrete, with a metal roof. Some view each pair as the tablets, while others find them to resemble factory turbines (figure 3.3). Moreover, smaller vaults built from brick appear as decorations on the entrance's concrete façade. The

combination of an industrial design with a faith symbol expresses abstracted faith symbols built with the use of new building technologies and reflects modernism.

This section analyzes the requirement of the synagogue to be oriented toward Jerusalem, as well as the seating arrangement, which is determined by the spatial relation between the Ark and the bimah, by the congregation's origin (e.g., Ashkenazi or Sephardic), and by their denomination (e.g., Orthodox, Conservative, Reform). A separated seating area for women in Ashkenazi and Sephardic Orthodox synagogues[92] is supposed to be designated either in a balcony/gallery above the main hall (figure 1.2) or by a divider called a *mechitzah* (figure 3.4). This arrangement also accommodates the perception that prayers for men are an act of spirituality and religious ritual that embeds the worshiper, while prayers for women are only spiritual and often only an acoustical experience, as the visual aspect is usually blocked.[93]

Before detailing the interior specifics, it is important to note that modern American synagogues of the 1950s and 1960s served as cores of Jewish life beyond just prayer houses. This idea followed the 1940s vision of Reconstructionist Rabbi Mordecai Kaplan (1881–1983).[94] He saw the synagogue as a community center that also includes sports, cultural, and social activities.[95] It is interesting to note that though this seemed like an innovative idea at the time, it already appeared in antiquity when the synagogues of Babylon served as centers of Jewish life in addition to places of praying.[96] The synagogues' program included the praying space and the community's activities areas. In the 1950s, architect Eric Mendelsohn was one of the first to include in his designs of American synagogues a school, a social hall, a kitchen, and community offices, reviving the traditional concept of combining religious activities and educational programs with social activities as part of the complex's functional program. The challenge for modern architects in America was the integration of all these functions (e.g., the praying wing, the education wing, and the social wing, as well as an administration wing) into one cohesive community center complex.

Figure 3.3. Temple Oheb Shalom in Baltimore, Maryland (1957), designed by Walter Gropius and Leavitt Associates: The main façade, inspired by the Decalogue, resembles factory turbines. Note the new addition/entrance on the side of the façade.

Figure 3.4. TriBeCa Synagogue in Manhattan, New York (1967), designed by William Breger: An example of a *mechitza* separating men's and women's seating in the sanctuary

These complexes became the trademarks of congregations, especially in the suburbs, and served as their proud institutions. The buildings manifested the rebirth of Jewish life after the Holocaust and the start of the process of belonging to America. Though the synagogues of the 1950s were built as complexes for religion, education, and social activities, the focus of the buildings was always on religion. During the late 1960s, congregations continued the process of Americanization, and synagogues shifted from religious to educational centers.[97] Congregations developed new programs such as school complexes for children and adults, music and art centers, and Jewish community centers[98] that attracted young families from the suburbs and cities and catered to their individual needs. Professor Kay Kaufman Shelemay emphasizes that these programs "generated a rich array" of the arts, especially sacred and secular musical activities.[99] The described shift highlights the synagogue's role as a social institution in American Jewish life.

Design Concepts of the Synagogue's Interior

This section introduces the main and general design concepts of synagogues' interiors in three subsections: the relation between the Ark and bimah and their orientation, the idea of a flexible design that caters to changes in occupancy, and the inclusion of art in the building. These concepts are common to all types of synagogues and are dominant in their sanctuary designs, while the variations and specific design details are illustrated in the examples in chapters 4 and 5.

The Axis between the Ark and the Bimah and Their Orientation

In all types of synagogues, the most important concept that defines the religious service and allows it to be communicated to the congregation is the axis between the synagogue's two focal points: the Ark and the bimah.[100] The Ark (*Aron Hakodesh*) is a cabinet where the Tablets of Law, the Ten Commandments are contained in the Tabernacle (*Ohel Mo'ed*). In synagogues, the Ark holds the Torah scrolls, while the second focal point of this axis is the bimah, a rostrum (stage) where the Torah is read (figure 3.5). The bimah is a freestanding feature representing the movement of the Tabernacle.[101] According to the Jewish Kabbala, the bimah symbolizes the altar, while other scholars compare it to Mount Sinai from where Moses read the Ten Commandments.[102] It is supposed to be made of wood to resemble the wooden pulpit from where Ezra read the Law (Nehemiah 8:4). Usually, it is covered with a decorative cloth so the Torah will not touch the mundane wood. It is central to the space, and its relation to the Ark determines the relationship between the space and the worshipers, the

Figure 3.5. Fifth Avenue Synagogue, New York City (1959), designed by Percival Goodman: An example of an Ark and a bimah

Figure 3.6. Baltimore Hebrew Congregation, Baltimore, Maryland (1953), designed by Percival Goodman: The bimah, Ark, eternal light, and menorah

entrance(s), as well as the seating arrangement.[103] The architecture of these elements, especially the bimah, "has the capacity to encapsulate all the theological and liturgical traditions of a congregation"[104] (figure 3.6).

The location of the Ark is always oriented toward Jerusalem, either standing at the end wall of the synagogue or in a niche in the wall called the *heichal*. Often, two columns frame the niche, reminiscent of the columns in Solomon's Temple.[105] The Ark's location points the worshipers toward Jerusalem in their prayers, as is said in Psalms (16:8), "I have set the LORD always before me." The Ark is considered the symbol of God's presence in the synagogue. As such, worshipers should face the Ark and, in that way, face the holy and the divine spirit (Isaiah 45:15). In addition, the book of Daniel tells that he was praying and thanking God three times a day facing Jerusalem. It is interesting to note that the seats of the congregation's leaders (the rabbi and the cantor) are placed on each side of the Ark facing the worshipers.

However, when reading the Torah from the bimah, they stand facing the Ark—Jerusalem. Thus it can be interpreted that they are part of the people and not part of the sacred location of the Ark.

The bimah's location was developed through history and was determined by the congregation's denomination and their ancestral traditions and rituals. Two major types of traditions can be identified. The Ashkenazi Jews used a central location of the bimah, where the worshipers sit around the bimah in a u-shape format facing the Ark.[106] Typically, the central location of the bimah was defined by four decorated columns, a special decorated ceiling above, and a hanging chandelier. This definition of the bimah space was lost once the central arrangement was developed into a theatre design,[107] where the bimah is located close to and in the front of the Ark. The theatre arrangement enhances the focal point of the synagogue, where all members face both the Ark and the bimah at the same time.

The second type of bimah location is on an axis facing the Ark, which is mainly used by Sephardic Jews. The bimah is situated in the middle of the sanctuary or at the opposite end of the space, on the other side of the Ark. The worshipers sit on both sides of the bimah, which allows them to view each other and the reader/rabbi/cantor in the middle. The bimah is elevated and can be reached by a few steps. This provides a better view of the bimah and better acoustics. In addition, and similar to the historic Ashkenazi arrangement, the bimah is surrounded by four columns that determine its setting and includes a special decorated ceiling above it and a hanging chandelier. Synagogues in Muslim countries included, in addition to the four columns around the bimah, a lantern with windows above it that introduce light for reading the Torah.[108] Thus the emphasis on the centrality of the bimah in these synagogues creates a space within a space, with enhanced light and acoustic qualities.

The prominent modern architects selected for this book[109] designed their synagogues in the Ashkenazi theatre seating arrangement, in which the bimah is located on the stage in front of the Ark and the worshipers are seated in rows facing both. In this case, the bimah essentially merges with the platform before the Ark and produces a unified pulpit (figure 3.7).[110] This unification calls for the bimah to serve as both a liturgical and nonliturgical lectern.[111] Still, some of the congregations asked to break this unity and include an additional lectern to be used only for nonliturgical announcements such as sermons (see chapter 5). In addition to the bimah, the Conservative and Reform synagogues include an organ and a choir. These are located either behind the Ark as in the case of Belluschi's Temple B'naj Jeshurun Synagogue (see chapter 5), or in a gallery opposite the stage of the Ark and the bimah, as in the case of Yamasaki's North Shore Congregation Israel Synagogue (see chapter 4). This change to include

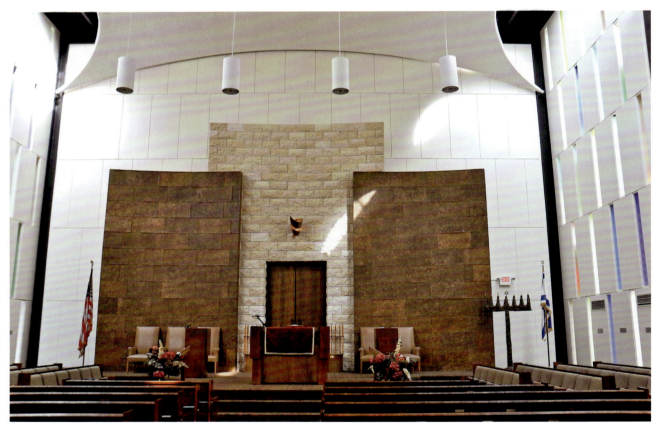

Figure 3.7. Philip Johnson's Kneses Tifereth Israel Synagogue in Port Chester, New York (1956): The current bimah in front of the Ark designed by Michael Berkowicz (2005)

instrumental music in liturgical services called for some acoustic measures that were not necessarily a major consideration in synagogue design. The focus has always been only on the rabbi for speech and the cantor for singing. Therefore, the bimah's position was also acoustically meaningful. Locating it in the middle of the congregation solved the issue, and when the bimah was moved to the stage in front of the Ark, the design tended to push it forward, closer to the congregation. Today, most of the bimahs and pulpits rely on the addition of an audio system.

Flexible Design of the Synagogue's Sanctuary

As mentioned before, an essential synagogue design requirement is the need for a flexible sanctuary space. The sanctuary supposes to serve as a daily chapel, as a sanctuary for Shabbat services, and as a space for expanding numbers of worshipers during the high holidays. The Union of American Hebrew Congregations (Reforms) emphasized in a 1946 pamphlet on "Synagogue Building Plans" the need for flexible rooms to expand seating accommodations for worshipers. In the same year, the United Synagogues of America (Conservative) also published a "Manual for Synagogue Building Committee," edited by Stanley Rabinowitz. This manual included various architects' proposals (especially Percival Goodman's) as examples of positioning the social hall close/adjacent to the sanctuary with a divider between them to be open during high holidays for additional seating (see Goodman's design concepts in chapter 5). Most architects in mid-twentieth-century America followed Goodman's concept and designed partitions, such as sliding doors, to divide the sanctuary for different occasions or to open it to an adjacent social hall. This arrangement of a space flowing into another space was defined as an "open plan"[112] or "expanding synagogue" to host the overflow of worshipers during high holidays.[113]

Other architects designed a separate small chapel in addition to a large sanctuary as part of the complex (e.g., Eric Mendelsohn, Percival Goodman, Sidney Eisenshtat). While the large sanctuary serves for Shabbat and holiday services, the small chapels serve for daily prayers, often for Shabbat prayers, and sometimes for intimate family celebrations. In Mendelsohn's Park Synagogue, the chapel also serves for adult study of the Torah.

Openings and Light

Light is one of the most dramatic features in the design of houses of worship, as it puts humans in touch with the eternal.[114] The Illumination Engineering Society's (IES) standards for houses of worship require that light reveals the sacred space while highlighting the building's architectural and artistic values. It established four major categories and their quantities of light. Mollie M. Clarahan[115] looked at these categories as layers of light and defined them as (a) task lighting (functional) for the pragmatic and mundane needs of a specific faith (e.g., reading the sacred texts, performing rituals to be observed by those present, and ensuring safety in the building); (b) accent lighting (spiritual) that draws the worshipers' eyes to brighter areas and highlights specific features such as religious items of importance; (c) architectural lighting (functional and spiritual) that adds to the drama of the service by illuminating the sanctuary and its symbols, which can be defined as the ambiance of the sacred place; and (d) celebration light (spiritual) that represents the divine. The four categories of lighting design in houses of worship are expressed in synagogues as follows. Task and architectural (ambiance) lights are the main concepts of lighting design in synagogues. Task light is important for the worshipers' requirements to read, recite prayers, and participate in the service. The light on the bimah is also critical for reading the Torah and often calls for skylights above the wooden pulpit (figure 3.2). Architectural light highlights the sacredness of the synagogue's sanctuary to become a beacon of light. This ambiance/atmosphere light is significant as a metaphor for enlightenment. The prophet Isaiah saw light as the "LORD shall be unto thee an everlasting light, and thy God thy glory" (Isaiah 60:19). Accent lighting is less pronounced in the design of the synagogue due to the lack of iconography. Yet it is common to include twelve windows as symbols of the twelve tribes of Israel.[116] Indeed, during antiquity, most synagogues included three windows on each side of the building. This was an inspiration for new synagogues as well, along with the celebration light associated with the Shabbat, certain holidays, and festivities. All categories agree that light offers "a hopeful sanctuary in a shadowy void, a safe-haven in the ontological night, a friendly harbour in the cosmic sea."[117]

There are no specific guidelines for the use of glass in synagogues. The prophet Isaiah talked about light as a feature to honor God (Isaiah 24:15). As such, openings were considered a symbolic element that honored the Temple. By the Halacha and the Kabbalah, soft light was distributed in the High Temples of Jerusalem via transparent and opaque glass windows. The transparent ones were located high above eye level to prevent worshipers from looking outside and being distracted from their prayers and studies.[118] Following the High Temple designs, historic synagogues used transparent glass at the top, mainly above the bimah,[119] and opaque glass for the rest of the windows. Painted or stained glass openings were not common and were added later in time. In modern times, examples include Percival Goodman's combination of opaque and transparent glass walls in the B'nai Israel Synagogue in Millburn, New Jersey, and the stained-glass windows in the eastern wall of his Shaarey Zedek Synagogue in Southfield, Michigan.[120]

Other modern American architects such as Eric Mendelsohn and Minoru Yamasaki introduced a new concept of light in synagogue design. They used transparent glass in the sanctuary's windows to stream natural light into the sanctuary (see the next chapter). The architects believed that connecting the sanctuary with nature on the outside brings God in. This notion corresponds to Frank Lloyd Wright's position that nature is God and "nature is all the body God has by which we may become aware of Him."[121]

Modern architects viewed lighting design in houses of worship similarly to Clarahan's idea of multilayering. They used different techniques in their lighting design, taking into consideration the movement of the sun and the elements that create shadows. Their design avoided glare and let soft light stream into the sanctuary, creating a special mood in the space. Frank Lloyd Wright introduced soft light that is distributed evenly in Beth Sholom Synagogue. The layers of glass and plastic produce white opaque light since he believed that God would create the colors of light (see chapter 4). Minoru Yamasaki, in his design of North Shore Congregation in Glencoe, Illinois, used amber gilded glass to fill the slits between the concrete fan shell vaults in the walls and the roof (see chapter 4). His combination of transparent glass in the lower windows, amber gilded glass in the slit windows, and an opaque skylight introduces changes in the reflection of light on the white walls and on architectural details. These reflections create a play of light and shadows on the smooth walls, generate warm tones, and increase spiritual experiences.

The Inclusion of Art in Synagogues

As mentioned in the beginning of this section on synagogues' interior design, another important contribution of modern American synagogues is the introduction into the sanctuary of abstracted art, which elevated the artwork from decorated functional religious elements to abstracted artistic contributions.

The inclusion of art in synagogues depends on the strictness of the interpretation of the second commandment: "Thou shalt not make unto thee any graven image, or any likeness of anything that is in heaven above, or that is in the earth beneath, or that is in the water under the earth" (Exodus 20:4). Jews throughout history interpreted this law to restrict any artistic creation in synagogues.[122] This meaning was intensified by the verse "With Me, therefore, you shall not make any gods of silver, nor shall you make for yourselves any gods of gold" (Exodus 20:20). Thus the idea was to avoid art that may depict the image of God and the Holy that may tempt the worshiper to return to paganism, or later to turn to Christianity. Though the Talmud (Jewish Law) was never clear about the inclusion of art in the synagogue and did not mention it as an "outright forbidding attitude,"[123] the negative interpretation toward art remained. This attitude stemmed from the ascetic frame of mind that the Torah is the "only truly worthwhile intellectual pursuit."[124] In addition, periods of hostility from the gentile world prevented Jews from glorifying the exteriors of their synagogues. However, these restrictions did not limit the expression of Jewish liturgical practice and "Jewishness"[125] in the interior design and decoration of synagogues. This was justified by the Halacha's request to beautify God's surroundings.[126] Regardless, the synagogue's interior was assumed to be simple in order to not distract the worshipers[127] and to withstand the threats of idolatry to monotheistic Judaism.[128]

The work of art in the Second Jerusalem Temple was based on Ezekiel's account of the art in the First Temple. It focused on the *cherubim* (carob) and palm trees, which symbolize the power and presence of God and survival in the desert.[129] In addition, Ezekiel's description includes two faces—one of a man and one of a lion.[130] Ancient synagogues in the Holy Land included stone decoration at the entrance façades and mosaic floors in the interior.[131] Seven of these floors have been discovered in Israel. All consist of biblical scenes, the zodiac (representing a calendar), the image of the synagogue's Ark and its surroundings, and the menorah. Figures 3.8a and 3.8b illustrate such a mosaic floor from the late fifth to early sixth century found in Zippori, an ancient town located on a hill in Lower Galilee, Israel. It was the home of Talmudic scholars from the end of the second century. Figure 3.9 shows the mosaic floor in Beit Alpha Synagogue from the beginning of the sixth century. It is located in the Beit She'an Valley, in the northeast of Israel. The entire floor of the prayer hall is paved in mosaic. It consists of a personification of the four seasons of the zodiac along its circumference. This mosaic also depicts figurative images describing the "offering of Isaac" biblical story. The synagogue building was designed as a typical synagogue of the time. It measures almost sixty-one by fifty feet and consists of a courtyard (atrium), a vestibule (narthex), and a prayer hall that faces Jerusalem.[132] The walls are constructed from undressed stone, with plastered inner and outer faces. These synagogues'

floors are great examples of the inclusion of art in synagogues. Some claim that the mosaics inspired the relations of art and architecture in modern American synagogues.[133]

Another example of a period when art was expressed in synagogues is the ancient synagogue of Dura Europos in Syria. It was discovered by archeologists in 1932 and revealed exquisite wall paintings that could not be reached or seen from 256 CE when the city fell into the hands of the Persians.[134] Numerous scholars studied these paintings and their meanings in Jewish learning, especially their relationship to Ezekiel's description of the "vision of the valley of dry bones" (Ezekiel 37).[135] Other scholars focused on the paintings' influences on Jewish and Christian art.[136] The archeological findings and their interpretations illustrate the importance of art in synagogues. However, from the third century, the fear of idolatry pushed the fundamentalist rabbis to reject figurative paintings, mosaics, and sculptures. They based it on Leviticus 26:1, which prohibited idols and grave images. Avram Kampf claims that external political pressures and a strong central control "brought about hardening" of this attitude.[137]

With the gradual disappearance of the fear of idolatry later in history, the use of art increased in popularity.[138] In 1870, Rabbi Leopold Löw studied postbiblical literature and the different interpretations of the second commandment (Exodus 20:4) forbidding the worship of man-made things representing god or gods.[139] The results of his analyses showed that Jews exhibited a need for art in their synagogues but that the attitudes of Jewish theology were still discouraging this endeavor.[140] As such, at the end of the nineteenth century and the beginning of the twentieth century, art and artifacts in synagogues were confined only to liturgical objects and were considered functional religious items. These were labeled as Judaic art and craft.[141] Examples of this type of artwork include the covering of the Torah scrolls in multiple layers to protect and beautify the scrolls. Figures 3.10 and 3.11 show Torah scrolls that are covered with a curtain (called the mantel) and protected with an ornamented silver case adorned with a crown (known as the *keter*). The *keter* is typically made of silver that rests on

Figure 3.8a. A synagogue in Zippori, Israel (late-fifth century/early sixth century): A mosaic floor

Figure 3.8b. A synagogue in Zippori, Israel (late-fifth century/early sixth century): The zodiac image in the mosaic floor of the synagogue

Figure 3.9. A sywnagogue in Beit Alpha, Israel (sixth century): A mosaic floor

Figure 3.10. Park Synagogue, Cleveland, Ohio (1953), designed by Eric Mendelsohn: An example of Judaica art pieces protecting and glorifying the Torah scroll

Figure 3.11. Temple Mount Sinai in El Paso, Texas (1962), designed by Sidney Eisenshtat: An example of a Judaica art piece protecting and glorifying the Torah scroll

two wooden shafts, which extend above the scrolls. The crown symbolizes honor and respect for the Torah. It is believed that "the visibility of liturgical elements . . . confirms the sanctity of the space."[142] Art in houses of worship should be "liturgical significant rather than just aesthetically pleasing and decorative."[143] The symbols found in the Judaic artistic items were inspired by the Torah and Jewish life (e.g., the tablets of the Ten Commandments, the Star of David, pomegranates).[144]

As mentioned previously, the topic of art inclusion in synagogues appeared already in nineteenth-century scholarly writings, as part of a reevaluation of traditional Jewish attitudes toward aesthetics.[145] However, the significance of artwork in synagogues and its acceptance by congregations and their leaders started to be notable in post–World War II America, reflecting in part the Jewish search for identity.[146] This search expressed the quest for art's "humanization and enhancement"[147] as influenced by the events of the Holocaust, the establishment of the State of Israel, and the realization of the American value of freedom of religion.[148] During that period, modern

Reform rabbis supported the inclusion of figurative art, artistic expressions of Jewish history, art depicting stories of the creation, and so forth. Reconstructionist Rabbi Mordecai M. Kaplan wrote about the aesthetic elements to be included in the synagogue, as they enhance the "religio-poetic feeling."[149] He continued to preach that artists such as sculptors, painters, glass-workers, and tapestry weavers should enlist the aid of the architects to beautify the place of worship.[150] Indeed, modern American synagogues exemplify the mutual relationship between religion and art as lifting the Jewish soul.

Abstract art includes a range of options, from a strict purism to simplification of forms, and from partial elimination to total dissolution. In many ways, it was easier for congregations to accept abstract art, interpreting it in their own religious and cultural versions, while deciphering the second commandment with varying degrees of severity.[151] Traditional themes have been woven into abstracted art's spirituality, mystery, and democratic values.[152] Synagogues include phrases from the Old Testament in Hebrew on the exterior above their entrances and in the sanctuaries above the arks. I argue that the Hebrew signage adds to the familiar feeling of the worshipers and to the confirmation of the sanctity of the building. Often, in modern synagogues, an abstract art piece serves as a context for the selected phrase (see later Henri [Nehemia] Azaz's sculpture on the façade of Chicago Loop Synagogue in Chicago, Illinois).

The common artwork in modern American synagogues follows the liturgical motifs and includes elements such as the Ten Commandments, the Star of David, and the menorah to reflect traditional symbols. Usually, the Decalogue (Tablets of Law) is centrally posted on the wall behind the stage (figure 3.6). In the case of Mendelsohn's Park Synagogue in Cleveland, Ohio, the tablets are posted outside on top of the dome of the sanctuary. As mentioned earlier, architect Walter Gropius used the Decalogue as his inspiration for the form of the building itself (figure 3.3). For Gropius, art and abstracted faith symbols were an organic part of the structure.[153] Another example of those motifs being interpreted by modern architects and artists includes the entrance façade of Percival Goodman's Baltimore Hebrew Congregation (figure 3.12). It illustrates the Decalogue in the center of eight panels that were designed in 1953 by sculptor George Aarons (1896–1980). These sculptural reliefs express the ethical ideas of Judaism.[154] The side façade of the same synagogue was designed by Goodman using the menorah and the Star of David in concrete as

Figure 3.12. Percival Goodman's Baltimore Hebrew Congregation, Baltimore, Maryland (1953): The main façade with a Decalogue in the center of eight panels that were designed as sculptural reliefs by sculptor George Aarons (1953)

Figure 3.13. Baltimore Hebrew Congregation, Baltimore, Maryland (1953): Percival Goodman's design of the side façade with concrete menorah and Star of David.

Figure 3.14. Percival Goodman's Baltimore Hebrew Congregation, Baltimore, Maryland (1953): The façade's menorah and the Star of David as seen from the sanctuary

symbols of the exterior and the interior (figures 3.13 and 3.14). These traditional elements link the exterior with the interior.

The Star of David serves as a key symbol of Judaism and is a visual image of Jewish identity.[155] It is made of two equal triangles overlapping each other and creating six points of a star. The Kabbalistic book of the *Zohar* (3:73a) states that the triangle represents the connection between three knots: God, Torah, and Israel. The Kabbalah illustrates each of the six points as an emotion, a flow of energy that allows us to "imbue pure cerebral activity with warmth and grace."[156] It is believed that the twelve lines of the Star of David represent the twelve tribes of Israel, each creating a unique emotion. Others interpret the six sides of the star as God's ruling over the universe, protecting the people from all directions.[157] Some designers introduced this symbol as the basis for the geometry of the building and integrated its shape into the structure (e.g., the floor plan of Frank Lloyd Wight's Beth Sholom Synagogue, Elkins Park, Pennsylvania [1956]; Pietro Belluschi's Temple B'rith Kodesh, Rochester, New York [1964][158]). Others used the Star of David as decorative artwork on the façade of the synagogue or as an artistic motif integrated into the interior.

Another important symbol is the menorah, a sacred candelabrum with seven branches representing the spiritual light of the Jews and their freedom. It is described in the Old Testament that the original menorah was made by the craftsman Bezalel Ben-Uri and placed in the sanctuary of the Tabernacle (Exodus 37:17–24). The exact description of how to create the menorah appears in Exodus 25:31–32, 39–40, where it states, "You shall make a Lampstand (Menorah) of pure gold; the Lampstand shall be made of hammered work." The menorah was used in the Holy Temples in Jerusalem and eventually became the symbol of the Jewish nation.[159] The removal of the menorah from the Second Temple by the Romans, and its displacement from Jerusalem to Rome in 70 CE, symbolizes not only the destruction of the Temple but also the loss of the Jewish people's freedom. The menorah became part of the collective memory of the Temple, its destruction, and the value of freedom. In modern art, the menorah also reflects imagery of "the galaxy of stars, the fellowship of man, and a towering mast at sea."[160] It always stands on the side of the Ark and often decorates the Ark. Its strong image and relation to the Ark can be seen already in the mosaic floors of the fifth-century synagogues in the Holy Land, where the menorah is situated on both sides of the Ark (top of figure 3.9). In modern America, often the menorah is also placed on the façade of the building either in its literary form (figure 3.15) or as an abstract piece, such as in the case of Beth Sholom Synagogue, designed

Figure 3.15. TriBeCa Synagogue in Manhattan, New York (1967), designed by William Breger: The menorah at the synagogue's entrance

by Frank Lloyd Wright, where the candleholders of the menorah are located on the roof's ridges. Often, the menorah is used to decorate the parochet (a curtain that covers the interior cabinet of the Ark), as in the case of Percival Goodman's Congregation B'nai Israel Synagogue (figure 5.38a). The parochet itself symbolizes the partition between the holy hall and the holy of holies space in the Tabernacle, and "represents the firmament."[161]

The collective memory of the lighting of the menorah in the Temple and the call for an eternal light as a spiritual symbol created the Ner Tamid (eternal candle), which is lit day and night in synagogues. Exodus 27:20 instructs, "You shall command the people of Israel that they bring to you pure beaten olive oil for the light, that a lamp may regularly be set up to burn." This rule of contributing oil or a lamp was literally interpreted by Jews as an act of honor.[162] The spiritual interpretation relates the eternal light to the Lord's presence and to the light that links the sanctuary to Jerusalem.[163] Others perceive the eternal light as a symbol of keeping alive the Jewish Law.[164] Later in history, an electrical fixture replaced the oil/candle and remains lit day and night. Hanging in front of the Ark, this fixture became an artistic object and a symbol of inclusion, an abstracted sculpture in the sanctuary (see chapters 4 and 5).

Architecture as Art and Framing Art in Modern American Synagogues

The study of art in modern American synagogues reveals two approaches of inquiry. The first focuses on the concepts of architecture as art, and the second on architecture as framing the art. The first approach implies that architects created artwork as integral parts of their buildings' architecture; the second approach suggests that architects provided the space/frame for the artwork and commissioned artists to integrate their artwork as part of the synagogues' architecture.[165] It is agreed that both approaches illustrate the architectural design of the synagogue as a work of art with no division between art and design. Chapters 4 and 5 detail the artworks

of each of the book's examples. For example, the first approach to the inclusion of art in synagogues is exemplified by the designs of Eric Mendelsohn, Walter Gropius, and Frank Lloyd Wright, demonstrating the architects' artworks as part of their holistic design approach. In addition to the buildings' designs, they created the interior architectural and liturgical details. These included the Ark, the bimah, the chairs on the stage, the eternal light, the menorah, the light fixtures, the pews, and even the calligraphy expressing the biblical verses mounted on the walls. Similar to some of the contemporary sculptors, painters, and other artists, those architects abstracted biblical motifs that served as inspiration for their artwork.

The second approach to the inclusion of art in synagogues shows the collaboration between architects and artists and illustrates how artists saw Jewish and biblical themes as extensions of their general imagery of abstract expressionism, an art movement that started in New York after World War II. This movement represented modernism and progressiveness, and was religiously neutral.[166] Robert Nelson claimed that abstract art, similar to modern architecture, showcased painting and sculptures in their "pure means and materials."[167] In synagogues, artists used Jewish imagery as a continuation of "their interest in the mythical and the spiritual."[168] They were inspired by motifs from the Old Testament, such as the Star of David, the menorah, and pillars of fire, and attempted to expand the meaning of specific Jewish liturgical themes to a more universal meaning of religious imagery.[169] For example, artist Herbert Ferber (1906–91) pointed out that his "burning bush" metal sculpture situated on the façade of B'nai Israel Synagogue in Millburn, New Jersey, appeals as a story to Jews and Christians alike.[170] Artist Ibram Lassaw (1913–2003) mentioned that his sculptures created for synagogues cannot be called synagogue art since his artworks for the synagogues were no different from his work prior to the synagogue commissions.[171] These sculptors departed from traditional techniques in metal sculpturing and used new direct-metal construction based on direct cutting, carving, or hammering of the metal.

Similar to the artists using new techniques in metal sculptures, artists working with stained glass continued to develop techniques based on traditional glass production. They renewed and developed the acid etching technique, a process "by which a resist is applied to glass before it is dipped into hydrofluoric acid. Once in the acid, the coloured surface that is *not* covered with resist is etched away, lightening or changing its colour. The surface underneath the resist remains shiny and untouched."[172] This technique increased the variety of effects within a single leaded area.[173]

Artists were given almost total freedom in designing and producing their work, which exhibited a collaboration with architects who provided a "minimalistic backdrop for modern art."[174] Avram Kampf claims that these cases showcase the "juxtaposition of works of art and architecture while preserving the autonomy of each."[175] In other words, art speaks with its own voice while being part of the architectural design. Architect, historian, and author Talbot Hamlin (1889–1956) mentioned this collaboration in 1952 as part of his guidelines for successful work between artists and architects. He highlights the importance of understanding and respecting the nature of each of the collaborators.[176] Examples of such collaboration are detailed in chapter 4 with Minoru Yamasaki's synagogue in Glencoe, Illinois, and in chapter 5 with the analyses of synagogues by architects such as Percival Goodman, Philip Johnson, and Sidney Eisenshtat.

The most influential collaboration between a synagogue's architect and artists is the modern expression of art in the exterior and interior of Percival Goodman's Congregation B'nai Israel in Millburn, New Jersey (1951), where the architect worked with American artists such as Herbert Ferber (1906–91), Robert Motherwell (1915–91), and Adolph Gottlieb (1903–74). Since this synagogue and its art are described in detail in chapter 5, I present here a different example that is not detailed later: the Chicago Loop Synagogue, designed by the Chicago architectural firm of Loebl, Schlossman & Bennett in 1957. The Orthodox congregation was founded in 1929 to serve Jews who lived and worked in downtown Chicago. Following a fire at their first synagogue, the congregation commissioned Loebl, Schlossman & Bennett to design their new synagogue. The architects were well-known for their Chicago religious architecture, including the 1929 monumental Temple Sholom on Lake Shore Drive. The architects designed the Chicago Loop Synagogue and its sanctuary with a restrained minimalistic modern style that characterized mid-twentieth-century architecture. They used brick, concrete, and granite for the walls as backgrounds for the artwork on both the exterior and interior. The architects collaborated with the Israeli sculptor Henri (Nehemia) Azaz (1923–2008) and with American painter/glass artist Abraham Rattner (1895–1978) to include abstracted art as an integral part of the synagogue.

Henri (Nehemia) Azaz's bronze sculpture hangs over the main entrance and welcomes the worshipers/visitors (figure 3.16). The sculpture, entitled *Hands in Peace*, includes an image of blessing hands and a blessing verse in Hebrew and English from the book of Numbers (6:24–26): "The Lord bless thee and keep thee; the Lord, make his face to shine upon thee and be gracious to thee; the Lord lift up his countenance upon thee and give thee peace." Once inside, a ramp path directs worshipers to the sanctuary on the second floor. As worshipers enter the sanctuary, they face the east wall of a stained-glass façade, designed by Abraham Rattner (figure 3.17). That wall distinguishes the synagogue from its surroundings and maintains the sacredness of the space.

Henri Azaz also designed the Ark and the eternal light in the sanctuary's interior standing on the east (to the left of the bimah) with the stained-glass wall in its background (figure 3.18). The bronze Ark cabinet is framed by a niche (*heichal*) of white/gray marble, which is the material of the bimah and the stand for the menorah. Thus the architects created the frame for the bronze sculptured Ark's doors as an integral part of the sanctuary. The eternal light hanging above the Ark is made from red glass and portrays fire with the color and the words "eternal light" in Hebrew, Ner Tamid.

The bimah (stage) is situated on the north concrete wall perpendicular to the glass wall on the east

Figure 3.16. Chicago Loop Synagogue in Chicago, Illinois (1958), designed by Loebl Schlossman & Bennett: An example of an art piece framing a phrase from the Old Testament above the entrance, designed by artist Henri (Nehemia) Azaz

Figure 3.17. Chicago Loop Synagogue in Chicago, Illinois (1958), designed by Loebl Schlossman & Bennett: The east wall is a stained-glass façade designed by artist Abraham Rattner.

Figure 3.18. Chicago Loop Synagogue in Chicago, Illinois (1958), designed by Loebl Schlossman & Bennett: The sanctuary

and the Ark (figure 3.18). This arrangement is not typical of sanctuary design, in which the Ark and the bimah are both facing Jerusalem. In this synagogue, the seating on the main floor is arranged in two directions: one section faces north to the bimah (stage), and the other section on the floor and in the balcony is angled to face northeast to look onto the Ark, the bimah, and the stained-glass wall behind the Ark (figure 3.18).

The glass wall is built of nine sections, each divided into nine small panels, and its composition depicts the theme from Genesis 1:3, "And God said, Let there be light; and there was light." It includes abstracted traditional images such as red flames to symbolize the biblical story of the burning bush, a large yellow hexagon that expresses the "unending light" (in Hebrew *ein-sof*), and more (figure 3.17). To enhance the light motif, Rattner included at the top of the wall seven celestial lights "set like diamonds into a mold."[177] Art historian Avram Kampf sees the *shin* branch in the middle of the wall as Jacob's ladder, descending from the blue background resembling the sky that balances the energy from the hexagon sun.[178] I argue that the balance between these images and other pieces of the glass wall is achieved by the entire glass composition, its colors, and its specific place on the east wall facing Jerusalem.

The collaboration between the architects and the artists illustrates how the simple, humble space of the sanctuary was designed to accommodate and highlight the artworks. The architects dedicated significant spaces for the artists to showcase their work as they located the Ark on the side in front of the stained-glass wall, which serves as its background. They hung the eternal light above the Ark as an integral part of the composition of the stained glass. The architects also framed the artwork in the synagogue in relation to the exterior surroundings of Chicago's downtown streets. They enhanced the significance of the exterior sculpture by hanging it above the building's entrance (figure 3.16). The entrance façade includes the back side of Rattner's glass wall, which is seen as a background for the Azaz's sculpture above the entrance (figure 3.16). The glass wall's

glory can be seen only from the inside. At night, when the sanctuary is lit, the glass wall image shines outside. In addition, it should be noted that the glass wall effectively blocks the noise and glare from the downtown street.[179]

Both artists Azaz and Rattner depicted universal themes of blessing and light that are combined with Jewish symbols and Hebrew letters. They aimed not only to beautify the synagogue and create its identity, but also to bolster worshipers' spiritual experiences. The analysis of such an example highlights the combination of modern abstracted architectural details and art as functional symbols, a mere biblical interpretation of the architect/artist, and as an inspiration for the congregation.

Summary

The analysis of synagogues' design principles expresses two modes of inquiry. The first focuses on the universal question of what makes a building sacred. The second introduces the main specificities of synagogue design.

The universal sacred perception of the cosmos and its creation is the basis for building a sacred structure, as there is a belief that the house of worship reflects the cosmos. This notion includes the interpretations of the four elements that are fundamental in the universe's construction: earth, air, light, and water. I linked these elements to buildings' materials and systems, which serve as the sacred foundations of houses of worship. This part of the chapter also introduced the horizontal and vertical axes that shape the cosmos and influence the geometry and form of the houses of worship, including synagogues.

The second inquiry into synagogues' design principles focused on the specific faith's (i.e., Judaism's) requirements and motifs. These are manifested in the interior of the sanctuaries and include the synagogue's orientation, the relations between the Ark and bimah and their effects on the seating arrangement, the flexible design to accommodate changes in occupancy during high holidays, light, and the inclusion of abstracted art in the synagogue. Each of those elements is designed in the modern mid-twentieth century as an abstracted interpretation of Jewish traditional symbols/meanings.

The two levels of investigation of the synagogues' design principles show that despite the notion that a synagogue is built for people to gather and should not reflect sacredness, the synagogue, as in other houses of worship, expresses "the culmination of humanity's attempt to reflect Divine presence."[180]

4 Modern American Synagogue Design
Key Developments

Lord, I love the house where you live, the place where your glory dwells.

(*Psalm 26:8*)

The study of mid-twentieth-century modern American synagogues reveals three key design developments that sustained synagogue architecture for decades. First was the departure from historicism and the introduction of a functional modern design that embraced abstracted symbols of Judaism. Indeed, all the synagogue designs exhibited in the 1963 exhibition *Recent American Synagogue Architecture* in New York City illustrated the departure from historicism and traditional synagogue designs by bridging modernism with Judaism.[1] The second key development was the attempt to design "The American Synagogue" that linked its symbols with the American landscape and its values of democracy and freedom of religion. The third development was the modernization of the concept of "cathedral synagogues," which was used in building synagogues in Europe during periods of emancipation and in America before World War II. These are grand monuments that convey importance and glorify the edifices as proud Jewish institutions. These three key trends were reflected in Orthodox, Conservative, and Reform synagogues. They illustrate changes in architecture that expressed modernist philosophy, theology, and liturgical art.[2]

Though the three developments were interpreted by architects in different ways, they all pushed the envelope of design and construction, geared toward structural integrity. They influenced the new aesthetics through the use of new materials (e.g., concrete, steel, and glass) and by employing new building systems and construction methods. As such, they can be found in many modern American synagogues.

This chapter introduces these key developments through the analysis of three synagogues that were among the first most prominent and influential in manifesting each of the developments:

- Eric Mendelsohn's design of Park Synagogue (Cleveland, Ohio, 1953). This was one of the first designs that attempted to cut ties with the traditional designs of synagogues and expressed the spirit of the time. It introduced faith requirements as part of modern architectural functionality.

- Frank Lloyd Wright's design of Beth Sholom Synagogue (Elkins Park, Pennsylvania, 1956). This combined universal sacred elements, local Native American art, and Jewish symbols to create "The American Synagogue." Similar to all Wright's houses of worship,[3] the design expressed the American value of freedom of religion.

- Minoru Yamasaki's design of North Shore Congregation Israel (Glencoe, Illinois, 1964). This introduced the modern interpretation of the "cathedral synagogue" as a grand institution. The design reflects the transition from the "spirit of the age" design concept to capture a sense of pride and eternity.[4]

The Departure from Historicism

Eric Mendelsohn's 1947 article "Creating a Modern Synagogue Style: In the Spirit of Our Age"[5] and his synagogue sketches and designs were among the first to reflect modern architectural concepts. They also captured the congregations' desires to depart from historicism.

In his writings, Mendelsohn emphasized how synagogue designs should apply modern architectural design concepts and utilize contemporary building construction to glorify God.[6] He (1887–1953) stated that "our temples should apply contemporary building-constructions and architectural conceptions to make the House of God a part of the democratic community in which he dwells."[7] He believed in the creation of a house of worship that reflects the Bible as "a living truth" and bridges the function and materiality of the synagogue with the spiritual experience it creates.[8] He expected the synagogue to serve as a symbol of the era we live in.

Mendelsohn's 1947 manifest was the first published testimony of how synagogue design should depart from historicism and the old-land traditions. His sketches illustrate his design idea of a dynamic building that balances mass, geometry, form, and faith symbols.[9] His approach to the design of a synagogue was to highlight man's material achievements while symbolizing the Jewish spirit in a majestic sacred space.[10] His work influenced other prominent modern architects to venture and bridge modernism and Judaism in their design of the American synagogue. Architect and artist Richard Meier declared in his book *Recent American Synagogue Architecture* (1963) that Mendelsohn has been a major influence in "altering the course of synagogue architecture."[11]

Indeed, Mendelsohn reinforced the use of modern architecture and highlighted the functional program of the synagogue as a changing task for the architect. In his view, the synagogue should serve as the core of community life and should include a religious center to lift the heart of man/woman and a community center for social and cultural gathering.[12] This concept is in line with Rabbi Mordecai Kaplan's 1940 vision to revive the early notion of a synagogue as a center for Jewish life. Mendelsohn's functional approach to the synagogue as a religious, cultural, and educational center influenced the design of mid-twentieth-century American synagogues as a whole.[13] The synagogue complexes inspired by his vision include four main units: the house of God (the house of worship); the house of the people (the assembly/social hall); the house of the Torah (the education wing); and an administration wing.

Although such structures became large complexes with various wings, Mendelsohn recognized the need to design them in human scale. He designed all parts of the building to cater to the congregation's needs. He also took into consideration the site and its environmental conditions. His designs utilized new building technology and construction methods. Mendelsohn claimed, "This period demands centers of worship where the spirit of the Bible is not an ancient mirage, but a living truth"[14] and "a fellowship warming men's thoughts and intentions by the fire of the Divine."[15]

Mendelsohn attempted to exhibit his manifest in six proposals and hundreds of sketches for synagogues in America from 1946 to 1953. When he passed away in 1953, only B'nai Amoona Synagogue in University City, Missouri, was built (1945–50), and three other synagogues—Park Synagogue, Cleveland Heights, Ohio (1946–53); Emanu-El Synagogue, Grand Rapids, Michigan (1948–54); and Mount Zion Synagogue, St. Paul, Minnesota (1950–54)—were under construction and completed after his death. Though many cite Mendelsohn's first built synagogue in America, B'nai Amoona Synagogue (today a Center of Contemporary Arts),[16] others established that Park Synagogue in Cleveland, Ohio, "probably represents the fullest expression of his [Mendelsohn's] vision"[17] and is "the most significant structure of its kind in our generation"[18] (figures 4.1 and 4.2). In 1947, before commissioning Eric Mendelsohn to design Park Synagogue, the synagogue's rabbi Armond Cohen visited Mendelsohn's show at the Human Art Exhibit in New York. Following this trip, he stated that the architect's designs were clear, bold, powerful, dynamic, and communicated the buildings' meaning.[19] As such, the rabbi was instrumental in commissioning Eric Mendelsohn to

Figure 4.1. Park Synagogue, Cleveland, Ohio (1953), designed by Eric Mendelsohn: Main entrance elevation

Figure 4.2. Park Synagogue, Cleveland, Ohio (1953), designed by Eric Mendelsohn: The sanctuary

design Park Synagogue and eventually became the architect's good friend.

Eric Mendelsohn's Park Synagogue, Cleveland, Ohio (1947)

In his book *Eric Mendelsohn's Park Synagogue* (2012), Walter C. Leedy Jr. describes the history of the synagogue's congregation, which was founded in the city of Cleveland, Ohio, in 1869 by a group of Orthodox Jewish Poles called Anshe Emeth. In 1916, Anshe Emeth merged with Congregation Beth Tefilo, adopting a new constitution in 1917 to become the largest Conservative congregation in the United States. Leedy Jr. writes about the congregation's move to Cleveland Heights, a Cleveland suburb. He details their attempt to purchase a site for building their synagogue, the commission of architect Eric Mendelsohn to design it, the history of the design phases, and the building's construction.

This section of my book focuses on the architectural analysis of Park Synagogue as one of the main examples of the departure from historicism and the introduction of a functional and symbolic modern synagogue.

The plan of the synagogue is laid out as a long triangle, catering to the site/lot constraints. The topography of the twenty-eight-acre woodland lot on a ridge overlooking Euclid Avenue influenced the site development and the synagogue building's plan (figure 4.3). The design is based on a central axis with a hierarchy of rectangles and circles that represent the various parts of the synagogue. The social, education, and administration wings accumulate into a climax of a dome that highlights the sanctuary of the prayer wing. Following the dome at the tip of the wedge of the axis, Mendelsohn located a small chapel that served the need for daily services during the week, with fewer members in attendance. The synagogue is "a composition in counterpoint, where

Figure 4.3. Park Synagogue, Cleveland, Ohio (1953), designed by Eric Mendelsohn: The complex site plan (Courtesy of Western Reserve Historical Society, Cleveland, Ohio)

Figure 4.4. Park Synagogue, Cleveland, Ohio (1953), designed by Eric Mendelsohn: The design of the synagogue along the site topography (the chapel at the tip of the site)

Figure 4.5. Park Synagogue, Cleveland, Ohio
(1953), designed by
Eric Mendelsohn: Main
elevation

the building's silhouette" caters to the site's topography[20] and to the congregation's needs (figure 4.4).

When Mendelsohn observed the construction of the building, he stated that the building rises in harmony with the land and "doesn't shake its fist at God."[21] The use of topography and a combination of geometrical forms is a clear departure from traditional synagogue designs, which usually were based on a rectangular volume positioned on the ground. His design created a harmony among all the building's elements and with the site conditions. All the building's parts are constructed with concrete blocks cladded with beige bricks that are linked with copper cornices as a horizontal trim around the building (figure 4.1). This link highlights the horizontality of the building and accentuates the vertical element of the copper dome above the sanctuary. Though the location of the dome is asymmetrical, Mendelsohn still achieved a balance of all parts, with the main entrance to the synagogue located between the domical part of the prayer wing and the horizontal cubical part of the foyer/assembly (figure 4.1). He continued the horizontal line with the educational wing, which has a separate entrance to the right of the praying and assembly wings (figure 4.5). These separations strengthen the modern horizontal design and are another expression of the departure from historicism, where houses of worship typically used a dome in the middle of the building.

Mendelsohn's holistic approach was illustrated by his design of the building's details, its landscape, and everything inside to "the last doorknob and door check."[22] Above the entrance he designed the Hebrew letters of the verse "Welcome in the name of God" as a welcome point (figure 4.1). He hoped that this quotation would elicit a positive response from the congregation as well as from the non-Jewish neighbors, as in the case of Architect Louis G. Redstone's B'nai Israel Synagogue in Pontiac, Michigan. There, the congregation and their neighbors adopted the philosophy of the quotation written on the synagogue's curved wall, "Behold how Wonderful and Pleasant it is for Brethren to Dwell Together."[23] Mendelsohn also included the Hebrew letter *shin* in metal as part of the doors' decor (figure 4.6). This letter became a motif in Mendelsohn's

Figure 4.6. Park Synagogue, Cleveland, Ohio (1953): Mendelsohn's use of the Hebrew letter *shin* as part of the décor of the entrance doors

detailed design. It symbolizes the first letter in one of the names attributed to God, *Shadai*, the first letter of the word *shalom* (peace), and the first letter of the Shema prayer, which is recited each morning and evening, "Hear Israel, The Lord our God, The Lord is One."

As mentioned, the focal point of the synagogue complex is the sanctuary's dome. Though it is not in the center of the complex, which does not claim a symmetrical design, it dominates the composition of the synagogue (figure 4.2). Mendelsohn was aware that a dome is a traditional and historic form used in houses of worship. However, he believed that his asymmetrical complex design with a shallow dome that "floats" above a glass wall beneath it enhanced the synagogue's modern design. Furthermore, the building's horizontality and the use of new building

Figure 4.7. Park Synagogue, Cleveland, Ohio (1953): Mendelsohn's sketch of the synagogue under the arc of the sky (Photo taken from a wall picture in Park Synagogue)

materials and systems (e.g., reinforced concrete) illustrate his departure from traditional synagogue designs. The dome in his view expresses unity and is a symbol of universality—a unity of the spirit of God and the unity of heaven and earth. Indeed, a typical feature in his sketches of potential synagogues (including Park Synagogue) is the arc of the sky, where a dome "disappears altogether and blends into the sky"[24] (figure 4.7). It should be noted that the arc in the sky also appeared in Mendelsohn's sketches of B'nai Amoona Synagogue in St. Louis (1945).[25]

Architectural theoretician and historian Bruno Zevi (1918–2000) interpreted the arc of the sky in Mendelsohn's sketches as a space "crowded with people gathered under the celestial vault."[26] In addition to the arc, a dome design was repeated in Mendelsohn's sketches of proposals for an English synagogue in 1934 among other synagogues,[27] and

for public buildings such as the Universum Cinema (Berlin, 1926–28),[28] and Palace of the Soviets (Moscow, 1929).[29] Zevi saw the dome as a static form that cannot express the fluent modern spatial layout of the synagogue.[30] However, he admitted that upon closer observation of this dome, it "floats" above the walls and creates a "centrifugal motion of the building volumes."[31] Mendelsohn enhanced the verticality and sense of height by adorning the dome with an exterior pinnacle of mosaic tablets that portray in stainless steel the Hebrew letters of the Ten Commandments (figure 4.1). I concur with Zevi's observation and see the juxtaposition of the horizontal axis of the building's parts and the vertical axes of the prayer wing converging within the dome.

The 680-ton semispherical reinforced gunite concrete dome with a diameter of 100 feet is only 4 inches thick (except for the beam around the base) and rises 65 feet above the floor. It is placed on only six concrete columns separated by a curved wall of fifteen-foot-high clear glass windows.[32] Rabbis in general did not approve of the transparent openings, since it was assumed that outside views distracted worshipers and interfered with services.[33] Still, Mendelsohn insisted on clear glass, which visually integrated the interior and the exterior and lit the space and its focal point. He believed that temples should reject the design of mystifying and dark sanctuaries, rather serving as symbols of faith in daylight.[34] Both Eric Mendelsohn and Frank Lloyd Wright believed that this relationship between the interior and exterior brings God's creation into the sanctuary. In addition, the synagogue's dome, which rests on the clear rounded wall, seems entirely detached, floating above the ground. It hosts the congregation and "protects" the synagogue's wooden mahogany canopy above the Ark (figure 4.2). The canopy references the nomad Tabernacle tent of the people of Israel during their travels through the desert. Bruno Zevi saw this interior space as "an architectonic scenario virtually in the open air."[35] The dome envelopes the congregation, in which everyone can easily see the synagogue's focal point of the Ark and the bimah (figure 4.8). Everyone can also hear the prayers while having a sense of "congregational unity."[36]

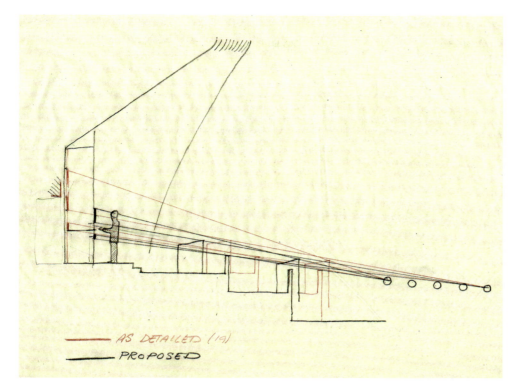

Figure 4.8. Park Synagogue, Cleveland, Ohio (1953): Mendelsohn's study of the canopy/Ark/bimah as the focal point of the sanctuary (Courtesy of Park Synagogue's archive)

The dome, the columns supporting the dome, the floor, and roof slabs are all constructed from reinforced concrete (figure 4.9). The dome's exterior is covered with felt and preformed copper sheets laid by the overlay method. The copper sheets developed a green patina throughout the years. In the interior, the domical ceiling is finished with twelve-by-six-inch acoustic tiles laid horizontally with staggered joints, which reduce the reverberation time, helping to contain sound and direct it toward the worshipers.[37] These tiles also create a floating cloud effect, which seems open to the sky. I concur with scholars who believe that the development of reinforced concrete, which counteracts outward thrust, aided in the construction of such a large dome.[38] Reinforced concrete, based on steel meridians, was utilized to construct a perfect hemicycle dome. The double curve at any one point of the dome made it a rigid structure despite its extreme thinness of only four inches.[39] As such, this dome separated itself from the traditional dome construction using innovative materials and systems. More details on the construction of the dome, including the building of the scaffolding, shores, and forms for the concrete work, can

Figure 4.9. Park Synagogue, Cleveland, Ohio (1953), designed by Eric Mendelsohn: The dome construction. August 4, 1949 (Photo taken from a wall picture in Park Synagogue)

be found in the 1954 document "The Architectural Concept of Park Synagogue."[40]

Mendelsohn enhanced the feeling of awe in the sanctuary by seating the congregation in a radial arrangement within the spherical profile of the dome (figure 4.2). The sunken edges of the sanctuary ceiling continue to the foyer and hold both the light fixtures that provide indirect lighting as well as the vents of the heating and cooling (HVAC) system. The reflector lamps that are hidden behind the canopy flood the dome with light,[41] which adds to the feeling of a floating dome. In addition, a soft light is added by lamps located at the sills of the glass windows. This design of a lower light shelf ceiling that continues beyond the sanctuary creates a functional holistic design and is an additional element of the departure from historicism.

The sanctuary's interior's finish material is wood, which creates a warm and human-scale atmosphere. The walls are finished with clear and stained maple, birch, and quarter-inch-thick, four-by-eight-foot mahogany sheets with butted joints.[42] Flex wood covers the large curved surfaces in the sanctuary, while plaster was used on metal lath and on gypsum blocks.[43] The wooden mahogany canopy over the Ark is perceived to "protect" the Ark and the bimah (figures 4.2 and 4.8). In addition, the canopy is interpreted as the symbol of the Tabernacle and the *Mishkan* (dwelling)—the first sanctuary of the Jews. The bimah podium is also made of mahogany and is incorporated into the *Mishkan*. It is built of three levels, corresponding to liturgical acts of the service (figures 4.2 and 4.10). The lower level is for delivering the sermon, the second level is for prayers and chants, and the highest level is dedicated to the Torah reading.

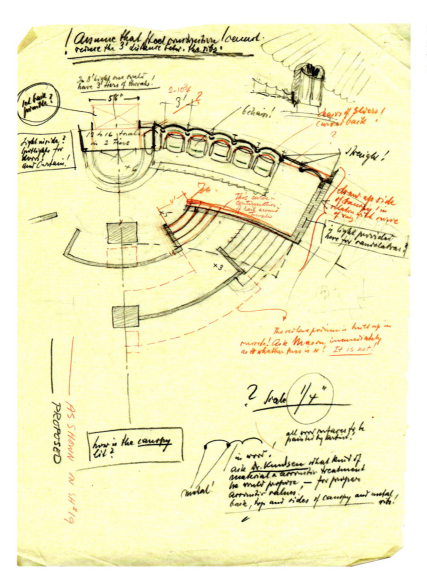

Figure 4.10. Park Synagogue, Cleveland, Ohio (1953): Mendelsohn's sketch of the three levels of the *Mishkan* (Courtesy of Park Synagogue's archive)

Figure 4.11. Park Synagogue, Cleveland, Ohio (1953): Ark doors, designed by Eric Mendelsohn

Figure 4.12. Park Synagogue, Cleveland, Ohio (1953): The bimah's background wall, designed by Eric Mendelsohn

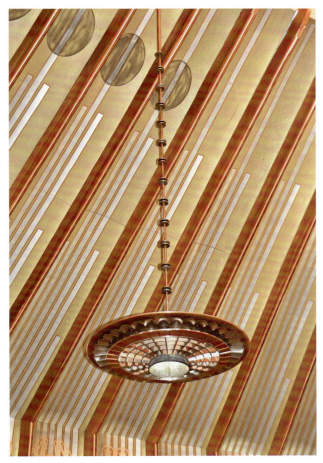

Figure. 4.13. Park Synagogue, Cleveland, Ohio (1953): The eternal light hanging from the dome in front of the Ark, designed by Eric Mendelsohn

As mentioned before, Mendelsohn used the Hebrew letter *shin* all over the *Mishkan*. It appears as the decor on the Ark's mahogany doors within the frame of the Tablets of the Law (figure 4.11). It also is shown on the fabric of the parochet—the Ark's curtain, which was woven by the artist Trude Guermonprez (1910–76) of San Francisco. Mendelsohn also used the letter *shin* in the design of the metal menorah (candleholder), which symbolizes light and freedom. In addition to the letter *shin*, Mendelsohn used the symbol of the Torah's crowns and the blessing hands illuminated in gold on the background panels of the bimah[44] (figure 4.12).

Figure 4.14. Park Synagogue, Cleveland, Ohio (1953), designed by Eric Mendelsohn: The foyer and assembly hall adjacent to the sanctuary (Courtesy of Park Synagogue's archive)

These crowns symbolize the four crowns mentioned in the Talmud:[45] the Torah, the Royalty, the Priesthood, and the Good Name. The latter was executed in brass, copper, and gold, and rests above the Ark (figure 4.11). This symbol is part of the Jewish tradition of blessing the good name of every human that glorifies the nobility of the Torah held in the Ark. Mendelsohn also designed the eternal light (Ner Tamid) fixture as a circular metal chandelier hanging with a metal chain from the ceiling in front of the Ark (figures 4.2 and 4.13). The disc-shaped eternal light is made of brass, copper, and the new material of the time—aluminum. It represents the infinite circle of eternity as well as the "eternal wisdom of the Torah."[46] In addition, Mendelsohn designed twelve chairs situated on the bimah stage for all who are called to read from the Torah, to represent the twelve tribes of Israel. Mendelsohn's detailed designs that interpreted faith symbols and biblical terms enhance the sacredness of the prayer wing spaces (e.g., the sanctuary and the chapel).

The plan of the synagogue shows that the foyer and the assembly hall were designed and built adjacent to the sanctuary (figure 4.14). When the sets of doors between the sanctuary and the two spaces are open, the combined area can host between eighteen to nineteen hundred seats, thus serving as an extension of the sanctuary, which includes only 984 seats. Mendelsohn believed "the foremost problem of a contemporary Synagogue was to devise an expandable and flexible plan."[47] The concept of extending the seating capacity of the sanctuary with

sliding/folding doors or partitions between communal spaces and the sanctuary was largely used by architect Percival Goodman and was adapted by architects during the 1950s–60s. This became one of the functional symbols of modern American synagogues. It should be noted that Architect Ben C. Bloch, in his 1944 article "Notes on Post-war Synagogue Design,"[48] already predicted that the "prayer hall will be designed to form a single unit with the social hall, and will be provided with a collapsible wall and reversible seats. The two rooms would be used separately on ordinary occasions and could be joined together for services on High Holidays."

Park Synagogue's fan-shaped assembly hall with its flat ceiling and roof was designed with a large span that was bridged with flat steel trusses, the longest of which is ninety-three feet.[49] It opens into a courtyard (figure 4.15) with fifty-eight-foot-wide and nineteen-foot-high stainless steel and plate glass doors to create the "courtyard of the temple."[50] It resembles the courtyards of the Tabernacles and the Solomon Temple.[51] One set of mahogany sliding doors connects the sanctuary and the hall, and another set connects the sanctuary and the foyer. When the doors are open, worshipers in the courtyard have a clear view of the bimah and Ark in the western part of the sanctuary. This orientation does not comply with the traditional view that the focal point of the sanctuary should be in the east. Mendelsohn explained this decision by saying that the earth is round, and therefore you always face Jerusalem.[52] This choice departed from the traditional orientation and later influenced other architects (see chapter 6 on the changes in Gropius's synagogue).

The prayer wing includes a smaller chapel to serve daily services that usually do not attract large numbers of worshipers. The chapel is located on the other side of the sanctuary at the tip of the triangular site (figure 4.4). Its location completes the axis of the complex and continues the horizontal pattern of the whole building. Its curved shape is built with the same material as the entire synagogue, and the copper horizontal trim that decorates the top of the walls reinforces the elegance and holistic design of the building. Mendelsohn designed the chapel's interior with the spiritual concept of a little

Figure 4.15. Park Synagogue, Cleveland, Ohio (1953), designed by Eric Mendelsohn: The courtyard, looking into the education and administrative wings

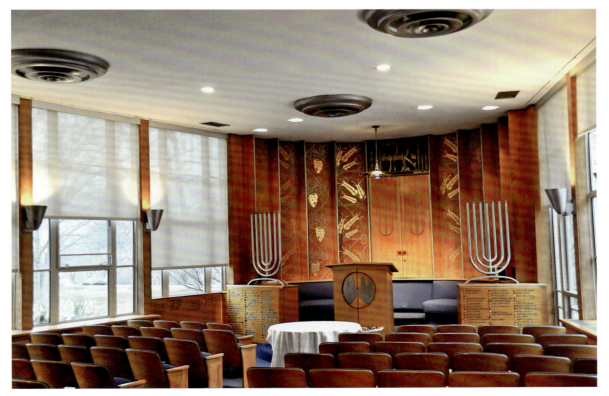

Figure 4.16. Park Synagogue, Cleveland, Ohio (1953), designed by Eric Mendelsohn: The chapel

sanctuary (Ezekiel 11:16; see chapter 3) and with a practical idea to serve as a wedding chapel (figure 4.16). At the chapel's entrance, Mendelsohn added an intimate study space for the few worshipers who assemble there after the morning prayers to study the Torah. Similar to the main sanctuary, the chapel has transparent large windows to bring in light and nature. Mendelsohn designed the panels in the background of the chapel's bimah using motifs of gilded sheaves of wheat and clusters of grapevines—symbols of bread and wine (figure 4.16). These also symbolize building a home for a couple getting married in the chapel. He continued the same décor motifs from the main sanctuary in the chapel. He introduced Jewish symbols to enhance the sacredness of the prayer wing's spaces. The letter *shin* appears on the Ark's wooden doors and serves as the basis for two menorahs. The blessing hands symbol is shown on the bimah's podium. His design of the eternal light is similar in its circular shape and materials to the eternal light in the main sanctuary, but smaller in scale. Above the chapel's Ark he posted a gold grill work with the Hebrew script *Adonai Echad* ("the Lord is One"), created by sculptor Viktor Ries (figure 4.16).

The other side of the domical sanctuary consists of the education and administration wings. Both are located around a courtyard at the base of the triangular site (figures 4.3 and 4.15). This arrangement enables natural light and air to penetrate the classrooms and offices. The school complex is a two-story building with twenty-one classrooms, a library, a school auditorium, and offices (figures 4.5 and 4.15), while the administrative wing consists of general offices, rabbinical studies, conference rooms, and fellowship parlors. The education and administrative wings are connected by a covered walkway to the main building.[53] They have operable round windows that resemble the circular geometry of the dome (figure 4.17).[54]

Figure 4.17. Park Synagogue, Cleveland, Ohio (1953), designed by Eric Mendelsohn: A round window in the administration wing

To conclude this section, we see that Mendelsohn bridged between Judaism and modernism as part of his manifest that synagogue designs should depart from historicism in a functional and sculptural architectural design. He saw the synagogue's architecture as a functional and spiritual program that sustained Judaism in an American present.[55] As many of the modern architects of his time, Mendelsohn believed in simplicity as a relief, not as a deprivation. He stated that his synagogues were "simple in structure, conception of space and ritual elements."[56] With his testimony and designs, Mendelsohn influenced other prominent modern architects, especially in the 1950s and 1960s.[57] Furthermore, his impact on the congregation was so successful that their rabbi Armond Cohen expressed his satisfaction in a private letter to Mendelsohn, stating that the building elevates the people.[58]

The congregation's pride and love for Mendelsohn's Park Synagogue continues to resonate despite the fact that many of the congregates moved to a different part of the city (e.g., Pepper Pike, Ohio). In addition to building a new synagogue, Park Synagogue East, the congregation still uses the original synagogue for Shabbat services, high holidays, special occasions, and adult learning. The congregation commissioned the local firm Centerbrook Architects & Planners to design a new building in their new vicinity, to host a sanctuary and a school. The project was completed in 2005 and fulfilled the wish of the congregation. It pays homage to Mendelsohn's synagogue while "proffering a dramatic modern welcome to its worshipers."[59] Centerbrook Architects were inspired by Mendelsohn's original design of the bimah in Park Synagogue from the 1950s (figure 4.3). Similarly, they designed the bimah with a wooden canopy above the Ark. Their new canopy abstracts Mendelsohn's wooden canopy above the original bimah (figure 4.18). The inspiration from Mendelsohn's design motifs creates a

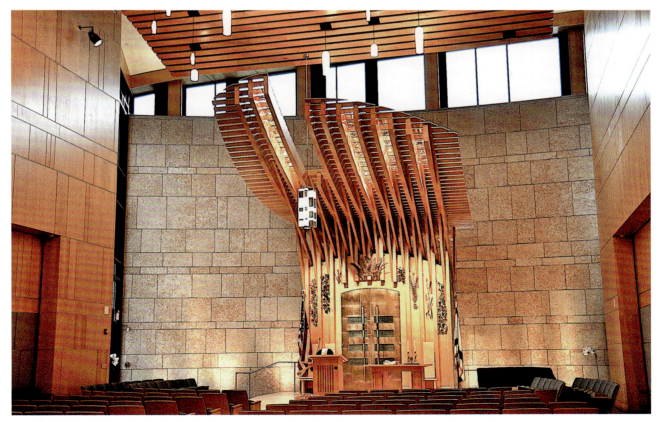

Figure 4.18. Park Synagogue East, Pepper Pike, Ohio (2005), designed by Centerbrook Architects & Planners: The bimah includes an abstracted wooden canopy above the Ark

space that reminds the congregation of their beloved original Park Synagogue.

The Design of "The American Synagogue"

The study of modern American synagogues reveals another key development: the attempt to design "The American Synagogue." This notion was first introduced by Frank Lloyd Wright (1867–1959) in his design of Beth Sholom Synagogue in Elkins Park, Pennsylvania (1954), Eric Mendelsohn considered Frank Lloyd Wright as the American architect who defined the character of America's architecture.[60] Indeed, Wright's design concepts, which expressed the American spirit and its landscape, were recognized by the American Institute of Architects (AIA). AIA designated many of Wright's projects, including Beth Sholom Synagogue in Elkins Park, as American cultural icons.[61] More so, this synagogue was listed on the National Register of Historic Places in 2007 for its unique architecture, engineering, and cultural value.[62]

Similar to Mendelsohn, Frank Lloyd Wright preached to depart from the traditional European design of houses of worship. While Mendelsohn focused on Judaism and synagogue designs, Wright reflected the departure from historicism in all of his designs of religious buildings, including Beth Sholom Synagogue (the only synagogue he designed).[63] He saw sacred architecture as an expression of American democracy, freedom of religion, the American landscape, and its indigenous spiritual roots. Thus Wright's sacred architecture, similar to his secular projects, was developed in harmony with the surrounding environment (the urban setting and the local culture), using the setting to frame and define the boundaries of his houses of worship. One example is the location on a major street of Unity Temple in Oak Park, Illinois, which Wright designed to be linear and parallel to the street. This composition also blocks the temple's interior from the street noise. Another example is his proposal for the Daphne Funeral Chapels in San Francisco, California, where the cubical urban background of the site frames the building and "helps to set apart and

distinguish the circular shapes of the sacred complex."[64] Wright designed more than thirty houses of worship for various religions and in different locations in the United States.[65] Only ten were built, including his only synagogue, Beth Sholom, which he called "The American Synagogue."

Frank Lloyd Wright's Beth Sholom Synagogue, Elkins Park, Pennsylvania (1954)

The Beth Sholom congregation was founded in 1918–19 in the city of Philadelphia. Their name, meaning "House of Peace," commemorates the end of World War I.[66] Moving later to the suburb of Elkins Park, the congregation purchased a property in 1949 and built their synagogue on a mount located on the highest point on the north side of the site (figure 4.19). The selection of this location followed the historic Jewish guideline that recommends building the synagogue on the highest location in the area (see the previous chapter).

Wright's design focused only on the religious function of the synagogue (the prayer wing). It is separated from the education and social parts, designed by a local architect Israel Demchick (1891–1980), a member of the congregation (figure 4.19).[67] The synagogue was designed in contrast to Demchick's rectangular brick/stone flat-roof buildings as a translucent pyramid-like structure with a span of 128 feet at the base (figure 4.20).

The location on the mount and the building's isolation on the site express the universal concept of separating the sacred from the mundane (see the previous chapter). In addition, this location makes the building look taller than its actual height. This perception is augmented by the surrounding background of the residential neighborhood on the lower streets. The optical illusion reminisces Wright's design of the path entering Unity Temple in Oak Park, Illinois. There, the segmented path creates the illusion of a longer journey from the mundane realm (the street) to the sacred realm (the temple).[68]

Joseph M. Siry's book *Beth Sholom Synagogue*[69] is devoted to the historic context of Wright's synagogue. The book describes the history of the

Figure 4.19. Beth Sholom Synagogue, Elkins Park, Pennsylvania (1954), designed by Frank Lloyd Wright: Site image (Courtesy of Beth Sholom Synagogue's archive)

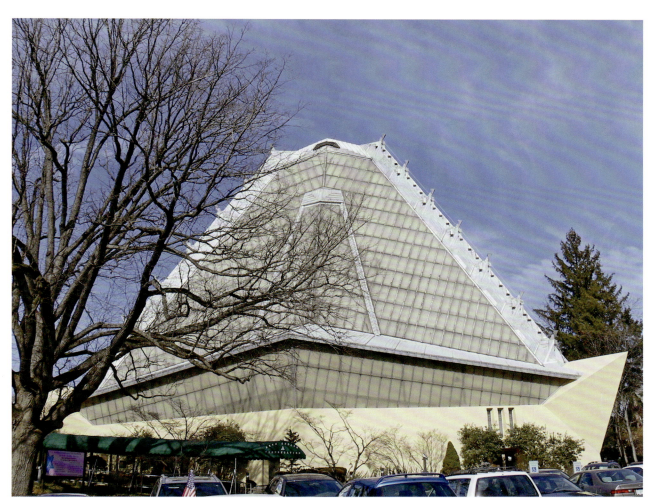

Figure 4.20. Beth Sholom Synagogue, Elkins Park, Pennsylvania (1954), designed by Frank Lloyd Wright: The building

congregation, the design process of their syna-gogue, and the built structure. My book *Frank Lloyd Wright's Sacred Architecture: Faith, Form, and Building Technology*[70] analyzes Beth Sholom Synagogue in the context of all Wright's sacred architecture and a conceptual model that illustrates the relations among faith, form, and building technology.[71] In my book, Wright's synagogue is illustrated as one of the key developments in the context of modern American sacred architecture.

As mentioned before, Wright's objective was to design Beth Sholom Synagogue as "The American Synagogue." This idea was reinforced by the congregation's rabbi, Mortimer J. Cohen, who envisioned that the synagogue would become the American symbol to commemorate the three hundredth anniversary of the arrival of the first Jewish settlers to the United States.[72] In a letter dated November 16, 1953, to architect Frank Lloyd Wright, the Rabbi outlines his vision for a synagogue as simple and modern in design. He asked for 1,200 to 1,500 seats and specified the program, his inspiration, and the budget.[73] He continues to describe the synagogue as a windowless structure, all air-conditioned with a glass and rotunda roof. He was concerned with acoustics in the sanctuary and mentioned that the walls would be acoustically treated. The rabbi saw the synagogue as a complex that includes a sanctuary, study rooms, meeting rooms, storage rooms, and a chapel. Wright embraced the Rabbi's vision and expressed it in a sketch that resembled a smaller version of his proposal for the Steel Cathedral, an all-faith chapel he had designed in 1925–26, which was never built.[74]

A major part of Rabbi Cohen's vision was a design of the synagogue as a modern Mount Sinai, the mount where the Ten Commandments were given to the people of Israel. His idea was to illustrate how the synagogue and the Jewish Law that was given on Mount Sinai had moved with the Jews from the ancient Tabernacle in the desert through history and finally reached the modern era of the New World. Mount Sinai plays a crucial role in biblical literature and is portrayed in modern interpretations as a mythical place of no return—a place that expresses God's revelation when given the Jewish Law (Exodus 19–24), which in turn is synonymous with light and

represents the Jewish people's collective memory.[75] This inspired Wright, who interpreted this symbol into a modern mountain of light[76] and called it a luminous Mount Sinai[77] (figure 4.20). Thus Wright catered to Rabbi Cohen's idea of bridging America with the ancient spirit of Israel.

Similar to Mendelsohn, Wright believed that architecture should express the era we live in. Thus, he introduced in his projects new aesthetics by utilizing modern materials such as steel, concrete, glass, aluminum, fiberglass, and their respective innovative structural systems. Wright not only understood the nature of each material and its potential structural strength and durability; he also saw them as influencing the form and image of the building. In his writing "In the Cause of Architecture, III–IX: The Meaning of Materials" (1928),[78] Wright specified each material and its influence on his design. For example, steel for Wright was a material of miracle tensile strength that expresses lightness and openness.[79] This image of steel is the image he attempted to achieve in the synagogue's sanctuary.

The building is based on a repeated triangular module that soars to the sky with a translucent pyramidal roof rising above the floor by approximately 110 feet (figure 4.20). The triangular shape appears on all of Wright's details (e.g., triangular bimah, triangular lamps, triangular speaker, etc.). The pyramid is supported by a steel tripod covered with stamped aluminum and anchored in a concrete bastion (figure 4.20). Terry Patterson claims that the use of the three materials makes the tripod's legs resemble more of a concrete construction than steel or aluminum. This in turn has "a fairly strong influence on the character of the synagogue."[80] In my visits to the synagogue, my impression did not follow Patterson's claim. I saw a light steel-and-glass building with steel columns holding the entrance canopy and a sanctuary covered by a pyramidal translucent roof hanging on a steel tripod anchored in concrete (figure 4.21). The 160-ton steel tripod's frame frees the sanctuary from structural elements and contributes to the open, spacious, and light image (figure 4.22). The cream-colored reinforced concrete bastion of the pyramid includes three tetrahedral

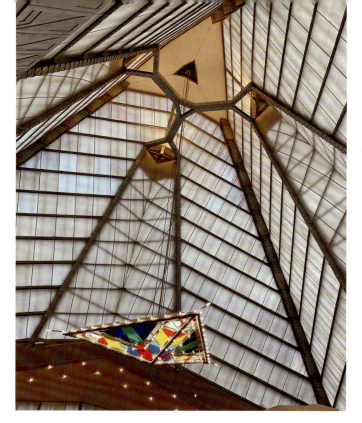

Figure 4.21. Beth Sholom Synagogue, Elkins Park, Pennsylvania (1954), designed by Frank Lloyd Wright: A zoom view on the interior tripod

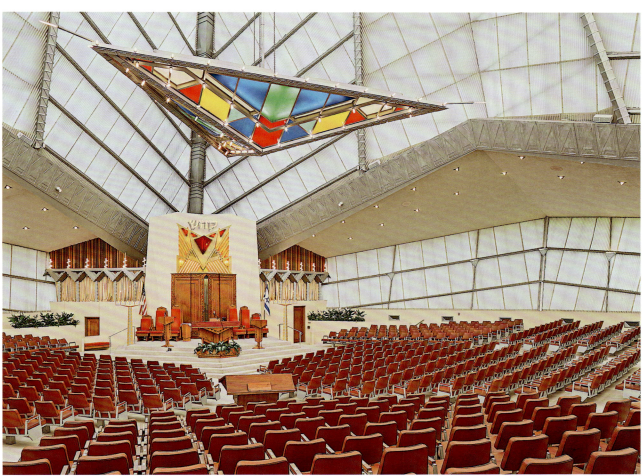

Figure 4.22. Beth Sholom Synagogue, Elkins Park, Pennsylvania (1954), designed by Frank Lloyd Wright: The sanctuary (Courtesy of John Milner Architects Inc.)

Figure 4.23. Beth Sholom Synagogue, Elkins Park, Pennsylvania (1954), designed by Frank Lloyd Wright: The concrete bastions

Figure 4.24. Beth Sholom Synagogue, Elkins Park, Pennsylvania (1954), designed by Frank Lloyd Wright: Natural light in the sanctuary—a view toward the back of the sanctuary

Figure 4.25. Beth Sholom Synagogue, Elkins Park, Pennsylvania (1954), designed by Frank Lloyd Wright: A view toward the bimah and the Ark

corners pointing upward and outward, which add to the lighter image of the building (figure 4.23).

The pyramid is a double-shell roof made of 2,100 square feet of white corrugated glass on the exterior and 2,000 square feet of cream-white fiberglass panels bound by aluminum strips on the interior (figure 4.22). Wright left a five-inch air space between the layers for insulation and as a barrier from the condensation accumulating on the roof. This air space also helps with the acoustics, as it blocks outside noise.

The synagogue's translucent roof became the main source of light. Though Wright's first proposals included stained glass, he rejected that idea, claiming that the presence of God through natural light would put "His colors on, for He is the great artist."[81] The sanctuary is filled with soft and diffused natural light that enhances varying colors and tones during different hours of the day and seasons (figure 4.24). Wright's lighting design intended that during the morning the sanctuary's light is celebrated with silver tones, while in the afternoon it changes to a gilded atmosphere. These tones enrich the spiritual atmosphere of the synagogue and the meaning of light. Wright also fulfilled the functional faith requirement to provide equal light for all one thousand worshipers to read and participate in services.

Wright introduced natural light during the day, while during the night spotlights and the triangular, colored chandelier, designed by Wright, lit the space (figures 4.22 and 4.25). The chandelier expresses the belief that only through a series of colors may God reveal himself to men.[82] The Jewish mysticism Kabbalah assigns each color with a special meaning: blue represents wisdom; green represents insight and understanding; yellow/gold represents beauty; red shows strength, courage, and justice; and cream/white shows mercy and loving-kindness. Rabbi Cohen reacted to the chandelier and its symbols, saying that the colors "flow out of the great White light, the Eternal, the *En-Sof*, that is God."[83] At night, the building becomes a luminous temple. The light from within shines onto the surroundings as a beacon of light for the community.[84] The notion of a beacon of light emphasizes the strength and confidence of American Jewry in building their institution as "The

American Synagogue," an expression of the American value of freedom of religion.

Rabbi Cohen, who worked closely with Wright on the design of the synagogue,[85] was quoted in the *New York Times* saying that the design was "the desert peak that was transformed into a mountain of light at the time of God's communion with the people of Israel."[86] Wright's wife Olgivanna concurred by saying at the opening of the building "the voices of God and Moses were called again to life."[87] Authors Henry and Daniel Stolzman called the building a Jewish symbol "heroic or metaphorical in tone." [88] Yet the idea of creating "The American Synagogue" called for "a 'new thing,' [where] the American spirit [is] wedded to the ancient spirit of Israel."[89] Architect and writer Peter Blake stated that a synagogue needs to proclaim the essence of Judaism itself and should be "indigenous to the soil and soul, the substance and spirit of America";[90] thus it should reflect "The American Synagogue."

During my visits to the synagogue, I was told that some see Native American symbols and art motifs of the tribes that used to live in the region integrated into the synagogue's symbols.[91] The belief is that Wright abstracted the Native Americans' tipi shape to become the pyramidal building and used some of their art details in the design of the synagogue. For example, the exterior decoration on the three sides of the tripod of the pyramidal roof consists of a menorah (a candelabra), a Jewish symbol of light and freedom, while the pattern of each of the menorah's seven candle holders is believed to be an abstraction of a Native American motif. In addition, a small metal menorah is placed on the concrete bastion (figure 4.26). The pattern of the tripod's menorah also appears as light fixtures in the entrance hall of the synagogue. This combination of Native American features with traditional Jewish symbols aimed to express the link of the building to its place and local history and in turn create "The American Synagogue." While this latter notion is considered an anecdote,[92] others claim that the pyramidal synagogue evokes the image of a vast desert tent, which can be interpreted as the new modern Tabernacle.[93] Some mention that Wright was inspired by ancient civilizations in his design

Figure 4.26. Beth Sholom Synagogue, Elkins Park, Pennsylvania (1954), designed by Frank Lloyd Wright: The exterior tripod as a symbol of the menorah with abstracted art patterns and a metal menorah

of sacred architecture,[94] using motifs from Mayan and Assyrian art, such as the stamped aluminum cladding of the tripod.[95] Scholar Vincent Scully Jr. claims that the synagogue resembles a cone of Astarte from Babylon.[96] As mentioned before, Wright and Rabbi Cohen saw it as the symbol of Mount Sinai.[97]

It should be noted that all anecdotes and scholarly interpretations show that Wright's conception of the building and its art was inspired by ancient symbols while pushing a futuristic image. Whatever the interpretation is, Wright designed the synagogue as a building "that people, on entering it, will feel as if they were resting in the very hands of God."[98] This is expressed in the building as a whole and in its details such as the entrance canopy, which symbolizes the outreached hands of the rabbi "calling the congregation to join together under one roof."[99] This concept is highlighted in a drawing exhibited by the synagogue where its plan is superimposed over Rabbi Cohen's hands (figure 4.27).

The synagogue's entrance on the ground level is placed halfway between two levels. From the vestibule, the worshiper can either ascend to the main sanctuary (figure 4.28) or descend to the Sisterhood Chapel, four lounges, and a lobby beneath (figure 4.29). The stairs on both sides of the sanctuary (figure 4.28 shows a ramp on both sides) create the worshiper's journey from the mundane to the sacred and evoke the "spiritual experience of reaching up to the divine light" in the sanctuary.[100]

Upon entering the main hall, one faces the focal point of the space, the bimah and the Ark (figure 4.25). The sanctuary's floor gently descends eastward toward it, and all seat sections are directed toward that area. The color of the carpet in the sanctuary is the color of sand, which symbolizes the desert in the vicinity of Mount Sinai where the people of Israel received the Ten Commandments. Wright designed the seats and all other features, details, and furniture as part of his holistic design approach, in which the whole is the equilibrium of its parts. Wright inserted

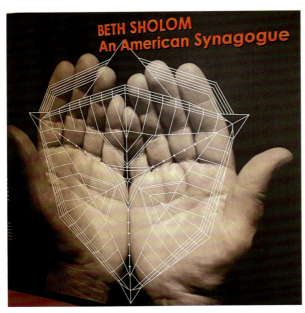

Figure 4.27. Beth Sholom Synagogue, Elkins Park, Pennsylvania (1954), designed by Frank Lloyd Wright: The synagogue's plan superimposed over Rabbi Cohen's hands (From Beth Sholom Synagogue's exhibit)

Figure 4.28. Beth Sholom Synagogue, Elkins Park, Pennsylvania (1954), designed by Frank Lloyd Wright: A copy of the main sanctuary floor plan (From Beth Sholom Synagogue's exhibit)

Figure 4.29. Beth Sholom Synagogue, Elkins Park, Pennsylvania (1954), designed by Frank Lloyd Wright: A copy of Wright's lower-level chapel floor plan (From Beth Sholom Synagogue's exhibit)

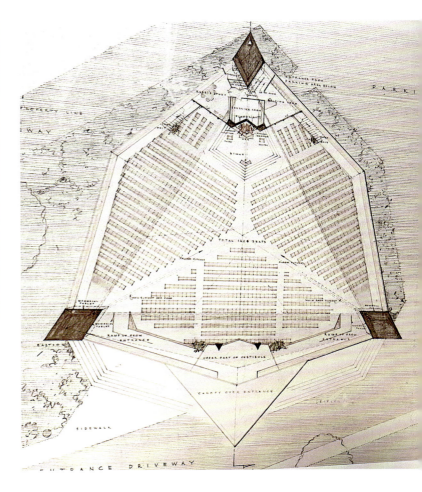

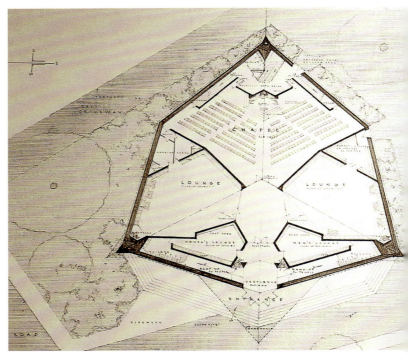

the Ark inside a twenty-foot-high cream-colored concrete triangular niche called the *heichal* (figure 4.25). He made the Ark's doors from rectangular wood panels that protrude out in a triangle form. Wright designed the eternal light (Ner Tamid) and set it on top of the *heichal*'s triangular walls as a crown (figure 4.25). The eternal light consists of a central crimson red lamp that is based on the geometry of the building's plan and of two crimson red triangular lamps on each side of the central one. These smaller lamps are in the shape of the rest of the triangular lamps in the building. The eternal light is set in a golden triangular abstracted background that resembles the lines of the pyramidal roof. Their composition expresses the wings of the *seraphim*, the flaming angels, crowded about God's presence (Isaiah 6:3). The wings were inspired by an image of a four-winged Assyrian cherubic figure that was sent to Wright by Rabbi Cohen on June 20, 1957 (the bottom part of figure 4.30). They embrace the word *Kadosh* ("Holy" in Hebrew). Wright designed the Hebrew word of *Kadosh* from metal in three layers, where each layer reflects its shade on the other (the upper part of figure 4.30). This strong image follows the biblical verses of *Kadosh, Kadosh, Kadosh* (Holy, Holy, Holy), as appears in Isaiah 6:1–3, "Holy, holy, holy is the LORD Almighty; the whole earth is full of his glory," and in Revelation 4:8, "And the four living creatures, each of them with six wings, are full of eyes all around and within, and day and night they never cease to say, 'Holy, holy, holy, is the Lord God Almighty,' who was and is and is to come!"

The bimah (the podium) is made of wood in a triangular form pointing out to the worshipers (figure 4.24). This form not only follows the building's triangular module but also creates an illusion of being closer to the audience and enhances the acoustic quality of the sermon. This type of stage and podium was used by Wright already in his 1938 Annie Pfeiffer Chapel in Florida, where the triangular podium and stage extend into the diagonally arranged seating.[101] Beth Sholom Synagogue's two original seven-candled menorahs that were supposed to stand on the stage on both sides of the bimah were moved to the chapel and were replaced with others (figure 4.24). As mentioned before,

Figure 4.30. Beth Sholom Synagog, Elkins Park, Pennsylvania (1954), designed by Frank Lloyd Wright: Upper sketch: Wright's design of the eternal light with the Hebrew letters of *kadosh*. Bottom sketch: An image of the four-winged Assyrian cherubic figure that was sent to Wright by Rabbi Cohen on June 20, 1957. (From Beth Sholom Synagogue's exhibit)

Wright designed a triangular chandelier in the center of the interior and hung it from the top of the tripod (figure 4.22).

In the lower level under the main sanctuary, Wright designed the sisterhood chapel, four lounges, a lobby, and restrooms (figure 4.29). The chapel was designed to host about three hundred seats and to serve daily activities and often Shabbat services (figure 4.31). Due to its location under the main sanctuary, the chapel has no openings and no natural light source. Still, Wright's lighting design is similar to his day lighting design concepts,[102] where he used multiple sources of light, including triangular light fixtures on the walls and ceiling and an imitation of a skylight over the bimah (figure 4.31). The latter was created as a light shelf that allows the light to reflect onto the ceiling and bounce down onto the Ark. More so, the change in the ceiling height enhances the chapel's focal point. As in the main sanctuary,

Wright designed all the details of the space, including the Jewish faith's elements. He designed the wooden Ark's doors; the triangular eternal light shining in crimson red; the podium of the bimah, which is a smaller version of the one in the main sanctuary; the two menorahs (candelabras), which were moved here from the upper sanctuary; and the chairs on the bimah, which are also based on a triangle pattern (figure 4.31). Some claim that the triangle is a symbol for the three fathers in Judaism—Abraham, Isaac, and Jacob—while others see it based on Native American art motifs and/or the Jewish association with Mount Sinai.

The design of the whole synagogue as a unique visible form that departed from historicism bridged Judaism with modern architecture to create "The American Synagogue." Samuel Gruber and Joseph Siry state that this synagogue broke the mold of modern synagogue design by pushing the envelope

Figures 4.31. Beth Sholom Synagogue, Elkins Park, Pennsylvania (1954), designed by Frank Lloyd Wright: The Sisterhood Chapel on the lower level

of aesthetics that created a sculptural architecture.[103] Wright reflected in his American synagogue the values of democracy and freedom of religion that allowed Jews to proudly exhibit their belonging to America. This design paved the way for other architects to sculpt their synagogue buildings, which eventually became "cathedral synagogues."

The Modern "Cathedral Synagogue" as a Grand Institution

The third key development of modern synagogue design—the evolution of modern "Jewish cathedrals"—occurred during the late-1950s and 1960s. These projects reflected the congregations' prominent institutions and pride. Rabbi Dr. Benjamin Elton of Sydney, Australia, describes the "cathedral synagogue" notion as a magnificent structure that evokes a feeling of awe in its exterior and interior[104]—a place where the congregants feel they have "arrived." This idea reminds of Wright's floor plan of Beth Sholom Synagogue, where he believed that the hands of the rabbi welcome the congregants entering their house of God. Rabbi Elton continues, "the grandeur of such edifices bestowed status on the Jewish community and enabled their house of worship to be counted amongst the leading public buildings of the area."[105] That was the case with synagogues in American suburbs built during the late-1950s and 1960s. American Jewry constructed their synagogues as important institutions that expressed their confidence in the American value of freedom of religion. Their pride was translated into grand expressionist sculptural buildings following the Biblical description of the Jerusalem High Temple: "What a fine sanctuary we have!" (Jeremiah 7:4).

Modernization of the cathedral synagogues permitted the architects to experiment with new aesthetics and building technology (materials, systems, construction). The buildings became concrete synagogue cathedrals filled with light. They diverted the focus of design from form driven out of functionality, which characterized synagogue design in the 1950s, to a focus on beauty and expressive forms.

Though these projects departed from historicism and embraced American modernism, they resemble the concept of the grand temples and churches in Europe, and the large hierarchical spaces of late-nineteenth and early-twentieth-century American synagogues (e.g., Sinai Temple, Chicago, Illinois [1876]; Temple-Tifereth Israel in Cleveland, Ohio [1923]; Temple Emanu-El synagogue in New York City, New York [1930]).[106]

Some criticized the new synagogue cathedrals as encouraging the individual and the congregation to worship the synagogue's sanctuary more than worshipping God. Indeed, in my visits to some of those synagogues, the main force enhancing my spiritual experience in the space was the feeling of awe that engulfed me when I entered the sanctuaries.

One of the prominent examples of the new design approach is Minoru Yamasaki's 1964 design of the North Shore Congregation Israel Synagogue in Glencoe, Illinois. In this project, Yamasaki (1912–1986), a Detroit-based American architect from the firm Yamasaki and Leinweber, continued the evolution of synagogue designs carrying from Mendelsohn and Wright.[107] In his design, not only did he push the envelope of aesthetics and building technology, but he also practiced his humanistic approach to design. He was influenced by the seminal books on architecture and humanism by Geoffrey Scott and Rudolf Wittkower,[108] in which humans are at the center of the physical realm and architecture becomes a body-building connection. The latter concept attempts to fulfill humans' "physical, psychological, social and cultural needs."[109] Yamasaki believed that in addition to human-scale design with humans at the core, architecture should express joy and beauty, be uplifting and truthful, provide order to the complexity of modern life, and arise from human physical, emotional, and spiritual needs "as ideally as is possible within the limits of a physical environment."[110] After studying Judaism and participating in special services such as Yom Kippur, Yamasaki indicated that "Judaism seems to place man and God side by side" and that man needs to believe in himself in order to believe in God.[111]

Minoru Yamasaki's North Shore Congregation Israel Synagogue, Glencoe, Illinois (1964)

The North Shore Congregation Israel was founded in 1920 as the North Shore Branch of Chicago's Reform Sinai Congregation. Rabbi Emil G. Hirsch traveled between the two and served both.[112] In 1926, the North Shore Branch separated from the Sinai Congregation and established their independent Reform congregation in Glencoe, Illinois.[113] They called themselves "North Shore Congregation Israel."[114] The need for a larger and permanent space toward the end of the 1950s resulted in the acquisition of a nineteen-acre lakefront property to build a large synagogue. Architect Minoru Yamasaki was commissioned to design the synagogue complex to include a prayer wing, administrative offices, and a religious school, and to plan it in three phases. Architect Alfred Alschuler Jr., from the firm of Friedman, Alschuler & Sincere, a member of the congregation, was part of the building committee. He was deeply involved as the resident architect in building the synagogue complex, especially the education wing.[115]

In 1959, Henry Goldstein, executive director of the board of North Shore Congregation Israel, wrote to the synagogue rabbi, its president, and the congregation's board an article entitled "The Architect and the Congregation."[116] In his writing, he described the challenge that the architect would face in designing a structure that would "break the silence of stone and steel" and combine within it "the glories of Israel's past, the melodies of its present, [and] the aspiration of its future."[117] He continued and claimed that the design should integrate the congregation's spirit and needs with an expression of vibrant grand forms that should reflect a song like a lyrical prayer.[118] This notion was one of the reasons that the synagogue's building committee selected architect Minoru Yamasaki out of ten candidates to design their synagogue. Yamasaki proposed a design that is a space of delight and reflection, in addition to its modern emphasis on function, budget, and order. His design objective was to introduce a poetic approach of serenity, surprise, and delight to the

synagogue's architecture that focuses on "the spirit of man [as] the candle of the light."[119] Similar to Mendelsohn and Wright, Yamasaki saw Judaism as a religion of light, rather than one of mysticism and darkness,[120] saying, "We must bring back the richness of sunlight and shadow, and of shadow within shadow to our buildings."[121] The climax of moving through light and shadows in the synagogue's complex is the sanctuary, which evokes an emotion of awe in a cathedral synagogue where modernism is interwoven with an ever-present thread of light (figure 4.32). Yamasaki's design followed the vision of the synagogue's Rabbi Siskin, who saw the building as a reflection of the congregation's desire to depart from historicism and emphasize light, while maintaining their traditions of faith.[122]

The synagogue is located on a nineteen-acre boulder site bounded by Lake Michigan, by Sheridan Road in Glencoe, and natural ravines (figure 4.33). Yamasaki positioned the synagogue perpendicular to the lake, so the sanctuary would face east to Jerusalem and each side of the sanctuary could provide a view of the lake and the landscape surrounding it. In addition, this orientation avoided the harsh winds from the lake. He worked with landscape architect Lawrence Halprin (1916–2009) on enhancing the existing wooden bluff facing the lake,[123] on screening the four hundred–car parking lot in front of the synagogue, and on creating a serene place in the suburb, which is "the Temple conception"[124] (figure 4.33). Author Dale Allen Gyure claims that Halprin's focus was on the worshipers' experience of nature, while Yamasaki's focus was on the experience inside.[125] I would not distinguish between the two; rather, I would emphasize the great collaboration between an architect and a landscape architect in creating a whole spiritual environment.

The synagogue complex forms a T-shape, which includes the sanctuary of eight hundred permanent seats perpendicular to the lakeshore, and an adjacent Memorial Hall as part of the prayer wing with terraces on each side of the hall parallel to the lake (figure 4.33). The Memorial Hall expands the seating in the sanctuary to include an additional one thousand seats for high holiday services. The other wings of the complex are parallel to the lake. On the

Figure 4.32. North Shore Congregation Israel Synagogue, Glencoe, Illinois (1964), designed by Minoru Yamasaki: The main sanctuary

Figure 4.33. North Shore Congregation Israel Synagogue, Glencoe, Illinois (1964), designed by Minoru Yamasaki: Aerial view of the synagogue's site (Courtesy of North Shore Congregation Israel Synagogue's archive: Photo by Reames Studio, Glenview, Illinois)

north side of the sanctuary, Yamasaki placed the educational wing, which includes a school of two stories[126] with eighteen classrooms and other related facilities, facing the lake. The school is constructed with reinforced poured concrete foundations, frame, floors, columns, and roof, with walls cladded with brick. On the south side, Yamasaki located a shorter wing for administration and service. The services of mechanical and electrical equipment, bathrooms, storage, and an archive are in the basement under that wing. Yamasaki intended to expand this area in the future to include a small chapel. Eventually, in 1982, a new chapel was designed there by local architects Hammond, Beeby, and Babka (see chapter 6). All three wings (prayer, education, administration/service) are connected with an enclosed glass arcade (figure 4.34), which faces east-west; the lake view is from the east and the entrance/parking is on the west. The arcade is constructed with pointed arch openings and vaults, continuing the Gothic architectural details of the sanctuary. Yamasaki was inspired by Gothic architecture for its grand monuments that integrated structure and aesthetics.[127]

However, like Frank Lloyd Wright, Yamasaki criticized it as being depressing. He stated that these structures made man in awe of God while reducing him to dust before God.[128] *New York Times* architecture critic Ada Huxtable saw Yamasaki's concrete design as a starting point for an ornamental style and as a means of transforming Gothic architecture into modern elegance.[129]

Yamasaki designed the synagogue utilizing precast concrete and thin-shell hyperboloid construction. He claimed that steel is a ready-made material that needs to be assembled, while he saw in concrete a construction material that can be molded with the architect taking charge.[130] He understood the plasticity of the material and used it to integrate form and structure into a sculptural architecture. This development represented a daring venture into a structural system that enables the spanning of large interiors, such as the eighty-foot width of the sanctuary. More so, it fulfilled one form of the modernist dream: it eliminated the distinction between roof and wall (figure 4.35).[131] The major structure is built of four pairs of reinforced concrete fan vault shells

Figure 4.34. North Shore Congregation Israel Synagogue, Glencoe, Illinois (1964), designed by Minoru Yamasaki: The enclosed glass arcade looking toward the school

Figure 4.35. North Shore Congregation Israel Synagogue, Glencoe, Illinois (1964), designed by Minoru Yamasaki: From the synagogue's construction site, showing no distinction between the roof and the wall (Courtesy of North Shore Congregation Israel Synagogue's archive: Photo by Reames Studio, Glenview, Illinois)

on each side of the building, with each pair weighing more than ninety tons (figure 4.36). The vaults end at the top with skylights as part of the wall/roof relationship. The precast concrete walls that fill the space between each pair of the fan vaults are made of a pointed arch and are nonstructural elements (figure 4.37). They are tied to the structure at three points—two on the floor and one at the ceiling (figure 4.38). The borders of each panel are glazed, which generates an image of lightweight precast elements. More so, the gilded color of the opaque glass fills the sanctuary with holy light (figure 4.32).

Some claim that the shape of the building was inspired by Yamasaki's impression of "the beautiful descriptions of nature he found in the [Jewish] high holiday services" and his interests in plant morphology.[132] His concrete building resembles a plant soaring skyward with the elegant curves of a calla lily plant's petals,[133] while the shape of the small windows at the baseline may be interpreted as artichoke leaves (figure 4.39 and 4.32).[134] Others referred to

Figure 4.36. North Shore Congregation Israel Synagogue, Glencoe, Illinois (1964), designed by Minoru Yamasaki: Northwest elevation showing the reinforced concrete fan vault shells

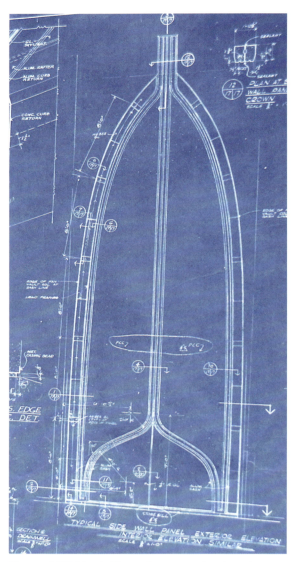

Figure 4.37. North Shore Congregation Israel Synagogue, Glencoe, Illinois (1964), designed by Minoru Yamasaki: Detail of a wall panel and the three ties (one in the ceiling and two at the floor; Blueprints from North Shore Congregation Israel Synagogue's archive)

Figure 4.38. North Shore Congregation Israel Synagogue, Glencoe, Illinois (1964), designed by Minoru Yamasaki: An interior detail of wall panel and a a tie point to the ceiling

Figure 4.39. North Shore Congregation Israel Synagogue, Glencoe, Illinois (1964), designed by Minoru Yamasaki: The sanctuary's lower transparent windows

the lower windows' design as hands in prayer (a universal symbol of prayer).[135] The end wall panels between the precast concrete structure as seen at the entrance and at the other side of the sanctuary facing the lake are made of site-poured concrete and weigh 150 tons.[136] The ends' white-washed concrete wall panels in between the structural vaults are interpreted as palm fronds between the lily stems (figure 4.40). As with the side elevations, the borders of the wall are glazed and make the wall look lighter. The gilded light coming from these glazed openings serves as a background to the sanctuary's stage and highlights the sacredness of the bimah and the Ark (figure 4.32).

The elegance of the sanctuary is based on Yamasaki's integration of concrete design with architectural light concepts (figure 4.32). He utilized the expressive concrete structure to design multiple sources of natural light and manipulated it with a combination

of transparent, opaque, and colored glass. The light in the sanctuary is diffused through the amber glass slits between the structural components and the wall panels. The light shines and creates a gilded atmosphere even during cloudy gray days (figure 4.32). The combination of amber glass in the walls, opaque skylights, and transparent lower windows creates the spiritual light, which enhances the sanctuary's sacred ambiance and helps reduce glare (figure 4.32). The task light in the space comes from the lower transparent windows and provides comfortable light for the congregation to move safely in the space and to participate in services (e.g., reading). These lower windows are shaped as Gothic pointed arches and enable natural light and views of the landscape surrounding the synagogue, including a glimpse of Lake Michigan (figure 4.39). With these openings, Yamasaki followed Mendelsohn's pioneering concept of bringing God's creation into the

Figure 4.40. North Shore Congregation Israel Synagogue, Glencoe, Illinois (1964), designed by Minoru Yamasaki: The synagogue's main entrance façade. The upper panel resembles a palm frond between the vaults that resemble lily stems. Glass separates them.

sanctuary. At night, the controlled incandescent and fluorescent lighting system that is installed between the inner and outer panes of the skylights achieves a similar effect to natural light and enhances sacredness.

The highlight of the interior is the synagogue's sanctuary of 80 feet wide and 126 feet long that rises 55 feet from floor level (figure 4.32). The proportion and symmetry of the rectangular sanctuary, with its defined axis leading to the focal point of the Ark and the bimah, emphasizes the sacred path/plan. The soaring height, with light shining from the amber glass between the structural elements and the walls and from the above opaque skylights, becomes the sacred verticality (figure 4.41). The architecture of the sanctuary, its details, and its inclusion of Jewish symbols bridge sacredness with Judaism in a lit concrete interior.

Figure 4.41. North Shore Congregation Israel Synagogue, Glencoe, Illinois (1964), designed by Minoru Yamasaki: Skylights

The most pronounced aspect in the interior is the Ark—the focal point of the sanctuary (figure 4.32). The architect collaborated with artist Lee DuSell (1927–) on the design of the bimah and the Ark. Yamasaki provided a niche in the concrete wall behind the stage for the artist to tuck in the wooden Ark decorated with a gilded leaf. The white-washed wall surface around the Ark wraps its cabinet and serves as the *heichal* (figure 4.32). This frame of a white wall embracing the cabinet is viewed as a white prayer shawl—the *tallit*—that embraces the rabbi, the cantor, and the worshipers who wear it. This is a very powerful image. Yet some criticize this design and the whole sanctuary as being "vaguely feminine" as part of the general criticism of Yamasaki's architecture.[137] This criticism should be viewed in the context of the time, when straight lines and harsh angles were considered masculine and appropriate. Still, I believe that the negative connotation should be changed and appreciated due to the following. First, Yamasaki mastered the plasticity of concrete and its possibilities in designing sacred architecture beyond straight lines and angles. Second is the way he bridged modernism with Jewish symbols. The latter can be observed in the Ark's concrete curved niche to express the *tallit* (the shawl wrapping the worshiper), which in Hebrew is a feminine noun. Third, Yamasaki's attempt to create divine presence in the sanctuary as associated with the Hebrew notion of the *schechina*. As mentioned in chapter 3, this word means the dwelling of the spirit and is written as a feminine word in the Hebrew scriptures and in rabbinic literature.

In addition, the powerful, white-washed wall in the background of the Ark includes the tablets of the Ten Commandments on one side of the Ark and a Hebrew verse from the Bible on the other side: "He has told you, O man, what is good; and what does the LORD require of you but to do justice, and to love kindness, and to walk humbly with your God." (Micah 6:8; fig. 4.32). Note that this verse is addressed to all humans, not just Jews. Furthermore, it shows that in order to honor God, one must honor every human being. This wall balances the sculptural Ark and acts as its frame. The Ark in

the middle of the wall shines under the slit of light above that wall, which frames the artwork. Thus, the architecture not only acts as art but also frames it (see this notion in chapter 3). This collaboration between the architect and artist illustrates how each had its own independent significance, but their strength is in the integration of the two.

In the center of the stage, four stairs covered with the same carpet as the sanctuary floor lead toward the stage in front of the Ark (figure 4.32). The move from the general sanctuary to the sacred of the holy Ark continues with three additional stairs made from white marble, accompanied by a white metal rail. The Ark is raised by another marble stair that leads to the marble podium of the Ark. In addition, a carpeted ramp on the side of the bimah was added for accessibility (see the left side of figure 4.39 and chapter 6). Yamasaki designed two carpeted platforms on each side of the sanctuary near the lower windows. They lead toward the stage as part of enhancing the focal point, as well as serving for additional seating as needed. The details of the marble stairs, its white metal rail, the stage, and the furniture of the bimah (e.g., wooden pulpits and marble chairs) follow the curves of the walls and the vault fans. Yamasaki's curved lines reflect continuity between the structure and its details—a design concept characteristic of Frank Lloyd Wright's sacred architecture.[138] The same pattern can be seen in the rail of the stairs to the choir/organ loft and the rail of the loft gallery (figure 4.42). The loft back wall, its slit of light on the side, the light of the skylight above, and the organ[139] itself all were designed with the same pointed arch detail of the whole synagogue (figure 4.43).

The analysis of Yamasaki's design of North Shore Congregation Israel Synagogue illustrates how modern expressive design in concrete evokes spirituality. It also shows his poetic approach to design, which was achieved through four major design concepts. First, there is a magnificent use of concrete as a sculptural material. The congregation appreciated Yamasaki's vaulted concrete fingers and saw them stretching to the sky like hands in prayer, curving gently to interlock at the pinnacle.[140] When I visited

Figure 4.42. North Shore Congregation Israel Synagogue, Glencoe, Illinois (1964), designed by Minoru Yamasaki: The stairs and their rail to the organ/choir loft

Figure 4.43. North Shore Congregation Israel Synagogue, Glencoe, Illinois (1964), designed by Minoru Yamasaki: The organ/choir loft

the synagogue, I first saw the impressive concrete entrance that looks like a fan or a palm frond; then, walking at the glazed arcade, the souring hyperbolic concrete side walls of the sanctuary appeared. This elevation made me admire the beauty of concrete beyond the brute and power of concrete sculpture. Second, when entering the sanctuary, I sensed Yamasaki's poetic design that created an awed spiritual space based on symmetry, human proportion, and light. Third, the space evoked a spiritual experience beyond a specific faith. His light design as drama and symbol created a "holy light" to uplift the spiritual experience of the worshipers. Light was perceived by the congregation as "delicate and almost infinite."[141] Indeed, during my visit to the synagogue, the sky was gray, the weather was rainy, and gray-blue stormy waves ran across Lake Michigan. Yet, when I entered the sanctuary, it was filled with natural light that shined in with golden tones, creating a holiness in the space. As the biblical verse from Genesis 1:3 says, "Let there be light." It made me feel in awe! The fourth concept that illustrates Yamasaki's special design is his successful collaboration with Lawrence Halprin, the landscape architect, and artist Lee DuSell, which helped create a cohesive sacred environment. These design concepts presented the idea of a synagogue cathedral that later was adapted by Yamasaki in his 1973 design of Temple Beth El Synagogue in Bloomfield Township, Michigan, and by other architects during the 1960s (see chapter 5). Yamasaki's modernization of the synagogue cathedral notion demonstrated his glorification of the synagogue to reflect the pride and confidence of the Jewish congregations. These designs expressed the key developments of departure from historicism and the creation of a unique American synagogue.

Summary

In conclusion, the three architects Mendelsohn, Wright, and Yamasaki managed to depart from traditional synagogue designs and introduce modern architecture that expressed Judaism in an American context. Their projects and the ones of those who followed them illustrate a structured conceptualization of three key developments. First was the departure from historicism, which became the major motif in Mendelsohn's writings and designs. His preaching expressed the congregations' post-Holocaust Jewish search for a new identity. Frank Lloyd Wright, like Mendelsohn, embraced modern design as a move away from historicism, attempting to create an American synagogue style, while Yamasaki based his synagogues on the two design concepts of Mendelsohn and Wright. Yamasaki's design departed from traditional synagogues by modernizing previous motifs of religious glory using new building technology and sculptural forms.

The three architects abstracted faith symbolism as well as universal sacred architectural elements that enhance spiritual experiences (e.g., the sacred paths to enter the sanctuaries, vertical elements, and light). Each of the architects reflected these concepts with some expressionist ideas[142] infused in their modern designs. They all interpreted the spirit of the period—departing from historicism—expressing modernism in symbols and function, looking at architecture as an art form. Mendelsohn's design of the Einstein Tower, in Potsdam, Germany (1924), is an example of expressionism[143] that often is mentioned as an organic design. However, his design of Park Synagogue in Cleveland (1947) exhibits a modernist approach rather than expressionism. The design of the synagogue was based on straight bold and horizontal forms that accumulate around a dome. Instead of a building soaring up, the dome blends with the sky while covering the sanctuary and protecting the congregation.

All three architects used light to express the holy in their synagogues. Mendelsohn created a strip of horizontal light underneath the dome and constructed the heavy large dome as "floating" above the sanctuary; Wright designed a pyramid of glass and plastic roof that distributes a soft light into the sanctuary; Yamasaki created details of light and shadow through vertical slits in the walls and skylights in the roof. Light became a symbol of spirituality that highlighted not only the building as an artistic project but mainly the abstracted Jewish symbols in the sanctuaries.

All three architects utilized innovative building technologies to create new aesthetics and to support the sacredness of the buildings. Their buildings attempted to realize the "dream envisioned by leaders not afraid to accept the challenge of change and growth"[144] and the dream of Jewish communities that were ready and open to accept progressive design concepts.[145] The designs responded to the time when Jews participated "in the momentous period of America's history"[146] and expressed the American values of freedom and democracy. Post-Holocaust Jews could build their pride and confidence through the exhibit of their modern institutions, including their synagogues.

To quote Mendelsohn, "The spirit of the Bible is not an ancient mirage, but a living truth. . . . It demands temples that will bear witness of man's material achievements and, at the same time, symbolize our spiritual renascence."[147] These sacred spaces were designed as landmarks in religious architecture with the idea for all to be transcendent for one moment away from day-to-day life. Rabbi Edgar Siskin of North Shore Congregation Israel stated in the congregation's annual report of 1963–64 that "the temple can lead us to God and to a deeper understanding of His ways if we will but enter often into its gates."

5 Pushing the Envelope
Architectural Illustrations

Now Bezalel and Oholiab, and every skillful person in whom the LORD has put skill and understanding to know how to perform all the work in the construction of the sanctuary, shall perform in accordance with all that the LORD has commanded. (Exodus 36:1)

During the 1950s and 1960s, the architectural design of American synagogues followed three trends: departure from historicism, the emergence of the American synagogue, and the surfacing of the cathedral synagogue.[1] These trends followed the evolution in modernism from a functional, bold, straight-lined, horizontal architecture, where form followed the function of faith, to expressive sculptural designs that glorified the synagogues as monumental institutions. This progression also highlighted the changes in the congregations' search for their Jewish identity.[2] Jewish self-perception shifted as Jews recognized the American value of freedom of religion and as Judaism became an accepted religion in America. This shift was expressed in the architecture of synagogues with dramatic and exceptional designs as modern places for worship. Moving outside the city, to either a suburb or a separate township, enabled congregations to build their synagogues from scratch and allowed them to adopt modernism as the new "progressive" architectural style.

This chapter includes an architectural analysis of five synagogues that were built during the 1950s and 1960s. They demonstrate the three key developments mentioned previously and illustrate additional specific design contributions that influenced modern American synagogues. These contributions highlight how architects pushed the envelope of synagogue aesthetics and building technology.

The selected synagogues follow the selection criteria described in chapter 1: they were built during the 1950s–60s, they continue to serve the communities as their houses of worship, and they were designed by prominent architects who were heavily involved in promoting the modern architecture movement in America. Some of these architects focused only on the design of modern American synagogues, while others influenced the design of other American houses of worship in the mid-twentieth century.[3]

The investigation of the synagogues in this chapter demonstrates how their designs bridged Judaism and modernism. They embraced the aesthetics of modern architecture, utilized innovations in building technology, and reflected the American Jewish context of the time (see chapter 2)—a context that was composed of the juxtaposition of the search for Jewish identity in America, the move of congregations to the American suburbs, and the development of the American modern architecture movement (figure 2.1).

The analyses of the specific design contributions of some of the following case studies show the introduction of the design concept "form follows function" that expressed the functional-industrial and minimalist modernism as seen in Philip Johnson's Kneses Tifereth Israel Synagogue in Port Chester, New York (1956). The analyses also illustrate the inclusion of abstracted modern art in synagogues and flexible design, as pioneered by Percival Goodman in his design of Congregation B'nai Israel Synagogue in Millburn, New Jersey (1950). These design solutions were followed by all other architects. Additional contributions relate to the utility of the cathedral-synagogue concept as a vehicle for pushing new building technology, such as the steel and concrete construction of Percival Goodman's Congregation Shaarey Zedek in Southfield, Michigan (1962). The case of Pietro Belluschi's Temple B'nai Jeshurun in Short Hills, New Jersey (1964–68) illustrates how the relation of building technology and form pushed the envelope of the aesthetical expression of the cathedral synagogues. This development often raised the question of the building's image: Is it a synagogue or a church? Finally, the study includes the introduction of sustainability in design, as expressed in Sidney Eisenshtat's Temple Mount Sinai in El Paso, Texas (1962).

Form Follows Function

Philip Johnson: Kneses Tifereth Israel Synagogue in Port Chester, New York (1956)

Philip Johnson (1906–2005) is regarded as one of the prominent architects who introduced modern architecture to America.[4] As described in chapter 2, in 1932, he was one of the organizers and curators of the *International Style Exhibition* at the Museum of Modern Art (MOMA) in New York City. He also copublished the exhibition catalog, which described the exhibited architects, the design concepts of the international style, and modern housing. His legacy spread from advocating "pure" modernism in America to postmodernism later in life, depicting his "eclectic thoughts and ideologies."[5] Johnson's approach to modernism was based on Sullivan's motif of "form follows function." His modern projects reflect bold "clean" horizontal lines, no ornaments, white color, and the use of steel and glass. His 1949 Glass House in New Canaan, Connecticut, and the 1958 Seagram Building that he codesigned with Mies Van der Rohe exemplify this approach.[6] Less known but influential was his modern design of Kneses Tifereth Israel (KTI) Synagogue in Port Chester, New York (1954), which is the focus of this section.

At the time that Johnson was fascinated with modern architecture, he was involved with profascist political ideology and activities in America.[7] He worked closely with US extreme right-wing politicians such as Alan Blackburn and Huey Long, authoring Nazi propaganda in support of Hitler and promoting anti-Semitism.[8] The Nazi party invited him to Germany for one of Hitler's parades and to visit the front in Poland. I mention these facts because they are relevant to the synagogue project that Johnson designed in 1954: Kneses Tifereth Israel (KTI) Synagogue in Port Chester, New York.

Johnson designed the synagogue free of charge, which raised some speculations both by Johnson's biographer Franz Schulze[9] and by those who mentioned it in obituaries following Johnson's death in 2005. Can his free-of-charge design be considered an act of atonement for his anti-Semitic and fascist behavior, or was it a mere reflection of monumentality to launch his career?[10] Ian Volner writes in his book *Philip Johnson: A Visual Biography* that "religious buildings would become a key component of Philip's practice, an opportunity for him to exercise his more grandiose impulses."[11] In an interview with Robert Stern, Johnson admitted that he followed his advisor, developer Robert C. Wiley, who said, "You have never built a big building. What does it cost you? What's that to start a career? You do it for nothing. It will help with your past—it will help you do other things."[12] Indeed, the synagogue project launched Johnson's career to become one of the leading architects in America. Other speculations relate to the commission of Johnson by the KTI congregation. Some claimed that the congregation did not know about the architect's past; others, such as Mr. Edgar Kaufmann Jr., an affluent member of the congregation, architect, and art historian,[13] claimed that Johnson apologized for his fascist past in front of the Anti-Defamation League of B'nai B'rith in New York City.[14]

Kneses Tifereth Israel Synagogue in Port Chester, New York (1956)

The original congregation that would eventually come to be known as Kneses Tifereth Israel (KTI) was founded in 1887 by a group of about twenty Jews in a private home on Pemberwick Road in Greenwich, Connecticut.[15] In 1927, the congregation merged with a group from the village of Port Chester, New York, and formed the Conservative KTI congregation.[16] In 1953, they commissioned architect Philip Johnson to build their synagogue, and until its completion in 1956, they used the Transverse Avenue Synagogue, which was sold in 1960. Johnson's synagogue sits on a low hillside up from King Street, originally surrounded by tall Jerusalem pine trees, which "soften[ed] the very large and austere" rectangular white building[17] (figure 5.1). After the death of Philip Johnson in 2005, most of the pine trees were cut to expose the building

(figure 5.2), and the building went through major interior renovations that are detailed later in this section.

The synagogue's floor plan is based on Johnson's previous proposal for a church that was never built. Most publications refer to his proposal for a church in Greenwich, Connecticut, which included a one hall box and a shallow-domed elliptical vestibule.[18] However, art historian Lindsay Cook claims that the design of the synagogue was also influenced by Johnson's proposal for Vassar College in Poughkeepsie, New York (1953), which was never built.[19] Johnson slightly modified his proposed single-canopy design around a sphere interior for the Vassar Chapel to serve as his initial sketch for the synagogue proposal.[20] Cook refers to Frank D. Welch's book *Philip Johnson and Texas*[21] and claims that the similarities of the initial proposals for both the Vassar Chapel and KTI synagogue can be traced visually to Johnson's contemporary design of St. Michael's Church in Houston, Texas. Henry-Russell Hitchcock added to the confusion by calling Johnson's proposal for Vassar Chapel the "un-built Greenwich church."[22] With that, Cook concludes that Hitchcock "unwittingly conflated the Vassar interfaith chapel, the KTI synagogue, and the Houston Catholic church."[23] In other words, there

Figure 5.1. Kneses Tifereth Israel Synagogue, Port Chester, New York (1956), designed by Philip Johnson: Façades surrounded by trees (Courtesy of Kneses Tifereth Israel Synagogue's archive)

Figure 5.2. Kneses Tifereth Israel Synagogue, Port Chester, New York (1956), designed by Philip Johnson: Today's façades with no trees

Figure 5.3. Kneses Tifereth Israel Synagogue, Port Chester, New York (1956), designed by Philip Johnson: Front façade

are different accounts of the origins of Johnson's synagogue floor plan and their influences. These attributions suggest that Johnson's design of houses of worship addressed a sacred space that is not necessarily affiliated with a specific religion.

Eventually, Philip Johnson abandoned those sketches and proposed a rectangular volume with inner dimensions of 140 feet long by 50 feet wide and 40 feet tall. However, he maintained the elliptical shallow-domed vestibule in the middle of the length of the rectangular sanctuary to serve as the vestibule entrance to the synagogue (figure 5.3). This oval-shaped space of twenty by thirty feet and almost twenty-five feet tall, on the outside, was constructed from concrete blocks and was covered by a concrete shallow dome. The structure of the dome is based on crisscrossed straight steel bars (e.g., horizontal ¾-inch and perpendicular 1½-inch bars). The bars are tied to a central 2½-inch steel elliptical ring (bent) that creates a skylight at the center of the shallow dome (figure 5.4). The skylight is covered with a glass cap.

The rectangular hall on the entrance floor serves as the sanctuary and the social hall, with a capacity to seat 840 to 1,000 people (figure 5.5). In addition, the floor includes bathrooms, a coat room, storage, and a kitchen. One straight flight of stairs directs worshipers to a daily chapel in the basement, which Johnson called the "praying room." Additional bathrooms and a broiler room are located in the basement. Johnson provided the praying room with four long vertical windows that light a simple, quite dim room (figure 5.6). He utilized changes in topography to create that source of light. However, since he did not refer to this space as a chapel, but rather as a room, he neglected to add a touch of spirituality and oriented it to the west side. As such, he did not comply with one of the faith requirements to orient the focal point of the space to the east—toward Jerusalem. Over the years, the congregation decorated the room by adding metal symbols to the wooden Ark, and installing decorative stained-glass panels on the walls on both sides of the Ark. These panels represent the different holidays of the Jewish calendar (figure 5.6).

Similar to Walter Gropius's design of Temple Oheb Shalom in Baltimore, Maryland (figure 3.3), Johnson's simple industrial construction corresponds to his design concept of modernism. It expressed the notion of "form follows function." The synagogue is built as a steel frame structure based on seven modules on the long sides of the rectangular façades (figure 5.3). The modules' frame is filled with whitewashed concrete panels on the outside and white painted wooden planks on the inside. They are pierced by 286 vertical slit windows of multicolored Belgian glass in five vertical tiers of alternating rhythms (figures 5.3, 5.5, and 5.7). Johnson was quoted in the synagogue's centennial brochure as saying that these slits bring

Figure 5.4. Kneses Tifereth Israel Synagogue, Port Chester, New York (1956), designed by Philip Johnson: The vestibule skylight

Figure 5.5. Kneses Tifereth Israel Synagogue, Port Chester, New York (1956), designed by Philip Johnson: The sanctuary and the social hall

Figure 5.6. Kneses Tifereth Israel Synagogue, Port Chester, New York (1956), designed by Philip Johnson: The chapel (praying room).

Figure 5.7. Kneses Tifereth Israel Synagogue, Port Chester, New York (1956): The slit windows of the main façade

Figure 5.8. Kneses Tifereth Israel Synagogue, Port Chester, New York (1956): The interior wall with its colored-glass slits

Figure 5.9 Kneses Tifereth Israel Synagogue, Port Chester, New York (1956), designed by Philip Johnson: Night image of the main façade (https://rabbi-careers.com/rouge_0)

"a pleasing luminous balance . . . which succeeds in providing relief from the aggressive purism of the architecture itself."[24] The pure colors of the glass slits transmit a "game" of light into the interior (figures 5.5 and 5.8). William Schack described this light in his article on modern art in synagogues: "In the morning sunlight pastel-soft violet, red, green, yellow beams stream through the air and lie aslant the floor in rich patches."[25] The light creates a spiritual atmosphere and enhances the architecture of the sanctuary. During the day, light shines through the colored slit openings and the concealed skylights and enhances the sacredness of the space (figure 5.5). During the night, the light from inside glimmers out in various colors of the slit windows.[26] These effects inspired the congregation and numerous scholars to call the building a "jewel box"[27] (figure 5.9). The short sides' façades are made of one steel frame filled with concrete blocks (figure 5.2).

In the interior, Johnson designed a secondary plastered ceiling concealing the building's concrete flat ceiling. (figure 5.5). The hanging ceiling is composed of seven canopies that create two rows of side skylights (figures 5.8 and 5.10). Johnson stated that the feature introduced a "more spiritual feeling into what has been a rather cold style of architecture

which we call modern."[28] He posited that "I have designed 'sails' of plaster that give a sense of containment to the space, and act as light buffers"[29] (figure 5.5). Art and architectural historian Vincent Scully (1920–2017) pointed out that these "sails" resemble the vaulting of small Roman baths, specifically those behind Hadrian's Villa.[30] Others, like Samuel Gruber (1938–), saw the vaulting as bays of a traditional

Figure 5.10. Kneses Tifereth Israel Synagogue, Port Chester, New York (1956), designed by Philip Johnson: Details of the interior skylight

longitudinal nave of a basilica, specifically the Roman Trajan's Basilica Ulpia.[31] This notion was backed up by Philip Johnson himself in his 1959 talk at Yale University, in which he stated that his passion was history and he admired Hadrian and Bernini, among others.[32] Some claim that the canopy ceiling was based on the white vaults that Johnson designed for the bedroom of his Brick House (1949), which later also appeared in the New York State Theater (now David H. Koch Theater) at Lincoln Center, New York.[33]

The congregation interpreted the seven sections of the canopy ceiling as the tent of Israel wandering in the desert and considered the number seven as a symbol of the seven days of creation. They also perceived the ever-changing light in the sanctuary as a factor that lifted their spirits and brought them closer to the divine. However, in a letter to Ms. Marjorie Tunick, one of the congregates, Johnson denied any intention to express faith symbols.[34] Johnson also mentioned that his lighting design was only functional: "Again, there is no symbolic significance to the slits. They are devices for moderating the daylight glare." In the same vein, Johnson considered the synagogue's domed entrance as "merely a domed vestibule."[35] It seems that Johnson viewed only the functionality of the synagogue, leaving the symbolic interpretations to the congregation.

Johnson recognized the functional flexibility problem of the synagogue and its challenge. He stated that "the problem of designing the contemporary synagogue is a nearly impossible one," since the sanctuary needs to act like an accordion with a large capacity for high holidays and small numbers of worshipers for daily and Sabbath services.[36] His solution was to design flexible half-height partitions framed with aluminum and steel bracing to cater to the multiple functional needs of the congregation (figure 5.5). His design was criticized as inappropriate for intimate gatherings, and as having acoustical and heating/cooling problems that resulted in high utility bills. Still, it was praised for following the idea that "the best synagogues are the purest architecture, the most straightforward expressions of what a synagogue should be."[37] Robert Walker, a past president of KTI Synagogue, summarized this dichotomy by saying that if he looked at the building only from a practical standpoint, he'd tear the building down, "but as a piece of architecture and for its aesthetic value, I think it's awe inspiring."[38]

As mentioned before, Johnson believed that "form follows function" should also prevail in the design of

Figure 5.11. Kneses Tifereth Israel Synagogue, Port Chester, New York (1956), designed by Philip Johnson: Philip Johnson's painting hanging in the synagogue's social hall

houses of worship. In his point of view, this type of building can be designed with pure, simple, modern aesthetics. Johnson, similar to other modernists, perceived simplicity as the ultimate sophistication.[39] Yet he still included his painting to decorate the wall of the social hall, opposite the focal point of the bimah (figure 5.11).

Johnson designed the bimah by following the liturgical requirements at that time. The expectations called for a hierarchal arrangement in which the rabbi and the clergy are on an upper stage above the congregation. The bimah designed by Johnson was raised by six stairs placed on the side (figures 5.12 and 5.13). He also designed the Ark as a functional

Figure 5.12. Kneses Tifereth Israel Synagogue, Port Chester, New York (1956): The original bimah as designed by Philip Johnson and Ibram Lassaw (Courtesy of Kneses Tifereth Israel Synagogue's archive)

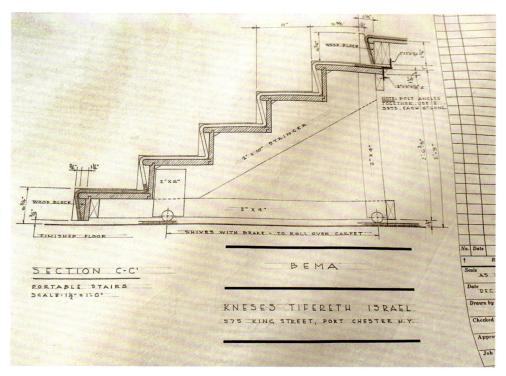

Figures 5.13. Kneses Tifereth Israel Synagogue, Port Chester, New York (1956), designed by Philip Johnson: A section drawing of side steps of the bimah (Avery Library's Drawings & Archives, Columbia University Libraries)

Figure 5.14. Kneses Tifereth Israel Synagogue, Port Chester, New York (1956): Philip Johnson's design of the synagogue's Ark and chairs; Ibram Lassaw's design of the eternal light and background wall (Pictures taken in The Jewish Museum, New York, New York)

wooden chest raised on a simple wooden platform, alongside two modest cubical chairs (figure 5.14). Some interpreted this freestanding closet as the traveling Ark of the ancient Tabernacle.[40] As suggested by Rabbi Joseph Speiser, Johnson included flat bronze letters on the Ark's door. Each letter represents a word taken from four phrases from books of the Old Testament (Zechariah 14:9, Proverbs 9:10, Psalms 34:15, and Ecclesiastes 12:13).[41] Furthermore, as all Hebrew letters have numerical values, the sum of all the letters placed on the Ark's doors equals 613, "equals the number of biblical precepts of commandments in the Torah."[42]

Johnson commissioned sculptor Ibram Lassaw (1913–2003) to work on the décor of the sanctuary's focal point. His work of art was expressive and symbolic, counter to Johnson's functional and simple design of the building and the features on the stage (e.g., the Ark, lectern, chairs). Lassaw designed the

eternal light, the menorah, and a large metal wire relief on the back wall as a background to the bimah (figures 5.12 and 5.14).

Ibram Lassaw was part of the abstract expressionist art movement that started in New York City during the 1940s and was known for its nontraditional art expression and techniques. As explained in chapter 3 of this book, abstract expressionist art in mid-twentieth-century America represented modernism and progressiveness, and was religious-neutral.[43] Many of the artists of that movement collaborated with architects on synagogue projects following architect Percival Goodman's commission of expressionist artists in his 1950s synagogue designs. Artist Ibram Lassaw collaborated with architects and created more than fifteen works for five synagogues.[44] His sculptured work was made of metal, and as did other sculptors of the time, he used a new technique of direct-metal cutting, carving, and/or hammering. It should be noted that he used these techniques for all his commissions, not necessarily only for synagogues.[45]

Lassaw designed for the KTI Synagogue a four-by-six-foot-and-ten-inch menorah made from hammered bronze by "drawing forth all the metal's sheen and glitter"[46] (figure 5.15). While his artwork for the sanctuary was sold after Johnson's death in 2005 to the Jewish Museum in New York City, the menorah still stands in the sanctuary. Avram Kampf claims that Lassaw's menorah seems primitive and spiritual since it "evokes an image of the first menorah fashioned by the biblical sculptor Bezalel, who used a crude mallet and cruder cutting tools."[47] The eternal light was also designed by Lassaw, who perceived it as a mystical light.[48] Lassaw continued to experiment with crude metal in his work for the KTI synagogue and set a precedent for other artists'

Figure 5.15. Kneses Tifereth Israel Synagogue, Port Chester, New York (1956), designed by Philip Johnson: Ibram Lassaw's menorah, still standing on the synagogue's bimah

treatments of eternal lights.[49] He designed it as a glowing sun hanging from the ceiling in front of the stage (figures 5.12 and 5.14). It is a round metal disc with a concealed light bulb at the center that radiates "sun rays" throughout the metal of the circle. It reminds us of the power of the sun as the eternal light of the universe and also the power of God's presence, as mentioned in the book of Psalms, "I have set the LORD always before me: because *he is* at my right hand" (Psalms 16:8).

Lassaw's third work of art in Johnson's sanctuary is an airy barbed-wire screen hanging on the wall behind the stage (figures 5.12 and 5.14). It is designed as a twelve-foot-high, thirty-four-foot-wide, and one-foot-deep composition of squares, rectangles, and spaces between them. Its lightness and delicacy helped counter the simple and pristine white architectural volume of the sanctuary. It is made of "bent, welded woven copper, brass and aluminum wires with interspersed rectangular forms of brazed bronze."[50] Lassaw entitled his work on the wall *Creation*. In a letter to Ms. Marjorie Tunick, a member of the congregation, he explained that "it is as a symphony structured in space rather than sound. It is an offering in praise and wonder of the living universe."[51] However, Kampf and others criticized all the artwork on the stage, including Johnson's designs, as "grotesque."

As mentioned earlier, following the death of Lassaw in 2003 and Johnson in 2005, the congregation became free to make changes in the synagogue and deal with the maintenance of the building. Maintenance issues included, for example, the replacement of the roof and skylights, the upgrade of the sound system, the addition of a new awning over the entrance, and installing a new front door. Since the synagogue departed from traditional design and exemplified the core concepts of modernism, the synagogue's renovations committee asked themselves the same question as the building committee fifty years earlier: "Do we want a really modern building?"[52] Howard Lavitt, one of the chairmen of the committee, stated in an article that there was great support from the community for the renovations: "It was really quite heartening."[53] The synagogue underwent major interior changes under architect Michael Berkowicz from Presentations Gallery firm in Mt. Vernon, New York. Johnson's bimah and its features (e.g., the Ark, the chairs, the lectern), and Lassaw's artworks, were replaced with new and more conservative décor (figure 5.16). The stage was lowered to accommodate changes in liturgical requirements (see chapter 6), and a ramp was added on the new bimah's side in accordance with the Americans with Disabilities Act (ADA). The more dramatic change was the replacement of Johnson's Ark and Lassaw's eternal light and his *Creation* wirework. As mentioned before, the original features and artwork, except for the menorah, were sold to the Jewish Museum in New York. The new Ark's niche (*heichal*) and the new bimah's background are made of large panels of Jerusalem stone, and the Ark can be reached through wooden doors. A new wooden lectern, wider than the original, was moved from the side to the middle of the bimah in front of the Ark, and a new smaller metal eternal light replaced the original "sun"-like eternal light that some saw as a symbol of worshiping the sun, which is part of paganism.

The sale and replacement of the bimah, Ark closet, and especially Lassaw's *Creation* wirework raise some questions: Did the modifications reflect a change in taste, as the original art no longer appealed to the congregation and "was vague in its message"?[54] Or was it because some congregants saw the barbed wire as a reminder of Nazi concentration camps, "which in turn made them wonder about Mr. Johnson's intentions"?[55] Thus, after more than fifty years, we are left with a beautiful modern volume and superb quality of light, but with a clouded history that became more pronounced since the publication of Johnson's biography in 1994 and later with Johnson's obituaries, which mentioned his antisemitic and racist past.[56]

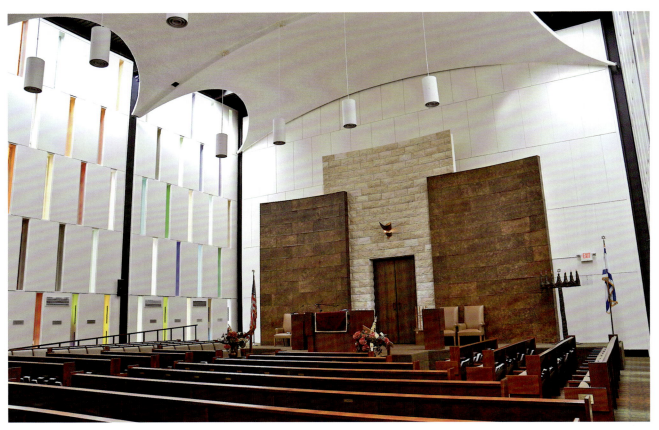

Figure 5.16. Kneses Tifereth Israel Synagogue, Port Chester, New York (1956), designed by Philip Johnson: Current sanctuary and bimah as designed by Michael Berkowicz

Abstracted Modern Art in Synagogues and Flexibility

Percival Goodman: Congregation B'nai Israel Synagogue, Millburn, New Jersey (1950)

Architect Percival Goodman (1904–1989) was the most prolific synagogue architect of the modern time. He designed more than fifty synagogues across the United States between 1947 and 1979. Goodman's designs departed from historicism and attempted to create the modern American synagogue by integrating modern American abstract art into his design. With that, he pushed the envelope of synagogues' aesthetics and translated "the modernist building vocabulary . . . into a language appropriate for religious buildings."[57]

The inclusion of art in Goodman's synagogue architecture was an integral part of his practice and the subject of most of his publications. He allocated part of the design's budget for art inclusion and hoped that the collaboration of architects and artists would be established as the norm in designing synagogues. Indeed, his approach influenced many other architects to include modern art as part of their designs of synagogues. In his publications, he and his brother, sociologist Paul Goodman, stated that architecture is part of the visual arts and can enhance the congregation's modern new self-awareness. They also acknowledged that none of the rising Jewish artists of modern times had ever worked in religious buildings, though they expressed their interest in interpreting "Biblical archetypes, the Prophetic tradition, and the simple sublime spirituality of Jewish theology."[58] As such, Goodman commissioned Jewish artists to include their artwork in the design of his synagogues. He worked with emerging American avant-garde and abstract expressionist artists.[59] Among them were Adolph Gottlieb, Robert Motherwell, Herbert Ferber, Ibram Lassaw, and Seymour Lipton. Their works of art represented a new style that was regarded as "energetic, bold, and confident,"[60] and served the "eternal unfoldment of the Jewish spirit."[61] Goodman believed that the work of the architect and the artist(s) would create an "atmosphere of sober joy as befits a celebration of the Creator. [As such], the light is clear, the air pure, the color gay rather than somber."[62] As shown in chapter 4, Eric Mendelsohn, Frank Lloyd Wright, and Minoru Yamasaki also shared Goodman's idea to design a synagogue as the Lord's new song.[63]

Percival Goodman's pioneering collaboration with artists and his publications[64] prompted artists, architects, and scholars to discuss this relationship. For example, artist Gyorgy Kepes (1906–2001), in his publication *The Language of Vision*,[65] emphasized the importance of the power of art and architecture to communicate social and spiritual values. Painter Lionel Reiss (1894–1986) talked about the realization of religion and art as essential to Jewish survival.[66] Other architects and artists discussed the synthesis of art and architecture in an article "Views of Art and Architecture: A Conversation," published in the journal *Dædalus*.[67] These discussions included two major ideas. First, art can be found in the architectural work itself.[68] See, for example, Frank Lloyd Wright's Beth Sholom Synagogue in Elkins Park, Pennsylvania (chapter 4). The second notion in their discussions refers to the need for contemporary art in architecture to exhibit its expressive objective(s) and be integrated into the building's design.[69] The latter was the design approach of Percival Goodman, who believed in the collaboration between architects and artists, where architecture is enhanced by the art while framing the art to have its "place to breathe and unfold"[70] (see chapter 3 for more details).[71]

Percival Goodman's second most important design contribution to modern American synagogues was his emphasis on community activities "with a corresponding diminution in the facilities for worship."[72] Similar to Eric Mendelsohn's synagogues, Percival Goodman designed synagogue complexes serving as community centers that included the prayer wing and social and education wings. To accommodate the congregations' needs for a flexible solution for their prayer services and cater to all other activities, Goodman applied insights published by Rachel Wischnitzer-Bernstein, an architect and art historian.[73] She outlined the suggestion of Ben Bloch to design the synagogue's social hall or school adjacent to the sanctuary with partitions dividing the spaces. Eric Mendelsohn designed both the social hall and lobby of his 1949 Park Synagogue in Cleveland, Ohio, to be opened to the sanctuary for the high holiday services, with a small separated chapel for daily services. Percival Goodman promoted and used this solution in all his synagogues, including his 1950 design of Congregation B'nai Israel Synagogue in New Jersey. To accommodate the variation in occupancy at the different services (e.g., few participants for daily services, medium attendance for Shabbat services, large occupancy for high holiday services), Goodman designed the social hall and/or the lobby adjacent to the sanctuary with dividing partitions/doors to be opened, extending the seating for the larger services. Small separate chapels were designed for daily services (see examples later in this section). This arrangement is different from Philip Johnson's synagogue in Port Chester, New York, where he designed one sanctuary hall divided by a small partition. Goodman's full-height partitions that can be opened between designated spaces followed his modern design concept of creating a dynamic flow between spaces. This flexible, functional/practical design influenced generations of architects

who "replicated [it] countless times throughout the nation."[74]

During the 1950s, Goodman attempted to commemorate the Holocaust in his synagogues (see chapter 1). His most known synagogue of that period is Congregation B'nai Israel, in Millburn, New Jersey (1950), which is analyzed in this section. In the 1960s, he followed the development of cathedral synagogues and designed sculptural monumental steel and concrete structures. His most known synagogue along this concept is the 1962 Congregation Shaarey Zedek Synagogue in Southfield, Michigan, which is analyzed in the next section. This and his other expressive projects of that period translated traditional monumental synagogue designs into modern institutions that showcased Jewish confidence in belonging in America.

Congregation B'nai Israel, Millburn, New Jersey (1950)

The Conservative Congregation B'nai Israel was founded in 1924 under the name of Congregation B'nai Yisroel.[75] They purchased ground on Lackawanna Place in New Jersey and completed construction of their first synagogue in 1925. In response to the growth of the congregation, by

Figure 5.17. Congregation B'nai Israel Synagogue, Millburn, New Jersey (1950), designed by Percival Goodman: Main façade with Herbert Ferber's sculpture

1942 they employed their first rabbi—Rabbi Melvin Keiffer.[76] Later that year, he was replaced by Rabbi Max Gruenewald, who emigrated from Germany after his synagogue in Mannheim was destroyed during the 1938 Kristallnacht pogrom.[77] He was instrumental in building the 1950 Congregation B'nai Israel Synagogue and worked closely with architect Percival Goodman (figure 5.17). The rabbi's main influence was expressed in commemorating the Holocaust through the synagogue's sanctuary design. Goodman used dim light in the space and mounted an English script on the sanctuary's wall as a remembrance: "To the heroes and martyrs, the known and unknown who died for the sanctification of the Divine Name" (figure 5.18). Underneath this text, he designed two niches within the brick wall of the sanctuary. They contain two small pieces of marble cornerstones retrieved from Rabbi's Gruenewald synagogue in Mannheim, Germany, that was destroyed by the Nazis. These eye-level cornerstones and their inscriptions accent a sense of memorial in the space. While the Holocaust memory was strong, the rabbi also promoted a modern synagogue design that he saw as a redemption from persecution.[78] Though Goodman was a secular Jew, his sense of Jewish identity was awakened by the Holocaust. He once characterized himself as "an agnostic who was converted by Hitler."[79] Goodman designed the Congregation B'nai Israel Synagogue in Millburn, New Jersey, as a modern and modest complex—a

Figure 5.18. Congregation B'nai Israel Synagogue, Millburn, New Jersey (1950), designed by Percival Goodman: The sanctuary hosts two marble stones retrieved from the Rabbi's destroyed synagogue in Germany, a remembrance mounted script, and Stars of David.

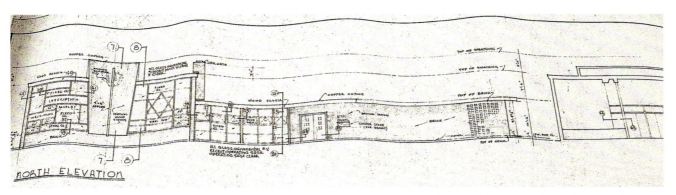

Figure 5.19. Congregation B'nai Israel Synagogue, Millburn, New Jersey (1950), designed by Percival Goodman: A drawing of the main elevation (Courtesy of Congregation B'nai Israel Synagogue archive)

horizontal "set of low, sprawling boxes in glass, brick and light wood that exemplified Modernism and the aspirations of American Jewish communities after the war"[80] (figure 5.19). The synagogue marks a drastic departure from traditional European synagogue architecture, allowing the congregation to detach themselves from their memories of horror.

In a manuscript entitled "The New Synagogue," Goodman described Judaism as a horizontal religion since all parts of life are holy.[81] In his point of view, horizontality made it possible to design all parts (wings) of the synagogue complex as a whole. The building would host all activities that are considered "a hymn in His Praise."[82] The horizontality of the building was kept in Goodman's addition of a school wing to Congregation B'nai Israel Synagogue in 1962, and during its major renovation and expansion in 2011.[83] The synagogue is one story tall with two skylights on each side of the main aisle of the sanctuary, while the school is a later addition of a two-story building built by Goodman in the same style and material (brick, wood, glass) as the prayer wing (figure 5.20).

Architect Goodman commissioned artist Herbert Ferber (1906–91) to design an abstract sculpture for the exterior main façade. Rabbi Gruenewald asked that the sculpture would symbolize the "burning bush" that never consumes and reflects the fate of the Jewish people.[84] In order to highlight this sculpture, Goodman used architecture to frame the art. He designed a natural cypress wooden vertical piece that projects out of the horizontal brick and glass wall for hanging Ferber's sculpture (figure 5.17). Indeed, Ferber mounted to that wall his twelve-by-eight-foot sculpture, which was designed of copper and brass covered with soldered lead.[85] He used a new direct-metal technique based on direct cutting, carving, and hammering the metal. Ferber, as his counterpart artist, emphasized the process of working with metal, rather than the polished product.[86] In this sculpture, the rough surfaces elicit a kinesthetic response from the flames, which capture the visual attention of the worshipers.[87] Sculptures that evolve from historic liturgical subjects are considered some of the most effective art forms for modern synagogues.[88]

Figure 5.20. Congregation B'nai Israel Synagogue, Millburn, New Jersey (1950), designed by Percival Goodman: The school wing was an addition designed by Perceval Goodman in 1962

Figure 5.21. Congregation B'nai Israel Synagogue, Millburn, New Jersey (1950), designed by Percival Goodman: The sanctuary—a view of the horizontal façade from the interior, on both sides of the Ark

As illustrated in the original elevation's drawing (figure 5.19) and in the image of the façade (figure 5.17), the wooden projection piece designed for the sculpture is flanked by two huge horizontal translucent walls made of blue-green frosted glass. Their mullions are arranged in Mondrian-like style,[89] forming a horizontal view. The horizontal part is decorated with a Star of David made of the same metal as the glass mullion and two boards with Hebrew and English inscriptions also framed by the same metal mullions. Goodman left the glass pane translucent to showcase the sanctuary's menorah that can be seen from the outside (figure 5.17). This is an interesting relationship between the exterior and interior that supports Goodman's design concept of creating a rhythm between parts of the building (figure 5.21).

In the interior, Goodman collaborated with two additional American abstract expressionists: painter, printmaker, and editor Robert Motherwell (1915–1991), who designed a mural at the synagogue's entrance; and painter, sculptor, and printmaker Adolph Gottlieb (1903–1974), who designed the Ark's curtain (the parochet). The design of the mural respects the orange wooden-planked wall designed by Goodman (figure 5.22).[90] Motherwell explained that the mural itself became the wall, which glows

Figure 5.22. Congregation B'nai Israel Synagogue, Millburn, New Jersey (1950), designed by Percival Goodman: Robert Motherwell's mural at the entrance

in harmony with the rest of the entrance walls. The eight-by-six-foot mural was painted orange in oil on Masonite boards. It offers a semiabstract decorative design and includes symbolic images of a white menorah, a gray-blue Ark holding a white surface with twelve dots representing the twelve tribes of Israel, the Ten Commandments tablets in gray, and Jacob's ladder to heaven in white, which introduces a vertical movement (energy) to the painting. These abstracted images that were not figurative and religiously didactic were criticized by many of the congregation members who did not understand the painting. They saw it as a wall decoration and not as a work of art "at which one pauses to observe and study."[91] I believe that the beauty of the abstracted mural is in its ability to trigger the imagination and art interpretations. For example, looking at the mural, I have interpreted the Ark symbol as open Torah scrolls ready to be read, or scrolls holding the mystical Kabbalistic symbols of sacred geometry and astronomy.

The sanctuary was designed by Goodman in a human scale and constructed with brick walls that are adorned with Hebrew inscriptions cut out of wood (figures 5.21). The proportion of the space and the warm colors of the brick and wood create an intimate sanctuary. To accommodate the flexible design requirement, Goodman located the social hall adjacent to the sanctuary and used dividing doors between them. He also opened the sanctuary to the corridor, which leads to a smaller social hall that serves the school activities. When the doors and dividers are open, both halls serve as an extension to the sanctuary and can accommodate larger occupancies during high holidays services, festivals, or family celebrations (e.g., Bar Mitzvahs or weddings).

As mentioned before, this was one of Goodman's first synagogues to use a flexible design solution. A separate chapel for daily use serves for smaller gatherings (figure 5.23). Note that the chapel was designed in the same style as the whole synagogue—an intimate proportional room with horizontal opaque windows and a parochet for the Ark resembling Motherwell's mural.

The main sanctuary's bimah and the tall Ark are located in front of the horizontal blue-green translucent glass walls of the main façade. In the original design, the lectern was placed on the stage, but later it was moved down to the center of the worshipers' seating, facing the Ark (figure 5.21). The change in the ceiling height creates a skylight that directs the eye to the focal point—the Ark—which is located in the middle of the stage.

The Ark is a tall, narrow, vertical wooden cabinet covered from floor to ceiling with a nineteen-by-eight-foot curtain (parochet) designed by artist Adolph Gottlieb and handmade by the women of the congregation as a quilt from Italian velvet appliqué (figure 5.24).[92] Gottlieb's idea for this piece of art was to express a "universal and continuity of human existence."[93] The curtain is rich with colors that compose a glowing collage. Gottlieb used rectangular and circular shapes to include traditional

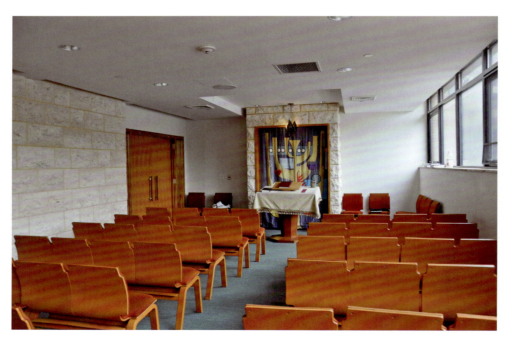

Figure 5.23. Congregation B'nai Israel Synagogue, Millburn, New Jersey (1950), designed by Percival Goodman: The chapel

Figure 5.24. Congregation B'nai Israel Synagogue, Millburn, New Jersey (1950), designed by Percival Goodman: Adolph Gottlieb's parochet of the Ark

of the artwork, all three artists preserved Jewish traditional symbols and expressed them in a modern abstracted way that was integrated into Goodman's design of one of his first modern synagogues.

Goodman's design of Congregation B'nai Israel in Millburn, New Jersey (1950) illustrates his unique contribution to the design of modern American synagogues. He added American art to lift the soul of the congregation and to enhance the sacredness of the flexible, functional design. In the next section, I analyze another of Goodman's synagogues, which is part of the development of the "cathedral-synagogue" design concept.

These two synagogues reflect not just Goodman's design evolution but also the changes in Jewish identity and perception in the American context. The first synagogue portrays architectural concepts of Holocaust memorials as interwoven within modern American architecture and art, while the second synagogue evolved to express the post-Holocaust triumph, showcasing a cathedral synagogue as a core testament of Jewish life in the new land of America.

Cathedral Synagogue: Steel/Precast Structural System

Percival Goodman: Congregation Shaarey Zedek, Southfield, Michigan (1962)

This congregation was established in 1861 by seventeen followers of Traditional Judaism who withdrew from the Beth-El Society in Detroit, Michigan, to found the "Shaarey Zedek Society."[94] It was one of the pioneering congregations of the Conservative Judaism movement in the United States. They joined the national organization of Conservative Judaism, the United Synagogues of America, in 1913. In 1961, during the centennial annual meeting of the congregation, most of the members approved the recommendation to build a new synagogue on a forty-acre site overlooking the River Rouge and Highway I-696 in Southfield, Michigan, a suburb of Detroit. Today, the river is not visible due to over-vegetation,[95] but the synagogue's sanctuary is clearly visible from the highway.

symbols that he abstracted. These contain columns of the Jerusalem Temple; a crown with its jewel-studded rim; a lion's paw; pomegranates; twelve small, rectangular abstracted images of the symbols of the twelve tribes of Israel; the Shield of David; the Ten Commandments tablets; and more. It is interesting to note that at first the congregation found the composition and its symbols strange, but with time they accepted the design. This can be attributed to their ability to decipher the familiar traditional symbols and the fact that members of the congregation were part of the art making.

The pioneering collaboration between architect Goodman and the different artists in this synagogue became the example to follow. Despite the diversity

Figure 5.25. Congregation Shaarey Zedek Synagogue, Southfield, Michigan (1962), designed by Percival Goodman: The synagogue's soaring roof out of the horizontal part of the building

Figure 5.26. Congregation Shaarey Zedek Synagogue, Southfield, Michigan (1962), designed by Percival Goodman: A model of the synagogue's complex (Courtesy of Congregation Shaarey Zedek Synagogue's archive)

Figure 5.27. Congregation Shaarey Zedek Synagogue, Southfield, Michigan (1962), designed by Percival Goodman: The sanctuary's soaring roof with its five double projections signifying the Ten Commandments

The new synagogue was designed by architect Percival Goodman from New York City with Detroit's Albert Kahn Associates as the resident architects and construction supervisors. It was the congregation's sixth building, and it is an excellent example of the evolution of synagogue design from a functional, bold, straight-lined horizontal design to an expressive, sculptural building. It also exhibits innovations in building technology, such as the extensive use of a steel structural system and the construction and use of precast concrete in building a cathedral synagogue. Congregation Shaarey Zedek "remains one of [Goodman's] most assertive projects embodying Goodman's work at the peak of his career."[96]

Though Goodman's 1962 Congregation Shaarey Zedek Synagogue is mostly horizontal, its focal point—the sanctuary—soars to the sky. It dominates the synagogue's form, creating an image of a vertical structure (figure 5.25). This design also follows Goodman's concept of a dynamic movement between parts of the buildings, as the vertical element "climbs" up from the horizontal spaces of the synagogues but does not overpower the structure (figure 5.26).

The soaring 108-feet tall concrete diamond-shaped sanctuary is based on an innovative steel structural system (see details later). This vertical part of the synagogue embodies the sanctuary (figure 5.27). It is perceived as Mount Sinai, where the Ten Commandments were given to the people of Israel. The five double projections on the soaring façade, as well as on the marble that frames the Ark inside, signify the Ten Commandments (figure 5.28). Others see the soaring roof as clasped praying hands. This symbol is universal, and as such, it is also used in church designs (see, for example, Frank Lloyd Wright's Unitarian Meeting House, in Shorewood Hills, Wisconsin).

Goodman followed the 1960s design of striking, expressive concrete cathedral synagogues (e.g., Minuro Yamasaki's synagogue in Glencoe, Illinois)

Figure 5.28. Congregation Shaarey Zedek Synagogue, Southfield, Michigan (1962), designed by Percival Goodman: The sanctuary's interior. Note the marble Ark with its five double projections signifying the Ten Commandments.

but based it mainly on steel construction. Congregation Shaarey Zedek Synagogue was designed as a large, monumental complex (figure 5.26). It serves prayer with a main sanctuary and separate chapels (including one for the school); it contains a social wing that has two main social halls on both sides of the main sanctuary; and it hosts an educational wing of a school that includes kindergarten, elementary, and high school classes, and a library. These multiple activities called for a large monumental lobby at the entrance to the synagogue, which becomes the threshold of the journey from the outside world to the sacred. The lobby is a hundred feet long and thirty-six feet wide and connects the main sanctuary and the chapel. From the lobby, you can enter the sanctuary, the social halls, the school, and the administration offices. In addition, Goodman designed a symbolic gate, prior to the synagogue's main entrance, as the first threshold to separate the worshiper from the parking lot (figure 5.29).

The gate consists of a large horizontal concrete canopy that rests on two major concrete columns in a V shape. It is decorated with a phrase written in Hebrew, "Open to me the gates of righteousness. I will enter into them. I will give thanks to Yah" (Psalm 118:19).

The sanctuary is designed as an elongated diamond-shaped space (figure 5.28) that is flanked by two equilateral triangular spaces serving as the social halls. These halls are separated from the sanctuary by three-inch-thick folding wooden panels. One hall contains a stage and is used as an auditorium. The other serves as a dining room with an adjacent kitchen (figure 5.30). When open and connected, the three spaces occupy approximately 32,000 square feet and can host up to 3,600 people.[97] The trapezoidal plan enables the bimah to be situated within 120 feet of all seats. This helps worshipers see the focal point and enhances the acoustics in the sanctuary.

Figure 5.29. Congregation Shaarey Zedek Synagogue, Southfield, Michigan (1962), designed by Percival Goodman: The entrance's front concrete canopy

Figure 5.30. Congregation Shaarey Zedek Synagogue, Southfield, Michigan (1962), designed by Percival Goodman: The social hall/dining room adjacent to the sanctuary

The sanctuary rises ninety feet at the front and descends to forty-five feet at the rear (figure 5.28). The bimah is composed of two levels (figures 5.28 and 5.31). The lower level rises by seven stairs and serves as the place for the lectern for reading the Torah, and it has chairs for the clergy. The second level is smaller in size and is raised by an additional three stairs. It serves to hold the Ark (figure 5.32). Thus the climb toward the Ark not only separates the worshiper from the surroundings, but also enhances the sacred verticality of the place. This design repeated itself in the interiors of cathedral synagogues and added to their monumentality (e.g., Yamasaki's synagogue in Glencoe, Illinois; Belluchi's synagogue in Short Hills, New Jersey). It also catered to the older doctrine of hierarchy between the clergy and the congregation.

The ceiling slopes up toward the focal point and frames the Ark. The effect of ribbing the ceiling along the walls is interpreted as a tent for praying—the Tabernacle (figure 5.28). Goodman utilized these ribs, which are framed with deep trussed steel arches, to hide the sanctuary's heating, ventilation,

and air-conditioning duct system.[98] The Ark is forty feet high and is made of polished golden Galilee marble imported from Israel. It reflects the colored light of the stained-glass windows that frame it (figure 5.28).

As in his other synagogues, Goodman collaborated with American artists to enhance the sacredness of the building. Artist Robert Pinart (1927–2017) designed the glass with abstracted patterns of the Tabernacle as described in the book of Exodus. Some interpret the patterns and their colors as the burning bush out of which God spoke to Moses (figures 5.28 and 5.33) Artist Jan Peter Stern (1927–) designed a stainless-steel sculpture in the center of the Ark (figure 5.33). This sculpture incorporates the eternal light (Ner Tamid), and its apex ends with a menorah. Again, we see here how architecture frames art and enhances the design of the Ark.

The major achievement of the design and construction of this synagogue is accomplished by its structural system and modern materials such as steel and precast concrete (both in the exterior and

Figure 5.31. Congregation Shaarey Zedek Synagogue, Southfield, Michigan (1962), designed by Percival Goodman: A drawing of the bimah (Avery Library's Drawings & Archives, Columbia University Libraries)

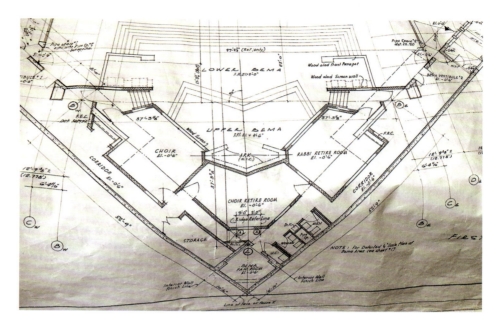

Figure 5.32. Congregation Shaarey Zedek Synagogue in Southfield, Michigan (1962): Percival Goodman's sketch of the sanctuary and its Ark (Avery Library's Drawings & Archives, Columbia University Libraries)

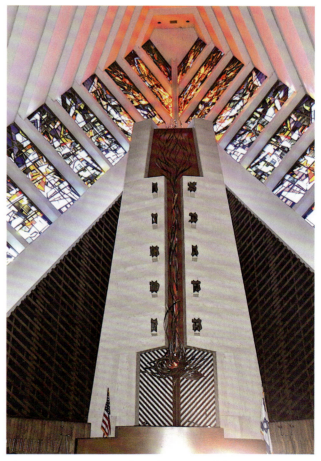

Figure 5.33. Congregation Shaarey Zedek Synagogue, Southfield, Michigan (1962): The marble Ark designed by Percival Goodman, framed by stained glass designed by Robert Pinart, which includes a stainless-steel sculpture within the center of the Ark designed by Peter Stern

interior of the sanctuary and its adjacent social halls).[99] The design of the sanctuary as part of the building is based on sets of steel and precast frames. Each diminishing in size and supporting the soaring roof, its stained-glass windows, the sanctuary's interior, and its marble Ark (figure 5.34). The main frames are "two hinged trussed steel frames of 11-foot depth and about 153-foot span," with 45-foot-long cantilevers at the high portion of the roof over the bimah[100] (figure 5.35). The roof of the sanctuary is formed by a series of three-hinged trussed arches of varying span and height, "springing from two frames located alongside the division lines between the central sanctuary and the adjacent Social Halls"[101] (figure 5.36). The flat roofs of these halls are made of conventional trusses and purlins. Six hundred tons of structural steel were used in construction, in addition to precast concrete elements and twenty thousand square feet of glass.[102] Part of the structural system includes exposed concrete beams with triangular trusses that resemble the contour lines of the Star of David (figure 5.25). The L-shaped concrete beams support the entrance lobby to the sanctuary and the social halls (figure 5.37).[103]

The steep roof of the sanctuary is covered with eighty thousand square feet of Follansbee Terne

Figure 5.34. Congregation Shaarey Zedek Synagogue, Southfield, Michigan (1962), designed by Percival Goodman: The frame supporting the precast mullions and the stained-glass windows around the Ark under construction (Avery Library's Drawings & Archives, Columbia University Libraries)

Figure 5.35. Congregation Shaarey Zedek Synagogue, Southfield, Michigan (1962), designed by Percival Goodman: The steel frame system of the sanctuary (Courtesy of Congregation Shaarey Zedek Synagogue's archive)

Figure 5.36. Congregation Shaarey Zedek Synagogue, Southfield, Michigan (1962), designed by Percival Goodman: The steel frame system of the sanctuary and social halls on both sides (Courtesy of Congregation Shaarey Zedek Synagogue's archive)

Figure 5.37. Congregation Shaarey Zedek Synagogue, Southfield, Michigan (1962), designed by Percival Goodman: Triangular precast concrete beams in the lobby

Figure 5.38. Congregation Shaarey Zedek Synagogue, Southfield, Michigan (1962), designed by Percival Goodman: The chapel's exterior, facing an inner courtyard

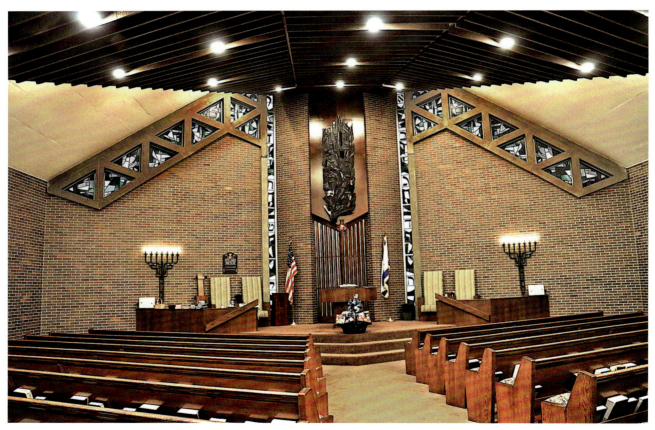

Figure 5.39. Congregation Shaarey Zedek Synagogue, Southfield, Michigan (1962), designed by Percival Goodman: The chapel's interior

metal roof decking "underlaid by insulation and solid wood planking spanning between the steel purlins. Wood battens form the backbone of the seams"[104] (figure 5.25). The terne metal sheets "form a weather-tight shield with unlimited life expectancy,"[105] do not need any pretreatment for soldering, are completely adaptable to paint, and have one of the lowest coefficients of expansion for roofing material.[106] In addition to terne metal's elegant looks, it is a highly workable material and costs less than a conventional metal roof.[107]

The main chapel, which hosts 250 seats, was designed with the same motifs as the main sanctuary but on a smaller scale. It is built with a conventional structural system that includes two exposed precast concrete trusses filled in with stained glass to support the steeply inclined roof slab over the chapel. The chapel's exterior and interior walls are cladded by bricks (figures 5.38 and 5.39). The school and the administration wings were also built with a simple structural system around a courtyard. The large windows of the school wing introduce a lot of light to the classrooms (figure 5.38).

Goodman's synagogue designs highlight the ethos of Judaism via a specific formal vocabulary.[108] The architecture was driven by Jewish requirements to include, in addition to the prayer space, social and educational facilities. Goodman saw this as an opportunity to frame synagogues as places for people to gather for multiple diverse activities as "a hymn in His praise."[109] His collaboration with artists augmented the synagogues' sacredness. Finally, Goodman demonstrated his thrust for innovations in an elaborate structural system based on steel and precast concrete construction in his Congregation Shaarey Zedek Synagogue. With this design, and similar to Minoru Yamasaki, Goodman showcased the cathedral synagogue as an innovative building technology development for the modern synagogue.

Cathedral Synagogue: Church or Synagogue?

Pietro Belluschi: Temple B'nai Jeshurun, Short Hills, New Jersey, 1964

As described in chapter 4, the "cathedral synagogue" became a popular design concept during the 1960s and served to glorify the synagogue as an institution for Jewish congregations across the United States. The monumental designs host, in addition to the prayer function, social and educational activities, acting as huge community centers. These synagogues utilized innovations in building technology and modern expression of aesthetics. Though congregations wanted to distinguish their synagogues from their neighbors' churches, the glorification of the cathedral synagogues often raised the question of whether the cathedral synagogue is a synagogue or a church. More so, art historian Susan G. Solomon, in her book *Louis I. Kahn's Jewish Architecture: Mikveh Israel and the Midcentury American Synagogue*, devoted a chapter to the question "Does it look Jewish?"[110] The congregations' need to distinguish their synagogues from other types of buildings in their surroundings resulted in the construction of cathedral synagogues that integrated "decorative arts with Jewish themes (e.g., the Star of David, the tablets of the Ten Commandments, and more) into their universal solutions."[111] The synagogues' exteriors exhibited modernism and showed that Judaism is a progressive religion that belongs in America, while the decorative arts in the interiors illustrated the link to Jewish traditions.

Like many modernist architects, Pietro Belluschi (1899–1994) applied the cathedral synagogue approach and used decorative arts to bridge between modernism and Judaism. Belluschi, an American Institute of Architects gold medalist and former dean of the School of Architecture and Planning at the Massachusetts Institute of Technology, is identified as a modernist architect with a focus on the regional architecture of the American Northwest. His designs attempted to link modernism to indigenous materials and highlight simplicity.[112] In his article "The Meaning of Regionalism in Architecture" (1955), he discussed regionalism and modernism as part of the changing world and globalization trends.[113] He concluded that regionalism can still be obtained by adopting humility and maintaining a human-scale design. He believed that the modern society of his time adhered more to technology and to the scientific process. Therefore, in his point of view, the design of modern churches of that period expressed the "decay of our spiritual heritage."[114] However, since society longs to find its spiritual experience, Belluschi advocated designing houses of worship on a "more human scale . . . to produce the kind of atmosphere most conductive to worship."[115] In addition, he believed that the architect needs to explore the relation with God and understand the nature of religion as an institution, which tends to glorify the spirit.[116] "To him, religion was a search for spiritual fulfillment. And designing religious buildings was itself an act of worship."[117]

Like other modernist architects (e.g., Eric Mendelsohn and Frank Lloyd Wright), Belluschi also believed that free people should express the time they live in. He quoted a pastor from Syracuse, New York, who claimed that congregations should "refashion their tradition in fresh new shapes and forms."[118] In the same article, Belluschi emphasized that a church design should focus on providing multiple visual experiences that can be enhanced by the effects of light and shadow within a proper scale. These ideas were reflected in his church and synagogue designs.

Like Percival Goodman, who emphasized in his synagogue designs the dynamics of the movement between spaces, Pietro Belluschi believed that the architect needs to create space sequences that instigate spiritual experiences rather than focusing on one traditional static space and image.[119] This idea was the basis for achieving transcendent quality in his church designs. Belluschi designed more than thirty churches of different denominations in various

parts of the United States, becoming one of the foremost church designers in the country.[120] He was an influential member of the Church Architectural Guild of America.[121] In the guild's national conferences on church architecture, members focused both on modern architecture as a response to the different liturgical changes and on the concept of regional designs. In Belluschi's church projects, he reacted to the changes in the liturgy during the late 1950s and 1960s that called for a closer relationship between the clergy and the congregation. This led to the design of new forms and new floor plans (e.g., a central plan for the sanctuary, instead of longitudinal naves). With that, he attempted to express the human spirit through an eloquent simplicity and understated elegance. Yet, in his synagogue designs, he was still influenced by the hierarchical order of the old ways and designed the bimah and Ark as pedestals standing above and removed from the congregation (see, for example, interior images of Temple B'Nai Jeshurun provided later in this chapter).

In addition to his many church projects, Belluschi designed five synagogues: Temple Israel, Swampscott, Massachusetts (1956–1959)[122]; Temple Adath Israel, Merion Station, Pennsylvania (1956–1959); Temple B'rith Kodesh, Rochester, New York (1959–1963); Temple B'nai Jeshurun, Short Hills, New Jersey (1964–1968); and United Hebrew Synagogue, St. Louis, Missouri (1986–1989). In all these synagogues, he created elegant monumental sanctuaries using concrete and/or steel construction with simple, warm-finish materials such as brick and wood. He claimed that these materials "may achieve beauty without ostentation and with economy of means. The architecture of the synagogue should be a fluent expression of the spirit of man."[123] All his synagogues were designed as cathedral synagogues with a central polygonal sanctuary. This followed Jewish liturgical requirements that were different from those he accommodated in his different church designs. After studying the Jewish customs, he designed his synagogues as a place of assembly, study, and prayer, and not only as a house of God, as is common in Christianity.[124] He designed "an explicit rationalized structure that met a clear transcendent purpose in distinctly Judaic terms."[125]

Four of his synagogues were designed with a high cupola structure rising over them. Natural light penetrates through the high drums to generate a stream of light from above that enhances the spiritual experience in the sanctuary. Though Belluschi used the drum effect in some of his church designs (see, for example, Portsmouth Abbey Church in Portsmouth, Rhode Island, 1952–1961[126]), he adapted this feature to his synagogue designs. He based the number of glass panels in the synagogues' drums on the Jewish numbers of the Ten Commandments or the twelve tribes of Israel. For example, Temple B'rith Kodesh in Rochester, New York, includes a sixty-five-foot tall, twelve-sided cupola sanctuary.[127] The Star of David was also introduced as the main decorative motif over the sanctuary's cupola on the exterior of Temple Israel in Swampscott, Massachusetts, and in a dramatic way in the interior of Temple Adath Israel in Merion Station, Pennsylvania.[128] He attempted to differentiate synagogues from church designs by utilizing decorative Jewish motifs. Susan

G. Solomon claimed that the decorations linked these monumental synagogues to Judaism rather than the architecture itself.

In this section, I analyze the less-studied synagogue of Belluschi's work. It is the only one that does not include a cupola on a drum: Temple B'nai Jeshurun in Short Hills, New Jersey. Its trapezoidal sanctuary embedded in a square space is covered with a slanted roof (figure 5.40). The brick exterior reflects Belluschi's regionalism concepts by blending the structure within the surrounding residential neighborhood and catering to the hilly wooded site. On its exterior, it does not portray any Jewish symbols to be identified as a synagogue. In the interior, except for stained glass with abstracted images, and the wooden screened *heichal*, Belluschi did not introduce Jewish symbols. Rather, he incorporated into the sanctuary the decorative arts brought from the congregation's second synagogue (discussed later). With that, he believed he connected the congregation to its history.

Figure 5.40. Temple B'nai Jeshurun Synagogue, Short Hills, New Jersey (1964), designed by Pietro Belluschi: The reddish-brown brick sanctuary's slanted roof meeting the other parts' flat roofs

Temple B'nai Jeshurun, Short Hills, New Jersey (1964–1968)

In 1848, a small group of families from Central Europe settled in Newark, New Jersey, and founded the Orthodox Congregation B'nai Jeshurun, which translates to "Children of the Upright."[129] They built their first synagogue in 1858. A second synagogue was erected in 1868. Over the decades, the congregation moved from Newark to Short Hills, a township/suburb in New Jersey, and built the current synagogue during the mid-1960s.[130] The most important change in Congregation B'nai Jeshurun's history occurred at the turn of the twentieth century when the congregation evolved from its original Orthodox Judaism to become one of the leading Reform congregations in the United States.[131]

The major difference between Orthodox and Reform Judaism is in the extent that followers adhere to the strict Halacha way of life.[132] The Reform movement has "enabled the Jewish people to introduce innovations while preserving their tradition."[133] It affirms the three central Kabbalistic cores of the faith: God, Torah, and Israel. The Reform tradition assumes that the Torah is a God-inspired living document that allows adaptations to changes in time. Note that this notion was also part of architect Eric Mendelsohn's manifest, in which he referred to the Torah as a living truth (see details in chapter 4). That allowed the Reform and Conservative congregations to be more open than the Orthodox and accept the designs of cathedral synagogues during the 1960s. The glass entrance to the current synagogue expresses the congregation's openness to inviting all kinds of worshipers. In Reform synagogues, as in the Conservative ones, female and male members sit together, as opposed to Orthodox synagogues, which maintain separate seating arrangements for men and women. In addition, Reform synagogues include an organ and/or choir, which are not accepted in Orthodox synagogues.

On October 30, 1960, during their annual meeting, Congregation B'nai Jeshurun approved the hiring of modernist architect Marcel Breuer to design their synagogue in their new (current) site in Short Hills, New Jersey.[134] Marcel Breuer (1902–1981), together with his partner Herbert Beckhard (1926–2003), proposed a synagogue composed of four structures connected by a corridor seen from the outside. The sanctuary was designed in the center as the tallest part, using a radial system of concrete folded-plate arches rising to twelve skylights. The other parts consisted of a three-story school, a chapel, and a two-story assembly building.[135] Concrete folded plates

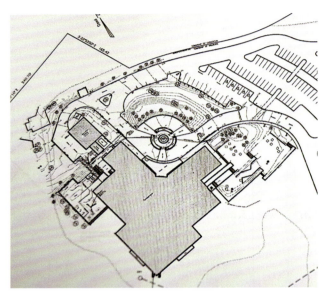

Figure 5.41. Temple B'nai Jeshurun Synagogue, Short Hills, New Jersey (1964), designed by Pietro Belluschi: Site plan (Courtesy of Temple B'nai Jeshurun Synagogue's archive)

Figure 5.42. Temple B'nai Jeshurun Synagogue, Short Hills, New Jersey (1964), designed by Pietro Belluschi: Landscape in front of the synagogue's entrance

also were part of the façades, which exhibited the architects' modern industrial modular approach.[136] In 1963, the congregation declined to build Breuer's project due to the significantly high costs of construction that exceeded their budget.[137] In the same year, the new building committee itemized a specific budget and selected architect Pietro Belluschi out of thirty potential architectural firms to design their synagogue. Belluschi recommended the local architectural firm of Kelly & Gruzen to work with him as associate architects and architects of residence.[138]

The temple is located on a twenty-two-acre, heavily wooded site in the rolling hills of New Jersey. It is a triangular site with a frontage of approximately 1,200 feet. Belluschi utilized the topography and designed the entrance level with the sanctuary as the central piece on the high side of the site, with two wings on both sides that create an L-shape plan. A floor below includes the school, and below that we find the building's utility spaces (figure 5.41). On the synagogue's main level, Belluschi designed a large parking lot separated from the building by a circular landscaped courtyard, including outdoor seating and a fountain facing the main entrance (figure 5.42). The site also includes the Ruth Pilchik Biblical Garden, with memorial rocks inscribed with the names of the twelve tribes of Israel, and the Harriet and Milton Perlmutter Family Outdoor Chapel (figure 5.40).

The central position of the sanctuary is accentuated by its slanted metal roof, which meets two flat roofs of the adjacent wings (figure 5.40). The building was constructed of fireproofed steel, with smooth-faced reddish-brown brick exteriors that are part of the region's construction. The use of traditional local materials (e.g., brick and wood) corresponded to Belluschi's attempt to apply his regionalism design approach, where local materials and traditional construction are encouraged.

As mentioned previously, the plan of the entire synagogue is based on three layers, creating an L-shaped building. Figure 5.43 illustrates the floor plan of the entrance level with the sanctuary and its two wings. The sanctuary plan is a square

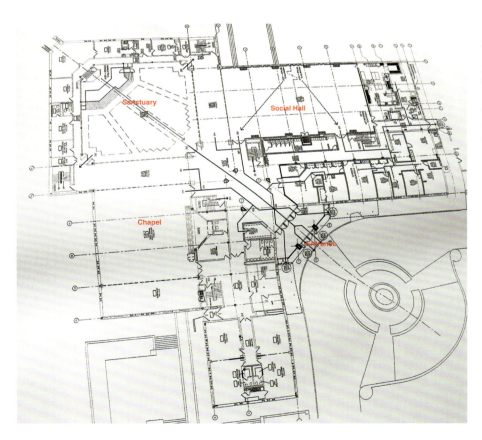

Figure 5.43. Temple B'nai Jeshurun Synagogue, Short Hills, New Jersey (1964), designed by Pietro Belluschi: The main (entrance) floor plan (note the axis between the entrance and the sanctuary's focal point; Courtesy of Temple B'nai Jeshurun Synagogue's archive)

positioned on a central axis. The axis stretches from the synagogue's entrance to the focal point, the bimah, which is located at the far edge of the square. Consequently, the main entrance to the sanctuary is at one of the square's corners. The axis within the sanctuary is highlighted with a strip of light. The bimah is highlighted by a vertical strip of stained-glass panels positioned behind the Ark (figure 5.44). The sanctuary seats one thousand worshipers on the main floor and the balcony.[139] Belluschi designed on the left of the sanctuary the Newman Chapel and on the right the Steiner Assembly/Social Hall. These spaces are separated from the sanctuary by moving partitions. When open, the combined spaces seat 2,700 people.[140]

The chapel's top hexagonal skylight provides natural light above the bimah and the Ark (figure 5.45), and its ceiling is artificially lit with small bulbs creating a sense of a sky full of stars (figure 5.46). The hall is lit by simple ceiling fluorescent lights. Both the chapel and hall are lit by vertical slit windows. The chapel's windows are stained glass (figure 5.46), while the hall's windows are transparent.

The lower level, beneath the sanctuary, is the educational component of the synagogue. It includes a library and seventeen classrooms around an

Figure 5.44. Temple B'nai Jeshurun Synagogue, Short Hills, New Jersey (1964), designed by Pietro Belluschi: The sanctuary's focal point—the bimah

Figure 5.45. Temple B'nai Jeshurun Synagogue, Short Hills, New Jersey (1964), designed by Pietro Belluschi: The chapel

Figure 5.46. Temple B'nai Jeshurun Synagogue, Short Hills, New Jersey (1964), designed by Pietro Belluschi: The chapel's stained-glass windows and ceiling lights

Figure 5.47. Temple B'nai Jeshurun Synagogue, Short Hills, New Jersey (1964), designed by Pietro Belluschi: The lower floor plan—the school around the youth lounge

Figure 5.48. Temple B'nai Jeshurun Synagogue, Short Hills, New Jersey (1964), designed by Pietro Belluschi: Vertical windows of the school from the exterior (one level below the main floor)

octagonal-shaped sunken common "Youth Lounge" (figure 5.47). All classrooms are lit by natural light that penetrates through vertical windows (figure 5.48). Stairs behind the Ark lead down to this level directly from the sanctuary.

The lowest level of the building was designed to hold the structure's utilities. It has the same shape as the other floors above it but is smaller in size. The utility floor has its own entrance (including for vehicles). Belluschi utilized the site's topography to create different levels, where he prioritized the main sanctuary at the top of the site. This followed the historic requirement that the temple (and then later the synagogues) be located at the highest point of the site/area. The worshipers "climb" toward the sacred place. This path continues in the sanctuary, where there are stairs to get to the holiest of the holy—the bimah and the Ark (figure 5.44).

The design of a sanctuary is expected to direct the worshipers toward the focal point of the spiritual place. Both Belluschi's seating arrangement and the light strips direct the attention of the worshipers to that focal point. The climax of this attention is the soaring eighty-foot-high strip of ten stained-glass panel windows, located behind the Ark (figure 5.44). Designed by artist Jean-Jacques Duval (1930–),

each panel depicts an abstract letter of the Ten Commandments—a Jewish symbol. The panels were made of faceted glass, which is the "process of grinding and polishing an object to give the surface a pattern of planes or facets."[141] The stained glass is one of the very few new art/craft pieces in the synagogue. The rest were brought from the congregation's previous synagogue in Newark.

Avram Kampf claims that Belluschi followed the same design concept as architects Frank Lloyd Wright and Walter Gropius, in which art is an organic part of the structure, though Belluschi was less strict.[142] I assume that the ideas to include stained glass as art in the synagogue and conform to the concept of light coming from above were probably influenced by Belluchi's church designs (see, for example, Belluchi's St. Mary Cathedral in San Francisco, California, 1963–1970[143]). In Temple B'nai Jeshurun, he designed transparent slit horizontal windows on the side walls (below the ceiling) converging into the stained-glass panels behind the Ark. They create an effect of a floating ceiling (figure 5.44). On the exterior, the side horizontal windows are beneath the metal parapet of the roof and above the brick walls. This simple solution resembles the horizontal strips of the international style. In

Figure 5.49. Temple B'nai Jeshurun Synagogue, Short Hills, New Jersey (1964), designed by Pietro Belluschi: The sanctuary's skylight from outside as part of the roof

addition, Belluschi included a skylight strip in the middle of the ceiling that also converges into the vertical stained-glass piece (figure 5.44). This central twelve-foot-high skylight slit stretches across the ceiling and runs as part of the slanted roof (figure 5.49). The highest point of the skylight converges with the stained glass behind the Ark, while the lower part starts at the entrance to the synagogue. Thus it highlights the axis that connects the entrance and the focal point of the sanctuary as shown on the floor plan (figure 5.43). The interior's effect of all light sources converging into the central stained glass behind the Ark is reminiscent of the interior of Belluschi's St. Mary's Cathedral in San Francisco (see the image sources in note 143).

The warm color of the reddish-brown brick walls, the laminated wood beams and steel trusses that support the metal roof and are exposed as part of the wooden ceiling the dark wooden pews, and the brown/orange carpet in the interior all help make the well-proportioned but monumental sanctuary

warmer and more intimate (figures 5.44 and 5.50). Furthermore, the balcony that wraps the sanctuary on four sides and embraces the main floor adds to the intimacy while enlarging the seating capacity in the space. The vents of the heating, ventilation, and air-conditioning (HVAC) system are part of the balcony design and look like small wooden towers (figure 5.50); other vents are located in a duct running above the partitions on each side of the sanctuary. With that, and similar to Eric Mendelsohn's Park Synagogue and Goodman's Congregation Shaarey Zedek Synagogue, Belluschi managed to design the HVAC system as an integral part of the sanctuary design.

The bimah is made of two levels (figure 5.44). The first level is separated from the main floor by seven stairs. It includes the main and larger lectern on one side for reading the Torah and a secondary lectern on the other side for announcements. The chairs for the clergy are on both sides of the bimah. The Ark is at the center of the second level

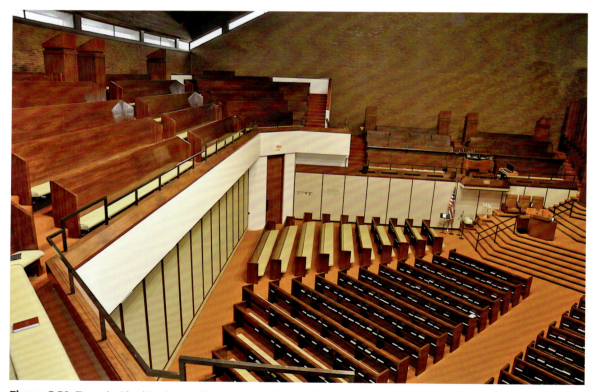

Figure 5.50. Temple B'nai Jeshurun Synagogue, Short Hills, New Jersey (1964), designed by Pietro Belluschi: The warm colors of the sanctuary's interior. Note the small wooden HVAC towers in the balcony and the vents above the partitions.

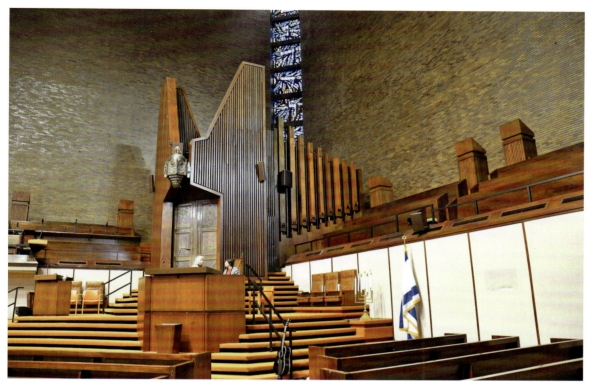

Figure 5.51. Temple B'nai Jeshurun Synagogue, Short Hills, New Jersey (1964): The Ark, the *heichal*, and the organ's pipes on its sides

of the bimah. The sacred closet is separated from the first level by four stairs and is positioned within a niche (the *heichal*) that is covered with a wooden screen (figures 5.44; 5.51). The shape of the upper front of the *heichal* resembles the wings of a seraphim.[144] The organ is located behind the Ark. Its wooden-covered pipes continue along the sides of the *heichal*'s wooden screens (figure 5.51). Thus the sanctuary's focal point is the Ark and organ, which appear as integral architectural elements of the sanctuary. The combination of an Ark with an organ emphasizes how far this Reform congregation has departed from Orthodoxy. It is also different from other Reform congregations, where the organ is located opposite the bimah (for example, see chapter 4, figure 4.43). The metal panels of the Ark's doors, the metal menorah, and the metal eternal light fixture were brought from the congregation's former synagogue in Newark (figure 5.51). Belluschi highlighted the eternal light, as he positioned it in the front center of the Ark niche (the *heichal*) and in the center of the stained-glass panels behind

it (figure 5.44). The older Jewish craft pieces maintain the Jewish symbolism in the sanctuary and link the congregation to their specific history. Belluschi claimed that the synagogue is not so much a house of worship but rather a place of assembly, study, and prayer.[145] I see Belluschi's focal point as an attempt to link church motifs such as stained glass and a central organ with the Jewish required elements of the Ark, menorah, and eternal light, creating a unity to express a house of God.

In an article in the *Baltimore Sun*, Edward Gunts quoted Belluschi's architectural concept as a struggle "between sky and earth, spirit and matter, logic and emotion, aesthetic and morality."[146] In the same article, architect Eduardo Catalano described Belluschi's religious building designs as touching the sky while anchored in the earth. I would add that Belluschi expressed the spirit of man in all his designs of houses of worship. Therefore, his many church motifs appeared in his synagogue designs. It fared well in his design of the cathedral synagogue of Temple B'nai Jeshurun, as his client was a Jewish

Reform congregation that was open to accepting his design, which included an organ as a centerpiece of the sanctuary. The notion of modern Reform cathedral synagogues can also be seen as a development from historic nineteenth-century European grandeur temples and large monumental early twentieth-century American synagogues. Most of the modern American cathedral synagogues of the mid-twentieth century embraced modern liturgical and architectural concepts that freed the designs from the previous formal geometry and symmetry, from hierarchical religious dogma, and from heavy ornamentation. It also pushed the envelope of new materials and systems that often influenced the shape of the synagogues.

Bridging Modernism and Sustainability with Judaism

Sidney Eisenshtat: Temple Mount Sinai, El Paso, Texas (1962)

Pietro Belluschi introduced regionalism as an approach to the design of houses of worship. It focuses mainly on the physical context of the region and its vernacular architecture. It emphasizes place-making as counter to modern architecture, in which universal progressive qualities highlight modernism as placeless.[147] Architect Sidney Eisenshtat's design of Temple Mount Sinai in El Paso, Texas (figure 5.52), can also be considered a regional design. The analysis in this section reveals that his design was actually a modern practice of sustainable architecture long before the term *sustainability* became popular. Rabbi Floyd Fierman, in his dedication of Temple Mount Sinai in 1962, concluded that the hope of the congregation is that the synagogue and its art exhibits the monumental beauty of this oasis in the desert.[148]

Architect, critic, and historian Kenneth Frampton (1939–) talks about sustainable architecture as one of his six guidelines for regionalism and critical-regionalism design.[149] The focus of these approaches is on local conditions and responsiveness to local climate. I claim that sustainable architecture as defined today comprises all elements of regionalism

and critical regionalism. It is considered an environmentally responsive architecture, and in addition, it contributes to the social, cultural, and economic infrastructure of a region.[150] The UN World Commission on Environment and Development defined sustainability "as development that meets the needs of the present generation without compromising the ability of future generations to meet their needs."[151] Similar definitions are presented by the World and US Green Building Councils, which developed sustainable measures focusing on the built environment using rating categories for Leadership in Energy and Environmental Designing (LEED).[152] While the following analysis of Temple Mount Sinai in El Paso from the 1960s was not conducted using the specific criteria of the current LEED system, it still demonstrates Eisenshtat's regional and sustainable concepts in this synagogue's design.

Sidney Eisenshtat (1914–2005), a Los Angeles–based architect, devoted much of his practice to designing synagogues, Jewish academic buildings, and community centers. He became an influential architect of modern synagogues, especially in California and on the West Coast.[153] His synagogues are known for their innovative and modern designs and the use of new materials.[154] He posited that synagogues should be built from modern materials and systems, such as concrete and its thin-shell construction, which often shaped the expression of his designs. The archive of his work in the University of Southern California Libraries describes his projects as a legacy of minimalist architecture in the Southern California basin. In his design of synagogues, he bridged modernism, innovations in building technology, and what we call today sustainability with Jewish traditions and values. For Eisenshtat, an Orthodox Jew, the synagogue commissions "expressed his devotion to Jewish traditions and values,"[155] including the Jewish mystical philosophy of *tikkun olam*, "repair of the world," which highlights environmentalism as one of its principles.[156] Eisenshtat's sculptural expression of synagogue shapes was influenced by the region's cultural and environmental conditions and was enriched by his collaboration with artists as part of his overall architecture.

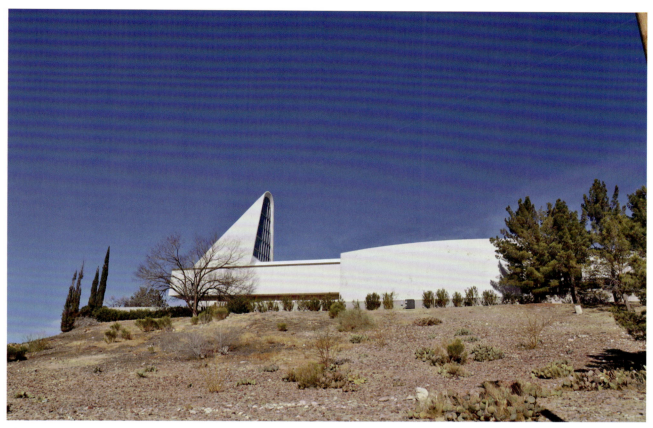

Figure 5.52. Temple Mount Sinai Synagogue, El Paso, Texas (1962), designed by Sidney Eisenshtat: The building

Two of his synagogues in Los Angeles became important landmarks in the city: Reform Temple Emanuel in Beverly Hills, California (1953), and Conservative Sinai Temple Synagogue located on the main street of Wilshire Boulevard (1960). In both buildings, Eisenshtat utilized the plasticity of concrete to create expressive monumental structures of cathedral synagogues that suited the glamour culture of Los Angeles and Hollywood. He based these synagogue designs on the pure geometry of a circle in the first and a triangle in the second. Similar to Frank Lloyd Wright, Eisenshtat repeated these "pure" geometric forms throughout the exterior and interior of each building.

The most impressive element of Temple Emanuel is its opulent, whitewashed concrete circular canopy that defines the synagogue's entrance (figure 5.53). It leads worshipers to a courtyard in front of the building entry doors. This design creates a separation from the mundane as one enters the sacred.

Figure 5.53. Temple Emanuel, Los Angeles, California (1953), designed by Sidney Eisenshtat: Circular canopy at the entrance and its courtyard

Figure 5.54. Conservative Sinai Temple Synagogue, Los Angeles, California (1960), designed by Sidney Eisenshtat: The building

Figure 5.55. Conservative Sinai Temple Synagogue, Los Angeles, California (1960), designed by Sidney Eisenshtat: The sanctuary with triangular ceiling and triangular stained-glass openings

Eisenshtat also used the motif of a concrete canopy and an entrance courtyard in his design of Temple Mount Sinai in El Paso, Texas (1962). In Los Angeles, the canopy catered to the enchantment culture of Hollywood and its film industry, while in El Paso, it was designed as a shading device.

Sinai Temple in Los Angeles is a massive concrete building based on a triangular geometry (figure 5.54). The building and its tower comply with modern architecture and Hollywood's glistening monumental culture. The synagogue became the largest Conservative synagogue in the city. It illustrates Eisenshtat's expressionist design, "full with color, rhythm, and dramatic angles."[157] Indeed, the rhythm of the triangles in the sanctuary's ceiling and the stained-glass triangular opening behind the Ark enhance that image and add to the sacred atmosphere of the place (figure 5.55). Stained-glass windows appear later as a major decorative piece in the synagogue's chapel in El Paso.

The two landmark synagogues, Sinai Temple and Temple Emanual, were the highlights of Eisenshtat's work in Los Angeles. However, Temple Mount Sinai in El Paso, Texas, is perceived as the peak of his career. Its design, like other synagogues of the 1960s, transformed the shape of the building to express more spirituality, community, and traditional values, while at the same time focusing on functionality and modernism. The synagogue as an institution exhibited American values, the congregation's Jewish identity and self-consciousness, and their confidence in living the American dream in the suburbs.

Temple Mount Sinai in El Paso, Texas (1962)

Mount Sinai Association was founded in 1887 to take care of a Jewish cemetery in El Paso and to aid the needy.[158] In 1890, El Paso Hebrew Sunday School was organized, and their first synagogue was built in 1900 for three hundred members.[159] In 1916, the congregation moved to their second synagogue, which was considered the first modern temple associated with the Union for Reform Judaism built west of the Mississippi.[160] During and post–World War II, Jewish members helped bring their families from Europe and other parts of the United States to

El Paso.[161] Following the growth of the congregation, in 1962 they decided to build a larger synagogue, which is the current Temple Mount Sinai building. They commissioned architect Sidney Eisenshtat from Los Angeles and the local architectural firm Carroll & Daeuble to design a modern synagogue on a large hilly site nestled into the Franklin Mountains.[162] The design of Temple Mount Sinai not only became part of the inventory of modern synagogues with an expressionist architecture of the 1960s, but also demonstrates a significant contribution to sustainable architecture of houses of worship long before the concept of sustainability became an accepted and desired part of design.

The first sustainable element expressed in the synagogue is the form of the building. It was definitely inspired by the region of the synagogue's site. Eisenshtat created a modern parabolic concrete "shell mountain" in the desert, which reflects the surrounding mountains (figure 5.56). This shell mountain established a local place—a synagogue that belongs in the region. Since mountains are considered habitats of God—"And I will lift up mine eyes unto the mountains" (Psalms 121:1)[163]—this sustainable measure can be considered a stewardship to God. The concrete shell (figures 5.52 and 5.56) is finished with mosaic pieces in white cream and variations of browns to express the terrain's color tones and ease the reflective glare of the white pieces (figure 5.57). Some saw the concrete mountain as a symbol of Mount Sinai. Rabbi Fierman wrote in his dedication of the building, "This tower is symbolic of the rabbi's outstretched arms. Its form represents the rabbi's gesture in invoking the priestly benediction. It records in concrete God's perpetual blessing upon His 'priest people.'"[164] These interpretations link Eisenshtat's modern concrete mountain with Jewish heritage and symbols. However, it should be acknowledged that some locals saw the shell as a nun's hat, linking it to Catholicism, the most prominent faith in the El Paso region,[165] thus emphasizing the synagogue's placemaking in the area.

An important sustainable design measure is the use of local landscape features. Indeed, Eisenshtat used the surrounding indigenous landscape in the development of the synagogue's site (figure 5.56).

Figure 5.56. Temple Mount Sinai Synagogue, El Paso, Texas (1962), designed by Sidney Eisenshtat to reflect the surrounding mountains

Figure 5.57. Temple Mount Sinai Synagogue, El Paso, Texas (1962), designed by Sidney Eisenshtat: The mosaic finishes of the concrete shell

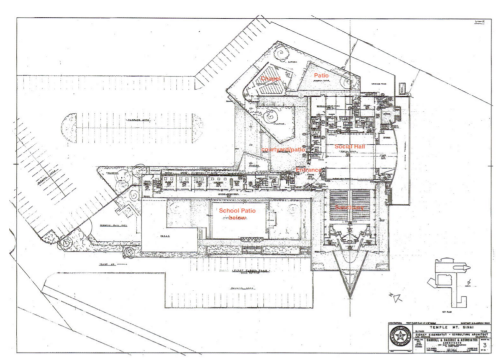

Figure 5.58. Temple Mount Sinai Synagogue, El Paso, Texas (1962), designed by Sidney Eisenshtat: The entrance floor plan with the synagogue, social hall, administration offices, chapel, and the two patios (Courtesy of In*Situ Architecture)

Figure 5.59. Temple Mount Sinai Synagogue, El Paso, Texas (1962), designed by Sidney Eisenshtat: The entrance courtyard

This design enhances the relationship of the synagogue with the desert. The landscape design also helps with sustainable maintenance of the land around the building. As part of the site development, Eisenshtat utilized the hilly topography and created three courtyards/patios: two at the entrance level and one on the level below (figure 5.58). The entrance multilevel paved courtyard serves as the core to connect the synagogue and its chapel (figure 5.59). A round bastion/canopy above the main entrance (figure 5.60) continues as a covered walkway that links the two buildings together, reminiscent of the round canopy entrance of Eisenshtat's Temple Emanuel synagogue in Los Angeles, California (figure 5.53). Temple Mount Sinai's bastion creates a shaded, covered walkway to protect the worshipers from the harsh sun of El Paso. The entrance courtyard serves as a threshold space separating the worshipers from the mundane when they enter the spiritual sphere (figure 5.59). The inscribed phrase "This is none other than the house of God"

on the entrance wall emphasizes this separation. This sign follows the verse in Genesis 28:17, where the gathering space for praying is termed *Beth Elokim*, which means a house of God. As mentioned in chapter 3, though the synagogue is a house of gathering—a house of the people—Jews still believe that God's spirit (the *shchina*) hovers over their house of worship, the synagogue.

The second courtyard is an indigenous local garden patio near the chapel. It separates the chapel from the service area (figure 5.58). The third courtyard is located on the lower part of the building and serves as a children's playground. The classrooms are positioned around it, while the administration's corridor overlooks it (figures 5.58 and 5.61). Courtyards are a sustainable feature, as they create shaded areas while allowing light and air to filter into spaces. The classrooms are shaded by the administration wing at the entrance floor above them, while a concrete screen protects the main-floor area that faces the courtyard from the direct desert light and

Figure 5.60. Temple Mount Sinai Synagogue, El Paso, Texas (1962), designed by Sidney Eisenshtat: The bastion/ canopy above the main entrance

Figure 5.61. Temple Mount Sinai Synagogue, El Paso, Texas (1962), designed by Sidney Eisenshtat: The lower courtyard with the school around it

Figure 5.62. Temple Mount Sinai Synagogue, El Paso, Texas (1962), designed by Sidney Eisenshtat: The sanctuary

glare. It should be noted that the definition of *critical regionalism* by Kenneth Frampton (2007) includes all of the above sustainable measures.[166]

At the entrance to the synagogue's complex, worshipers are exposed to the soaring parabolic concrete shell mountain, which serves as the focal point of the synagogue. It hosts the holy Ark in the sanctuary (figure 5.62). The exterior/interior relation continues into the sanctuary, where the tower is the source of light behind the Ark, enhancing the sacredness of the Ark. The sanctuary's vaulted ceiling and the procession toward the bimah direct the eye toward the focal point of the place—the Ark (figure 5.62). The vault that symbolizes the Tabernacle tent can be considered as shelter from the outside harsh environment of the desert. It definitely sheltered me from the harsh winds during my visit there. The concrete vault and walls also help with cooling/heating the building via thermal mass effect.[167] This effect is known and accepted as a sustainable measure in a hot-arid desert environment. The combination of this solution with an HVAC system that is installed throughout the building helps reduce the synagogue's utility bills.

The transparent window behind the Ark includes an inscription of the Ten Commandments. It lights the bimah and, as mentioned before, attracts the worshipers to focus on the synagogue's focal point (figure 5.62). The view outside from that window is to a deck/terrace looking at the local landscape, the Rio Grande Valley, and the desert beyond in the distance (figure 5.63). This terrace is secluded on the site and was designed for meditation within nature—a tribute to the sacredness of the synagogue.

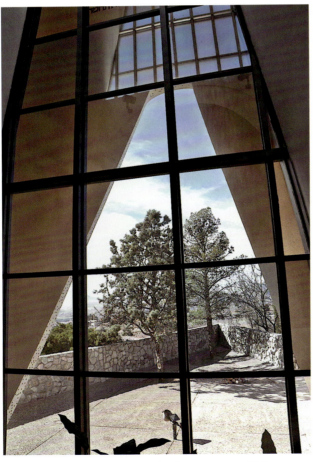

Figure 5.63. Temple Mount Sinai Synagogue, El Paso, Texas (1962), designed by Sidney Eisenshtat: A view outside from behind the Ark

Figure 5.64. Temple Mount Sinai Synagogue, El Paso, Texas (1962): The *heichal* designed by Sidney Eisenshtat; the Ark, the eternal light, and the menorah designed by Wiltz Harrison

In addition to the natural light from the window behind the Ark, light penetrates the sanctuary through colored-glass windows in the walls (see the lower left side of figure 5.62). The sanctuary's pastel-toned glass creates a natural, soft light that adds to the ambiance of the space. The thickness of the windows' niches creates some shade, while the color of the glass protects the space from the harsh glare of the desert sun. More so, these openings do not reveal the outside world and therefore enable worshipers to concentrate on their prayers. This notion follows the design of the opaque and colored openings in the High Temples of Jerusalem.

The use of natural light is another important sustainable design concept. At night, similar to the natural light, the electrical lights, which can be dimmed as required by sustainable lighting design, appear from various sources and provide enough light for the worshipers to read while enhancing the spiritual atmosphere in the sanctuary (figure 5.62). The light fixtures designed by Eisenshtat resemble the mezuzah, an important Jewish craft that relates to the blessing of a structure.[168] Thus Eisenshtat abstracted a Jewish symbol with a design that bridges modernism and Judaism in this synagogue.

Eisenshtat also designed the *heichal* on the bimah as a wooden vault. It hosts and highlights the Ark and the eternal light designed by artist Wiltz Harrison (1916–2001) of Texas Western College (figure 5.64). Harrison's art pieces and his menorah that stands separately are made from new direct-metal construction, which involves directly cutting, carving, or hammering the metal. Similar to Eisenshtat, Harrison departed from traditional techniques in metal sculpturing and followed the expressionist artists from New York City. Harrison's sculptures were influenced by his jewelry making: "Harrison exchanged his fine instruments and minute techniques of jewelers for the blow torch and of the artifact."[169] The Ark's doors are woven with a priestly breastplate, which symbolizes the sacred breastplate worn by the high priest of the Israelites, as described in the book of Exodus. Others see the colored pieces as leaves and the metal as their vines or branches (figure 5.64).

Eisenshtat designed the sanctuary for a capacity of 450 occupants with an adjacent social hall that is separated from the sanctuary by a wooden accordion-style partition (figure 5.58). When needed, the dividers can be opened to accommodate more worshipers. The synagogue complex's flexible design also accommodates the small numbers of people attending daily prayers in the morning and evening, and often Shabbat services. To cater to this demand, Eisenshtat designed a separate chapel as part of the complex, with an entrance on the left of the courtyard under the round canopy (figure 5.58).

The chapel was designed with concrete and stained-glass panels that are visible from the exterior. It soars upward to reflect the surrounding hills and express the place of the holy Ark, and the worshipers' yearning to be closer to the divine (figure 5.65). Some see it as emulating the Tabernacle of the wandering Israelites in the desert. The latter perception is reinforced by the shape of the interior, especially its sculptural ceiling (figure 5.66). The space illustrates the impression "that the worshiper is offering devotional prayers in a tent."[170] Eisenshtat designed the art glass panels, made from faceted glass set into a tinted epoxy resin.[171] As can be seen in figure 5.66, Jewish symbols are embedded in the stained glass: on the left side of the chapel facing the Ark, the glass art includes the menorah with its seven red flames, the Jewish symbol of light and freedom; on the right side, Eisenshtat depicted in glass the symbol of the tablets of the Ten Commandments, with the first ten letters in Hebrew to represent them. He also designed the chapel's Ark, the eternal light, and the lectern from oxidized metal[172] (figure 5.66). The Ark's doors symbolize the Shield of David and serve to shelter the holy from the mundane, while the decorative motif on all the metal artwork is the tree of life. In addition to the tree of life's universal meaning, which emphasizes sacred verticality, it also reflects the Jewish religious teaching. Rabbi Fierman considered these teachings as an ever-blooming tree that finds new thought and interpretations in each generation.[173] As in the main sanctuary, the art in the chapel expressed faith symbols in modern expressionist new techniques and reflects Jewish symbols.

Figure 5.65. Temple Mount Sinai Synagogue, El Paso, Texas (1962), designed by Sidney Eisenshtat: The chapel exterior

Figure 5.66. Temple Mount Sinai Synagogue, El Paso, Texas (1962), designed by Sidney Eisenshtat: The interior of the chapel

Summary

The selected cases are examples of the many synagogues that were built during the mid-twentieth century, many of which I have personally visited. They illustrate how architects pushed the envelope of aesthetics and building technology. They departed from historical styles of synagogues while embracing modernism and bridging it with Judaism. These synagogues reflect the search of congregations for their Jewish identity and eventually expressed their pride and confidence in belonging in modern America. Furthermore, these synagogues showcase special contributions to modern synagogue design. Examples include the articulation of the modern motto "form follows function"; the introduction of abstracted expressionist art into synagogue architecture; the development of a flexible solution to expand the capacity of worshipers in the sanctuary; the utility of new building materials, such as concrete and steel, and their appropriate structural systems; and the design of sustainable measures, which are believed to be part of God's guidance.

These cases may raise the question of how much the architects' religion influenced their design of the synagogue—a question that was presented in the introduction of this book. The analyses of the buildings in this chapter reveal that you do not necessarily have to be a Jewish architect to design a synagogue, a Jewish architecture. All architects, no matter their personal sets of beliefs (e.g., Pietro Belluschi was a Catholic architect; Percival Goodman and Sidney Eisenshtat were Jewish architects), included in their designs universal sacred architectural elements that generate spiritual experiences in the synagogues. They all used simple geometry and proportion, elegant materials and finishes, and applied light for dramatic effect in the spaces. This conclusion also illustrates the rabbinical interpretation that gentiles (non-Jews) can design and build a synagogue since it is a house of people, not a house of God like the High Temples in Jerusalem. Architect Percival Goodman stated, "I cannot deign to do honor to God; this is vanity, suitable for the heathen. The affirmation lies in the effort to make a place in which people can gather . . . to learn the tradition and its interpretation" and try to improve the meaning of "peace, justice, love, mercy."[174]

6 Adaptations and Changes

Preserve my life, for I am holy.

(*Psalm 86:2*)

I consider this chapter on adaptation and changes as an interim epilogue, which implies continuity within this domain rather than termination of the subject. Modern American synagogues are a continuous phenomenon. Congregations across the United States feel obligated to preserve their synagogues for future generations. They proudly maintain and preserve these institutions with attempts to continue enhancing the buildings' modernist design heritage. Their ongoing work on these mid-twentieth-century structures became part of the "preservation of the recent past" movement.

Recent publications on preserving the recent past (buildings from the 1950s to 1970s) focus mainly on preservation measures concerning the materials. Scholars and practitioners claim that the experimental materials of that period, such as concrete, steel, and glass, were integral in the creation of the modernist statement.[1] Some even look at concrete as a cultural phenomenon, as it is the material directly associated with modern architecture and serves as an image of a progressive medium.[2] Indeed, modernism is characterized by experiments in building technology that influenced the buildings' shapes. Therefore, scholars who address the conservation of modern heritage highlight the importance and challenges of preserving the building materials that were central to that time.[3] Following this focus,

guidelines were developed and workshops and symposia were organized to help those preservation initiatives. Some prominent examples are Docomomo;[4] the Association for Preservation Technology International's (APTI's) Technical Committee on Modern Heritage;[5] the Getty Conservation Institute's Conserving Modern Architecture Initiative;[6] and the International Council on Monuments and Sites' (ICOMOS) Twentieth Century Heritage International Scientific Committee, Madrid—New Delhi Document.[7] It should be noted that the Secretary of the Interior's Standards for the Treatment of Historic Properties from 1976 and the revisions in 1995[8] are also geared toward materials preservation.

Preserving materials and their details helps maintain the authenticity of the historic integrity of a building. Still, some claim that "authenticity relies on the continuity of the original design intent more often than on preservation of original materials."[9] However, when the original design is driven by the use of new materials, as in the case of modern architecture, the preservation of the original materials and their authenticity remain dominant in keeping the integrity of the modern design. There is a general agreement among preservationists that the preservation approach of the recent past "places importance on design and technology as a continuation of the original intent."[10] Thus it focuses on the original materials and systems, as they became synonymous with preserving modernism and its culture.

In addition to the maintenance of buildings and preserving materials, congregations faced other challenges beyond brick and mortar. Demographic changes, changes in liturgy, new building codes and regulations, and the need for new energy conservation strategies called for modifications in the synagogues. It was important to solve these challenges while maintaining the modern integrity of the original buildings.[11] However, very few publications or guidelines focused on these problems. This chapter attempts to illustrate these aspects of preservation and proposed solutions as part of the continuous effort to preserve modern American synagogues. With that, I present an additional aspect to the preservation of recent past buildings.

The different facets of the congregations' demographic changes called for administrative and religious adaptations, which were directly reflected in various architectural modifications. The first major change was triggered by the decline in attendance of services due to aging members. The second relates to the decline in memberships due to younger generations' waning affiliations with religion. The third demographic change was influenced by the move of members out of their synagogues' neighborhoods to establish congregations in newer suburbs around the city. Congregations became very creative in solving these challenges while maintaining the integrity of their original synagogues. Solutions included interior modifications, such as the construction of new smaller chapels, shifting the focus of the synagogue to education to attract young families, and providing options for adaptive use. The results of those architectural solutions also helped the synagogues comply with newer building codes and design guidelines such as the Americans with Disabilities Act (ADA), lower their energy utility bills, and cater to some liturgical changes, which focused on fostering a closer relationship between the congregations and their officiants.

Accessibility

The decline of memberships associated with aging members translated to practical issues of accessibility. Most of the original designs of modern American synagogues did not cater to elderly or disabled members. At the time of the synagogues' design and construction, most of the original congregations were comprised of young people who had recently moved to the suburbs to start new lives and fulfill the American dream. In addition, at that time, there were no design guidelines and/or references to the ADA, which was initiated only in 1990.

As the original members aged, accommodations were necessary to enable them to enter the buildings and participate in regular and special services. One example included changes in the way older congregants entered the synagogue. The 1987 addition of a new entrance from the parking lot to Walter Gropius's Temple Oheb Shalom in Baltimore, Maryland (1960), illustrates one of the solutions. Levin/Brown Architects from Owings Mills, Maryland, were in charge of the synagogue's renovations. As part of their designed additions, they provided a new entrance on the side of the building (figure 3.3). This change respected the original monumental main elevation.

Other examples include the common addition of a ramp and handrail to the existing main entrance as an option to access the original door. In the case of Eric Mendelsohn's Park Synagogue, such features were added, though in this case, it does not seem to respect the original design (figure 6.1). A more appropriate design of this type of solution can be found in the case of Frank Lloyd Wright's Beth Sholom Synagogue. In 2011, the firm of John Milner Architects Inc. from Chadds Ford, Pennsylvania, with architect Christopher J. Miller leading the project, left the main entrance of Beth Sholom Synagogue as is, adding a small ramp to an existing side entrance, replacing the outdoor stairs with a drop-off area (figure 6.2). Moreover, they also designed an elevator at the side entrance. This elevator serves the sanctuary level and the lower level's Sisterhood Chapel and accessible restrooms. Their respectful addition to the historic building was seen by the architects as "challenging both from the standpoint of preservation and technical feasibility."[12] The elevator was constructed in an area east of the sanctuary in order to minimize interventions to the original building and to provide access to both sanctuaries (figure 6.3).[13] The only changes that resulted from

Figure 6.1. Mendelsohn's Park Synagogue in Cleveland, Ohio: Addition of a ramp and handrails to the main entrance of the synagogue

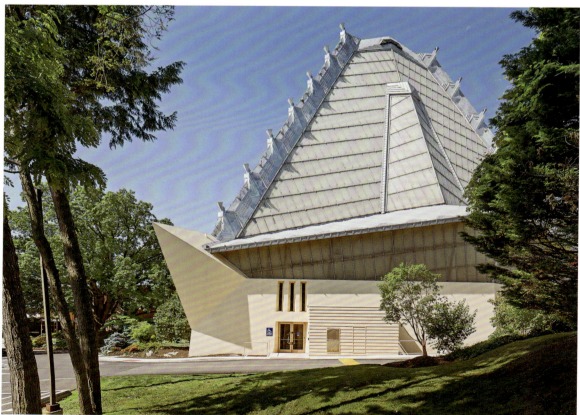

Figure 6.2. Frank Lloyd Wright's Beth Sholom Synagogue in Elkins Park, Pennsylvania: Addition of a small ramp to a side entrance and a drop-off area. Design by John Milner Architects Inc., 2011. (Courtesy of John Milner Architects Inc.)

Figure 6.3. Frank Lloyd Wright's Beth Sholom Synagogue in Elkins Park, Pennsylvania: Addition of an elevator on the east side of the synagogue. Design by John Milner Architects Inc., 2011. (Courtesy of John Milner Architects Inc.)

Area removed to raise door height

Low wall reconfigured

Before

Figure 6.4. Frank Lloyd Wright's Beth Sholom Synagogue in Elkins Park, Pennsylvania: Minor modifications in the main sanctuary with enlargement of the door from the east side of the synagogue and a reconfiguration of a low wall near the door. Design by John Milner Architects Inc., 2011. (Courtesy of John Milner Architects Inc.)

the installation of the elevator in the rear spine of the building were as follows: the dismantling of the rabbi's study; the replacement of one of the back stairs behind the Sisterhood Chapel with a ramp; the modifications to the south organ chamber; and the enlargement of an existing interior door in the main sanctuary, which visually had a minimal impact when viewed from the seating areas[14] (figure 6.4).

Another aspect to improve accessibility was to make the bimah reachable to all worshipers. One important part of Jewish services is the invitation of a worshiper to stand on the bimah and read parts of the Torah. This is an extreme honor for the member of the congregation and his/her family. In most Orthodox synagogues, the leader of the service is seen as an emissary of the community (*shaliach tzibur* in Hebrew), "rather than as a clergyman in position of special authority."[15] As such, the bimah is usually centrally located as part of the worship space and helps create a communal service. In contrast, Conservative and Reform sanctuaries are designed with a "theater seating" arrangement where the bimah acts as a high stage detached from the audience.[16] That means that access to a higher-level bimah requires stairs (see for example, figure 5.44). This arrangement reflects a hierarchical design of the sanctuary, which separates officiants and congregants and "introduce[s] a sense of greater decorum in worship services."[17] However, a high bimah makes it difficult for elderly and disabled members to participate in the service when called to step up on the bimah. An exceptional example of easy access to reach the raised bimah is North Shore Congregation Synagogue in Glencoe, Illinois. Architect Minoru Yamasaki designed stairs with a handrail and a side ramp to get to the bimah as integral parts of the original sanctuary in 1964 (figure 6.5). Yet rarely can we find other such examples from that period. Most of the modifications occurred much later. Examples include the 2005 renovations of Kneses Tifereth Israel Synagogue in Port Chester, New York. Architect Michael Berkowicz from Presentations Gallery firm in Mt. Vernon, New York, lowered the original high bimah

designed by Philip Johnson in 1954 and added a side ramp (figure 5.16).

The 2001 modification to Temple Oheb Shalom Synagogue in Baltimore is a dramatic example of creating a new accessible bimah. The original one was designed in 1960 by Walter Gropius (1883–1969) in collaboration with architect Sheldon I. Leavitt (1922–) from Norfolk, Virginia, as an elevated pedestal above the sloped-up seating area of the sanctuary (figure 6.6). The architects believed that this arrangement enhanced the feeling of ascent[18] and glorified the Ark and the officiants who served the congregation.[19] The wooden Ark of twenty feet in the shape of the tablets of the Ten Commandments was designed by artists György Kepes (1906–2001) and Robert Preusser (1919–92). Almost forty years later, Levin/Brown Architects renovated and

Figure 6.5. Yamasaki's North Shore Congregation Israel Synagogue, Glencoe, Illinois (1964): The original side ramp and railing going up to the bimah

reconfigured the sanctuary by reversing the location of the bimah to the rear side of the original sanctuary facing northwest and designing a new *heichal* from stone and a new metal and glass Ark (figure 6.7).[20] The change in orientation from the traditional east toward Jerusalem was already mentioned in chapter

4 with Mendelsohn's claim that God is all around us and, therefore, it does not matter where the bimah and Ark are located. Levin/Brown also reversed the seating to slope down toward the new bimah, which is lower and smaller in size and scale. This change provides accessibility and generates "more intimate

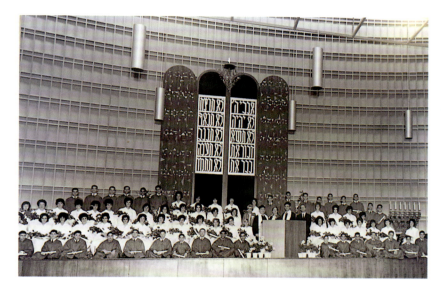

Figure 6.6. Temple Oheb Shalom in Baltimore, Maryland: The original design of the bimah by Walter Gropius and Sheldon Leavitt, as seen in a picture from 1962. Artists György Kepes and Robert Preusser designed the Ark. (The picture was taken from the synagogue's wall.)

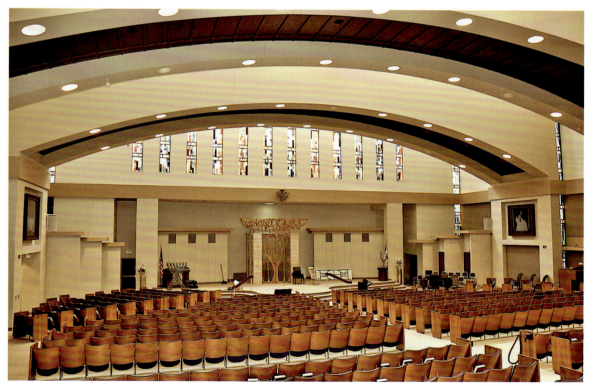

Figure 6.7. Temple Oheb Shalom in Park Heights in Baltimore, Maryland: The renovated sanctuary with a reversed bimah, a new Ark, and added vaults. Designed by Levin/Brown Architects, 2001.

worship experiences."[21] The new seating arrangement allows the worshipers to view and enjoy the original stained-glass windows designed by György Kepes. In the original design, the congregates sat with their backs to those windows.

The congregation exploited these changes to further "democratize" their synagogue. They canceled the hierarchy of reserved paid seats in the sanctuary. Now, the rule has changed to first come, first to choose their seats. Figure 6.6 also reveals that Levin/Brown inserted new false arches between each of the original barrel-vaulted segments to accentuate the original vaults. The complete replacement and redesign of the bimah help worshipers of all ages participate in the services and be honored when called to read the Torah. In addition, the new design fulfills newer building codes and design guidelines such as ADA requirements. Furthermore, it complies with recent liturgical changes in Conservative and Reform synagogues, where there is an attempt to bring officiants and congregants closer together "both spatially and psychologically."[22] This attempt called for the transformation of the bimah to help frame the new liturgical demands. My conversation with the rabbi and members of the building committee of Temple Oheb Shalom Synagogue revealed the gap between the congregations' generations. The older members wanted to preserve the sanctuary in its original design and to continue the traditional ways of service. They voted against the new renovations, though the modifications catered to their needs. The younger members see the new worship space and the various additions as an evolution, while attempting to preserve the integrity of the original modern design. They also hoped that the modified sanctuary and the changes in hierarchy of seating, which emphasize the close relation between the officiants on the bimah and the congregation, might attract new young families.

Acoustics

Congregations also face acoustical challenges in accommodating hearing-impaired aging congregants. In addition, younger members also expect the prayers and music to be livelier and to reverberate within the volume of the sanctuary. Though some modern architects treated acoustics as part of their original synagogue designs, their solutions had to be revisited and often the synagogues' underperforming audio systems had to be upgraded or replaced. In other cases, an audio system had to be added, and today most, if not all, of the recent past synagogues include these systems. The challenges of installing new speakers, microphones, and a control panel are both functional and aesthetic.

The study of practical audio concerns in synagogues unfolds into two issues. One relates to the general acoustical problems in houses of worship, where solutions have to cater to varied sounds (e.g., preaching, praying, singing, music). The second concern relates specifically to synagogues and their flexible designs. As explained in previous chapters, social halls were designed adjacent to the sanctuaries with partitions/dividers to be opened during high holidays and special festivities. The enlarged area and increased capacity of worshipers call for a multioutput audio system in order to accommodate the various activities. This can be seen in Percival Goodman's solution in Congregation Shaarey Zedek, Southfield, Michigan. There, the sanctuary as well as the adjacent social halls are served by an audio system and acoustic measures for noise reduction (e.g., Gold Bond acoustic ceiling tiles) that facilitate various activities in each of the spaces at the same time.[23]

The aesthetic aspect of installing a new audio system in the sanctuary should be sensitive to the original architectural design. An example of these considerations is the 2006–7 replacement of the old audio system with a new upgraded system in Pietro Belluschi's Temple B'nai Jeshurun in Short Hills, New Jersey. Monte Bros. Sound Systems Inc. of Dobbs Ferry, New York, designed and installed the new system.[24] The speakers on the bimah almost match the wood finish of the organ pipes and their width (figure 5.44). The same figure also illustrates the speakers located underneath the balconies. They provide coverage for the back pews on the main floor. Bob Pelepako from Monte Bros. said that "speakers were also hidden inside the structure to provide coverage for seats in the side balconies adjacent to either side of the organ pipes," and speakers were also positioned within the "spine" of the building, a set of wooden beams that run up the middle of the sanctuary, to help with the acoustics in the rear of the balconies.[25] Microphones are positioned on the two lecterns and on the left-side balcony above the organ player for the officiants seated there. Though their placement in the sanctuary is necessary for audio coverage for the diverse uses of the synagogue, they are visible, and in my point of view are not an elegant solution.

Additions of New Chapels

Decline in memberships due to fewer new members has been addressed via two solutions. First, congregations added new smaller chapels to cater to the lower number of members attending services. Second, congregations expanded their educational wings to attract young families with children to become members (see the next section).

The new chapels designed by local architects accommodate smaller groups of worshipers for daily and small Shabbat services, while the large original sanctuaries are used mainly for high-attendance

Figure. 6.8. Temple Oheb Shalom in Park Heights in Baltimore, Maryland: The new chapel. Designed by Levin/Brown Architects, 1987.

services of Shabbat and high holidays, festivals, and family celebrations like weddings. Some architects, such as Eric Mendelsohn, Frank Lloyd Wright, Percival Goodman, Pietro Belluschi, and Sidney Eisenshtat, designed smaller chapels as part of their synagogues' original designs (see chapters 4 and 5). Other architects, such as Walter Gropius and Minoru Yamasaki, did not include smaller chapels in their overall designs. The addition of new chapels to these synagogues not only catered to the smaller numbers of congregants attending services but also helped lower the rising costs of utility bills following the energy crisis of the 1970s. Heating or cooling the large original sanctuaries for the few members attending daily or Shabbat services became extremely expensive.

The Gordon Chapel at Temple Oheb Shalom Synagogue in Baltimore was designed and constructed in 1987 by Levin/Brown Architects (figure 6.8). Its design respects the original design of the exterior with four decorative arches that reflect the main façade of the original building where the arches are part of the structure (figure 3.3). As explained previously, this new part of the building enabled the creation of a new entrance to the building, accessible to all users. The chapel's interior was created as an intimate worship space made of oak and warm colors and includes flexible seating. The bimah is low (e.g., three steps up, with a small ramp) and is lit by a skylight above. The design is simple and does not compete with the designs of the original building or the main sanctuary.

Another example is the addition of the Perlman Sanctuary, a new chapel in Minoru Yamasaki's North Shore Congregation Israel Synagogue in Glencoe, Illinois. The chapel was designed by Chicago architects Hammond, Beeby & Babka in 1979. The congregation selected them following several interviews with local architects and after the office of Minoru Yamasaki Associates withdrew their name from consideration due to other commitments. The chapel was built as a cylindrical building at the edge of the original south wing of the synagogue. The circular praying space was embedded into a large rectangular social hall addition. Though the exterior of the chapel is round, in contrast to the straight lines used by Yamasaki, the architects attempted to respect the wishes of the congregation by using the same bricks of the south wing and integrating the new with the old on the outside (figure 6.9).[26] However, the chapel's entrance from outside was designed in a postmodern style, which contrasts with the original modern entrances to the synagogues and its wings (figure 4.40). In 2003, Minoru Yamasaki Associates proposed a change to the chapel's exterior entrance that would better integrate the chapel's exterior with the original synagogue's complex (figure 6.10), but it was not materialized.

The new chapel's interior was designed in a postmodernist style (figure 6.11) that completely contrasts with the modernist style of the original sanctuary (figure 4.32). As a postmodernist architect, Thomas Beeby looked to the great classical styles of European synagogues for inspiration. Specifically, he was inspired by the rich, traditional Sephardic synagogues of Venice.[27] Indeed, when I visited the chapel, I felt as if I returned hundreds of years back in history to a traditional historical European synagogue with eclectic details drawn from various styles. It was hard to understand the

Figure 6.9. Yamasaki's North Shore Congregation Israel Synagogue in Glencoe, Illinois: The addition of the chapel as viewed from outside behind the south wing

Figure 6.10. North Shore Congregation Israel Synagogue in Glencoe, Illinois: A new entrance to the Perlman Sanctuary—the chapel as presented by Minoru Yamasaki Associates in 2003 (Courtesy of North Shore Congregation Israel Synagogue's archive)

Figure 6.11. Yamasaki's North Shore Congregation Israel Synagogue in Glencoe, Illinois: The interior sanctuary of the Perlman Sanctuary—the chapel designed by architects Hammond, Beeby & Babka, 1979

A Shift in Focus to Education

The second solution to the problem of decline in memberships due to fewer new members was to refocus the congregations' attention on education. To attract new members, especially young families, congregations expanded the synagogues' educational wings. Synagogues' renovations included the addition of new classrooms and the retrofit of existing ones, while preserving the original integrity of the synagogue complex.

In 1962, Percival Goodman designed such an addition to the school he included as part of his 1950s design of Congregation B'nai Israel Synagogue in Millburn, New Jersey. The two-story school building became an integral part of the synagogue's complex. It maintained the horizontal lines of the synagogue and the original school, while also using the same construction materials (figure 5.20). As mentioned in chapter 5, the 2011 major renovations and expansion of the synagogue also included additions to the education wing. These were constructed with respect to Goodman's design.

A similar solution was introduced in 2003 by Minoru Yamasaki Associates, who added a new floor to Yamasaki's 1964 school of Congregation Israel in Glencoe, Illinois (figure 6.12). The firm utilized the site topography to add the new floor below the original existing classrooms. This elegant solution used the paved courtyard as a balcony and left the playground at the entrance level. The lower-level façade includes glass walls to bring daylight into the classrooms. Internal stairs were added at the end of the left corridor of the synagogue and serve as the entrance to the additional classrooms below. The school can be reached by the original entrance from the parking lot (figure 6.13) and by a new additional glass entrance from the courtyard (figure 6.14). The sensitive addition maintained the modern integrity of the original design and became an integrated part of the complex. It is plausible to assume that when the original architectural firm designs new additions, the architects are more attuned to the existing modern recent past building.

extreme difference in styles between Yamasaki's original sanctuary that took my breath away and the chapel that felt out of place. Author Samuel Gruber claims that just as the congregation willingly embraced modernism for their first sanctuary (1964), they chose to build the chapel in the newest postmodernist style at the time (1979).[28] Rabbi Herbert Bronstein expressed the wish of the congregation to feel a sense of sanctity that he claimed was lost in the large monumental original sanctuary, and therefore he welcomed the new chapel (see chapter 3). The architects believed that by selecting a different architectural style (i.e., postmodernism), their design does not compete with the original modern building. This approach is seen in preservation projects in which the style of a new addition contrasts with the original in order to highlight the existing building. Since architect Beeby did not regard Yamasaki's synagogue as a masterpiece,[29] it is hard to tell if this approach was his design intent.

Figure 6.12. Yamasaki's North Shore Congregation Israel Synagogue in Glencoe, Illinois: The addition of the lower floor to the school by Yamasaki Associates

Figure 6.13. North Shore Congregation Israel Synagogue in Glencoe, Illinois: The original entrance to the school from the parking lot, 1964

Figure 6.14. North Shore Congregation Israel Synagogue in Glencoe, Illinois: A new additional glass entrance from the courtyard designed by Yamasaki Associates

Adaptive Use

The decline of memberships due to migrations of members to newer suburbs of the city or to different cities/states also caused a decrease in the number of students attending the synagogues' schools. Consequently, it became harder to maintain monumental synagogue complexes with their large sanctuaries and education wings. Ideas of reusing parts of the building for new purposes other than their original functions emerged as means to save and preserve the synagogues. This is the case of Temple Mount Sinai in El Paso, Texas. In 2014, the congregation commissioned local firm In*Situ Architecture to assess the facility's condition and propose solutions to preserve and save the synagogue. In*Situ's architectural reports included a comprehensive assessment/analysis of the existing physical and spiritual conditions[30] of the synagogue's complex and site. Following these assessments, In*Situ recommended extensive maintenance work, which included

rehabilitation projects to deal with hazardous materials such as asbestos, address accessibility/ADA issues, and upgrade the parking and landscape. The second part of the reports included plans to save the building through adaptive reuse of the education wing that was hardly used at the time of the analysis and to utilize the large site of the synagogue. The firm offered two alternatives. The first option called for a conversion of the existing school to a charter school, while keeping a small religious school at the entrance level. This option also considered converting the school to a community center (figure 6.15). The plan did not require major adaptation to the lower floor, though it necessitated interior changes on the entrance floor. The administration offices would become classrooms for a small religious school of the synagogue's members. These offices would take the place of the existing multiple-use room, kitchen, and part of the social hall (figure 6.15). This proposed plan maintains the historic integrity of the synagogue complex and especially

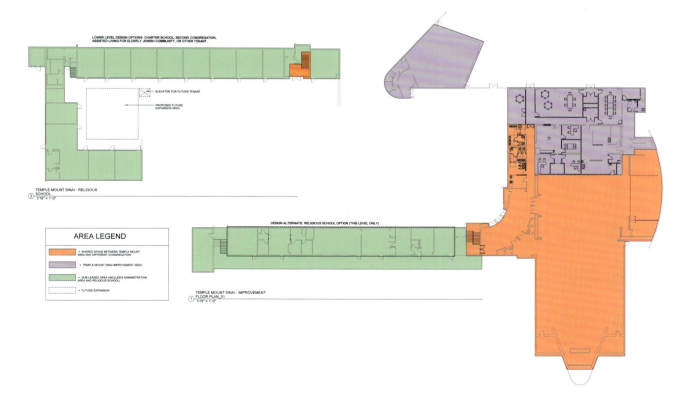

Figure 6.15. Eisenshtat's Temple Mount Sinai in El Paso, Texas: A design proposal for adaptive use of the school on the lower floor of Temple Mount Sinai in El Paso, Texas, and modification to the administration wing at the entrance level. Proposed by In*Situ Architecture, 2014. (Courtesy of In*Situ Architecture)

Figure 6.16. Eisenshtat's Temple Mount Sinai in El Paso, Texas: An improved site plan proposal with a design of a new neighborhood. Proposed by In*Situ Architecture, 2014. (Courtesy of In*Situ Architecture)

Figure 6.17. Eisenshtat's Temple Mount Sinai in El Paso, Texas: A design proposal for a housing prototype to be built on the synagogue's site. Proposed by In*Situ Architecture, 2014. (Courtesy of In*Situ Architecture)

of its sanctuary and the chapel. Thus Temple Mount Sinai can continue to serve the religious needs of the Jewish community.

The second option was a proposal for an adaptive use of the school. This option suggested turning the school into an assisted living facility for elderly Jewish community members. This proposed plan entails changes to the entrance floor, including the small religious school (figure 6.15). It also implies major modifications to the lower floor. However, it still maintains the historic integrity of the synagogue as a complex and specifically of the prayer wing. This proposal includes accessible solutions that would make it easy for the elderly to stay within the synagogue's complex and use the sanctuary and chapel for prayer and study. It also may encourage their families to join them for Shabbat and high holidays services and to celebrate their family festivities in the building. This proposal was an appealing solution since it had the potential to generate more revenue for the synagogue.

In addition, In*Situ architects suggested utilizing the large site of the synagogue to build a new neighborhood on the far side of the lot (figure 6.16). The housing development will include twenty-nine living units (sixteen townhouses and thirteen single-story houses), which will create revenues for the synagogue and hopefully will attract new members to join the community. Figure 6.17 illustrates In*Situ Architectures' proposed townhouses and single-story houses. This initiative would maintain the synagogue building's historic integrity but would change the suburban feel to a more urban environment. This change may hurt some of the historic integrity of the site, especially its sustainable measures (chapter 5). Still, I believe that if the planned neighborhood follows the original sustainable design of the synagogue and its landscape, it can blend as part of the synagogue's surroundings.

As of the time of this writing, the congregation has not decided which of the rehabilitation alternative(s) based on In*Situ's assessment reports to follow. Currently, they lease the school at the lower level to a Jewish preschool (figure 6.18) and follow In*Situ Architecture's suggestions for maintenance and repairs. These include sustainable measures such as replacing the whole HVAC system with a more efficient one, adding insulation to better sustain the extreme climate and help conserve energy, and working on water prevention improvement as appropriate to the region's desert conditions. These efforts help preserve Mount Sinai Temple in El Paso and its unique contribution to the sustainable design of synagogues. It should be

Figure 6.18. Eisenshtat's Temple Mount Sinai in El Paso, Texas: The existing/original school on the lower level turned into a Jewish preschool

noted that the mentioned maintenance and repairs are the first step in protecting a historic synagogue that belongs to the important inventory of modern American synagogues of the 1960s.

Summary

The maintenance and preservation work of modern architectural heritage corresponds to the contextual model I presented in chapter 2. As illustrated in figure 2.1, the intersection of the congregations' search for identity, their moves to the suburbs to build their American dream homes, and the rise of the modern architecture movement in America became the context of modern American synagogues during the 1950s and 1960s. The search for identity evolved from the questions of Jewish identity post-Holocaust to the realization of the American value of freedom of religion. It was expressed in the design of synagogues from a functional approach and sometimes as memorials to institutions reflecting self-confidence and pride. The desires of congregations to preserve their houses of worship express their admiration of these buildings and their modern heritage. Thus the context of the modern architecture movement in the mid-twentieth century turns out to be part of "preservation of the recent past" movement. Finally, the context of the American suburbs is still in the background of these buildings, as we saw in chapter 4 with the case of Eric Mendelsohn's Park Synagogue. Members who left the suburb continue to use the original building for Shabbat and high holidays services while building a new smaller synagogue in their new location with homage to the modern architecture of the original synagogue (figure 4.18).

Congregations and architects approached the various changes that occurred through time as preservation of the recent past beyond brick and mortar. They addressed issues of accessibility, acoustics, education, energy conservation, and more. The challenge was to address these changes while maintaining the modern historic integrity and keeping the modern Jewish heritage alive.

7 Concluding Remarks

Firmitas, utilitas, and venustas
(*Vitruvius, 40 BCE*)

The application of this book's conceptual model (figure 3.1) to selected modern American synagogues of the 1950s–1960s highlights the relationship between faith (Judaism), form, and the building technology of these buildings. It illustrates how architects bridged Judaism with modernism and utilized new building technology (e.g., materials, systems, and construction) to develop new architectural aesthetics. As described in chapter 3, Judaism focuses on the interior design of the synagogue, while the exterior is left open. Thus the interior's form is directly influenced by Jewish requirements. This form is enhanced by building materials and systems, which focus on creating the synagogue's spiritual ambiance. However, on the building's exterior, the focus is on a bidirectional influence of form and building technology. Usually form dictates the kind of building technology to use. However, in modern architecture, building technology often influenced the development of form. Pushing the envelope of these synagogues was expressed in the use of new materials such as steel and concrete and their corresponding structural systems and construction methods. These experiments with materials and systems enabled the designers to create new aesthetics with forms that sought to enhance the sacredness of those buildings and establish monumental institutions of American Jewry.

The modern shapes included the sacred path that helps the worshiper exit the profane world and enter the spiritual realm. This path continues inside the building and brings the congregates to the sanctuary—the sacred plan. The modern synagogue's plan, with a seating arrangement avoiding hierarchical design, creates unity and harmony. The sacred verticality in these modern synagogues is achieved by soaring roofs (see chapters 4 and 5) and mainly by light pouring into the sanctuaries from above (see chapters 3 and 4). The designs of the three-dimensional sacred spaces dictate the use of systems (e.g., light, acoustics, climate comfort), and in turn those systems, especially the treatment of light, enhance the dramatic effect of the spiritual experience in the sanctuaries.

Modern American synagogues exhibit the design concepts developed by Vitruvius, the Roman architect from the first century BCE: *firmitas*, *utilitas*, and *venustas*, meaning strength, utility, and delight/beauty.[1] The synagogues' *firmitas* is expressed in the simple fact that they are still standing and serving their original purpose—a house of worship, gathering, and education (chapters 3, 4, and 5). The synagogues' *utilitas* is exhibited in the preservation efforts to utilize the buildings and save them via various adaptations and changes (chapter 6). The *venustas* is reflected in the awe and spiritual feelings the synagogues and their sanctuaries evoke. It expresses the congregations' emotions of delight. The original congregations who commissioned and built their modern synagogues post–World War II and after the horrific events of the Holocaust felt pride and love toward their buildings. The synagogues served as "an active participant in community life"[2] and helped the congregation find their modern identity and "belonging" in America. These buildings were part of the American boom of houses of worship during the 1950s and 1960s that reflected the nation's religious mind-set (see chapter 1) and followed President Eisenhower's call for the American people to embrace their faith and belong to a congregation (see chapter 2). This delight continued through generations that preserved the modern heritage of their synagogues and relished the fact that their synagogues were unique as designed by famous modern American architects. In my field trips to all the synagogues depicted in this book, I felt overwhelming gratitude for the hospitality of the representatives of these congregations, who walked with me through their buildings and showcased their synagogues with love and pride.

I felt delighted by the familiar feeling I experienced when I read the Hebrew verses on the wall(s). It brought me a sense of belonging and pride. More so, some of these spaces evoked a sense of spirituality that transcended beyond my religious association (as discussed later).

My experiences of delight were accentuated by my direct exposure to the essence of the synagogues' architecture and their designers, as I "touched" and photographed original drawings signed by architects about whom I learned in architecture schools.

My sensation of admiration strengthened as I approached each of the buildings, being aware of how they soar to the sky to be closer to God and to be seen by humans. I appreciated how the modern architectural and construction details brought the *firmitas* and *utilitas* to become part of the *venustas*, giving credence to architect Ludwig Mies van der Rohe's summary of modernism when he claimed that "God is in the details."[3]

The climax of the spiritual delight in these synagogues is experienced when you enter the sanctuary and your breath is taken away. This is the point when the feeling of awe transcends into spirituality. Some scholars claim that spiritual emotions are evoked from the connection between one's religion and feelings.[4] Still, I experienced the feeling of awe in some of the synagogues regardless of my religious inclinations. In her PhD research, Nesrine Mansour investigated the common ground between religion and spirituality in a search for the source of the sacred.[5] Indeed, the synagogues' architects managed to enhance universal common elements of spirituality on top of the specificities of faith requirements in creating sacred spaces. In their designs, they have pushed the envelope of aesthetics and building technology and built the synagogues as spiritual spaces. These places evoke the sacredness of congregations' gatherings, which in Judaism is more sacred than the building itself (chapter 3). Their push in design reflected the modernism of their time, but as shown in the book, these buildings became timeless and continue to serve as the "focal point of the community's aspirations."[6]

Notes

Chapter 1

1. For example, the analyses and history of the religious, social, or cultural concepts of the phenomenon, or as the history of one specific synagogue or one congregation.

2. Shahram Shandiz, "Architectural Analysis: A Methodology to Understand and Inform the Design of Spaces" (Auckland, New Zealand: Unitec Institute of Technology, 2014); Simon Unwin, *Analysing Architecture*, 4th ed. (London: Routledge, 2014); Francis D. K. Ching, *Architecture, Form, Space, & Order*, 3rd ed. (New York: John Wiley & Sons, 2007).

3. Unwin, *Analysing Architecture*, 3, 9.

4. Unwin, *Analysing Architecture*, 11.

5. See the conceptual framework model in Anat Geva's book *Frank Lloyd Wright's Sacred Architecture: Faith, Form and Building Technology* (London: Routledge, 2012), 13.

6. Geva, *Frank Lloyd Wright's Sacred Architecture*, 29.

7. Margaret Grubiak, "Educating the Moral Scientist: The Chapels at I. I. T. and M.I.T.," Arris, *Journal of the Southeast Chapter of the Society of Architectural Historians* 18 (2007): 1–14.

8. Gavriel Rosenfeld, *Building after Auschwitz: Jewish Architecture and the Memory of the Holocaust* (New Haven, CT: Yale University Press, 2011).

9. Oscar Handlin, "Immigration in American Life: A Reappraisal," in *Immigration and American History: Essays in Honor of Theodore C. Blegen*, edited by Henry Steele Commager (Minneapolis: University of Minnesota Press, 1961), 8–25.

10. Michael Meyer, *Jewish Identity in the Modern World* (Seattle: University of Washington Press, 1990), 56.

11. David Morgan and Sally M. Promey, "Introduction," in *The Visual Culture of American Religions*, eds. David Morgan and Sally M. Promey (Berkeley: University of California Press, 1971), 10; Samuel Gruber, "Jewish Identity and Modern Synagogue Architecture," in *Jewish Identity in Contemporary Architecture*, eds. Angeli Sachs and Edward Van Voolen (Munich: Prestel, 2004), 30.

12. Michael Padwee, "Mid-Twentieth Century Synagogues in the United States: The Collaboration of Art and Architecture and a Request," *Architectural Tiles, Glass and Ornamentation in New York*, published May 1, 2016, and accessed June 7, 2019, https://tilesinnewyork.blogspot.com/2016/05/mid-twentieth-century-synagogues-in.html

13. Padwee, "Mid-Twentieth Century Synagogues in the United States."

14. Meyer, *Jewish Identity*, 57. Deborah Fripp points out that debates over how to teach about the Holocaust continue even today and focus mainly on teaching it either from the Jewish perspective or as part of the history of World War II. "This Synagogue Embraced a New Narrative for Teaching the Holocaust," ReformJudaism.org, accessed May 27 2019, https://reformjudaism.org/blog/2017/04/19/synagogue-embraced-new-narrative-teaching-holocaust.

15. Arnold Eisen, *The Chosen People in America: A Study in Jewish Religious Ideology* (Bloomington: Indiana University Press, 1983), 4.

16. Eisen, *The Chosen People in America*, 4.

17. Eisen, *The Chosen People in America*, 4.

18. Eisen, *The Chosen People in America*, 5.

19. Marc Raphael, *The Synagogue in America: A Short History* (New York: New York University Press, 2011), 12.

20. Philip Nobel, "What Design for a Synagogue Spells Jewish?" *New York Times*, December 2, 2001.

21. Jack Wertheimer, *The American Synagogue: A Sanctuary Transformed* (Cambridge: Cambridge University Press, 1987), 9.

22. Lance J. Sussman, "The Suburbanization of American Judaism as Reflected in Synagogue Building

and Architecture, 1945–1975," *American Jewish History*, 75, no. 1 (1985): 37.

23. Geva, *Frank Lloyd Wright's Sacred Architecture*, 16–28.

24. Richard Meier, *Recent American Synagogue Architecture: An Exhibition Catalogue* (New York: The Jewish Museum, 1963), 22.

25. "Form follows function," a design concept representing an architecture school of thought that started with the work and philosophy of architect Louis Sullivan. See, for example, Jackie Craven, "The Meaning of 'Form Follows Function,'" ThoughtCo., published August 1, 2019, and accessed July 7, 2020, https://www.thoughtco.com/form-follows-function-177237. It continued with other modernist architects such as Philip Johnson. See, for example, Steven Bradley, "Form Follows Function?," *Smashing Magazine*, published March 23, 2010, and accessed June 7, 2019, https://www.smashingmagazine.com/2010/03/does-form-follow-function/.

26. Geva, *Frank Lloyd Wright's Sacred Architecture*.

27. Samuel Gruber, *American Synagogues: A Century of Architecture and Jewish Community* (New York: Rizzoli, 2003).

28. *Torah*, the "old Testament," is defined as "the five books of Moses constituting the Pentateuch." See "Torah," Merriam-Webster, accessed March 19, 2019, https://www.merriam-webster.com/dictionary/Torah.

29. Jack Wertheimer described the growth of congregations in *The American Synagogue*, 7.

30. María Francisca González, "15 Facades That Push Conventional Limits: The Best Photos of the Week," *ArchDaily*, published November 12, 2017, and accessed April 25, 2020, https://www.archdaily.com/883386/15-facades-that-push-conventional-limits-the-best-photos-of-the-week.

31. Wertheimer, *The American Synagogue*, vii–viii.

32. Victoria Young, *Saint John's Abbey Church: Marcel Breuer and the Creation of a Modern Sacred Space* (Minneapolis: University of Minnesota Press, 2014); Jay M. Price, *Temples for a Modern God: Religious Architecture in Postwar America* (New York: Oxford University Press, 2013); Louis P. Nelson, *American Sanctuary: Understanding Sacred Spaces* (Bloomington: Indiana University Press, 2006).

33. Henry Stolzman and Daniel Stolzman, *Synagogue Architecture in America: Faith, Spirit & Identity* (Mulgrave, Victoria, Australia: The Images Publishing Group Pty Ltd., 2004); Gruber, *American Synagogues*.

34. Jay Price, *Temples for a Modern God*; Douglas R. Hoffman, *Seeking the Sacred in Contemporary Religious Architecture* (Kent, OH: Kent State University Press, 2010).

35. Joseph Siry, *Beth Sholom Synagogue: Frank Lloyd Wright and Modern Religious Architecture* (Chicago: The University of Chicago Press, 2011); Anat Geva, *Frank Lloyd Wright's Sacred Architecture*; Walter L. Leedy Jr., *Eric Mendelsohn's Park Synagogue: Architecture and Community*, ed. Sara Jane Pearman (Kent, OH: Kent State University Press, 2012).

36. Samuel Gruber, *American Synagogues*.

37. It should be noted that this chapter does not include the history of synagogue architecture, which can be found in many other publications.

38. Geva, *Frank Lloyd Wright's Sacred Architecture*.

39. Rabbi Dr. Benjamin Elton, "Cathedral Synagogues Still Have a Future," *The Jewish Chronicle*, published June 24, 2018, and accessed June 29, 2020, https://www.thejc.com/judaism/features/cathedral-synagogues-still-have-a-future-1.465950.

40. Minoru Yamasaki's quote in *The Architecture of Light* brochure by North Shore Congregation Israel (1960).

41. Percival Goodman designed more than fifty synagogues in the United States between the 1950s and 1970s.

42. Theodore H. M. Prudon, *Preservation of Modern Architecture* (Hoboken, NJ: John Wiley & Sons, 2008); Thomas C. Jester, ed., *20th Century Building Materials* (Los Angeles: Getty Conservation Institute, 2014); Adrian Forty, *Concrete and Culture: A Material History* (London: Reaktion Books, 2012).

43. Forty, *Concrete and Culture*, 14–15.

Chapter 2

1. David De Sola Pool, "Judaism and the Synagogue," in *The American Jew*, ed. Oscar I. Janowsky (New York: Harper and Brothers, 1942), 54.

2. Abraham J. Karp, *Jewish Continuity in America: Creative Survival in a Free Society* (Tuscaloosa: University of Alabama Press, 1998).

3. Abraham J. Karp, "Ideology and Identity in Jewish Group Survival in America," *American Jewish Historical Quarterly* 65, no. 4 (June 1976): 310–34.

4. Karp, *Jewish Continuity in America*.

5. Lance J. Sussman, "The Suburbanization of American Judaism as Reflected in Synagogue Building and Architecture, 1945–1975," *American Jewish History* 75, no. 1 (1985): 31.

6. Sussman, "The Suburbanization of American Judaism"; Karp, *Jewish Continuity in America*.

7. Gretchen Buggeln, *The Suburban Church* (Minneapolis: University of Minnesota Press, 2015), xv.

8. Buggeln, *The Suburban Church*, xxi; Albert I. Gordon, *Jews in Suburbia* (Westport, CO: Greenwood Press Publishers, reprinted, 1973), 7–9.

9. Gordon, *Jews in Suburbia*, 7–9.

10. Kathleen A. Tobin, "The Reduction of Urban Vulnerability: Revisiting 1950's American Suburbanization as

Civil Defense," *Cold War History* 2, no. 2 (January 2002): 1–32.

11. "Holocaust Encyclopedia," United States Holocaust Memorial Museum, accessed January 27, 2019, https://encyclopedia.ushmm.org.

12. "Holocaust Encyclopedia."

13. "Jewish Refugees during and after the Holocaust," My Jewish Learning, accessed May 27, 2019, https://www.myjewishlearning.com/article/jewish-refugees-during-and-after-the-holocaust/.

14. "Jewish Refugees during and after the Holocaust."

15. "The 1951 Refugee Convention," accessed July 15, 2022, https://immigrationhistory.org/item/the-1951-refugee-convention/.

16. Eric Mendelsohn, "Creating a Modern Synagogue Style: In the Spirit of Our Age," *Commentary* 3, no. 6 (June 1947).

17. Henri Tajfel ed., *Differentiation between Social Groups: Studies in the Social Psychology of Intergroup Relations* (London: Academic Press, 1978); Henri Tajfel and John C. Turner, "An Integrative Theory of Intergroup Conflict," in *The Social Psychology of Intergroup Relations*, eds. William G. Austin and Stephen Worchel (Monterey, CA: Brooks Cole, 1979), 38–48; Henri Tajfel, "Social Psychology of Intergroup Relations," *Annual Review of Psychology* 33 (1982): 1–39.

18. Henri Tajfel, "Social Categorization, Social Identity, and Social Comparison," in *Differentiation between Social Groups: Studies in the Social Psychology of Intergroup Relations*, ed. Henri Tajfel (London: Academic Press, 1978), 63.

19. Michael A. Meyer, *Jewish Identity in the Modern World* (Seattle: University of Washington Press, 1990), 8.

20. Otto Weininger, *Geschlecht und Charakter*, 20th printing (Vienna: W. Braumuller, 1920), 402, as quoted in Meyer, *Jewish Identity*, 41.

21. Meyer, *Jewish Identity*, 41.

22. Meyer, *Jewish Identity*, 101 (note 30).

23. Ashkenazim are those who came from or are descended of Jews from western, northern, and eastern Europe; Sephardim are those who originated from or are descended of Jews from Spain, Portugal, Turkey, North Africa, and the Middle East.

24. Meyer, *Jewish Identity*, 83.

25. Michael A. Meyer (1937–), Professor of Jewish History at Hebrew Union College–Jewish Institute of Religion in Cincinnati, Ohio.

26. Meyer, *Jewish Identity*, 8–9.

27. Meyer, *Jewish Identity*, 10.

28. Meyer, *Jewish Identity*, 33.

29. Meyer, *Jewish Identity*, 59.

30. Meyer, *Jewish Identity*, 59.

31. Abraham J. Karp, "Overview: The Synagogue in America – A Historical Typology," in *The American Synagogue: A Sanctuary Transformed*, ed. Jack Wertheimer (Cambridge: Cambridge University Press, 1987), 20.

32. Jay M. Price, *Temples for a Modern God: Religious Architecture in Postwar America*. (New York: Oxford University Press, 2013), 49.

33. Will Herberg, *Protestant-Catholic-Jew* (New York: Doubleday & Co. 1955), 274.

34. Herberg, *Protestant-Catholic-Jew*, 260.

35. Rabbi Louis Jacobs, "Modern Jewish History: *Haskalah*, the Jewish Enlightenment," *My Jewish Learning*, accessed July 2018, https://www.myjewishlearning.com/article/haskalah/.

36. Jacobs, "Modern Jewish History."

37. Jacobs, "Modern Jewish History."

38. Colleen McDannell, *Material Christianity: Religion and Popular Culture in America* (New Haven, CT: Yale University Press, 1995).

39. Charles Taylor, *A Secular Age* (Cambridge, MA: Belknap Press of Harvard University Press, 2007).

40. "Charles Taylor, Canadian Philosopher," Britannica.com, accessed January 2022, https://www.britannica.com/biography/Charles-Taylor.

41. Mike Stunson, "Majority of Americans Don't Belong to a Place of Worship in Historic Decline, Poll Finds," *Lexington Herald Leader*, published March 30, 2021, and accessed October 2021, https://www.kentucky.com/news/nation-world/national/article250289895.html.

42. *Rabbi Michael Knopf,* "What's Driving Jews Away from Synagogues? Not Dues, but 'Membership,'" *Haaretz*, published April 10, 2018, and accessed October 2021, https://www.haaretz.com/jewish/.premium-membership-is-stopping-jews-from-paying-synagogue-dues-1.5387705.

43. Charles Hirschman, "The Role of Religion in the Origins and Adaptation of Immigrant Groups in the United States," *International Migration Review* 38, no. 3, Conceptual and Methodological Developments in the Study of International Migration (Fall 2004): 1215.

44. Jack Wertheimer, in the preface to his edited volume *The American Synagogue: A Sanctuary Transform* (Cambridge: Cambridge University Press, 1987), claims that between 1945 and 1975 Jews continually pushed toward Americanization and social activism, while Abraham J. Karp in his overview of the same volume (p. 9) claims that Americanization had already been described by Joseph Krauskoff in his article, "Half a Century of Judaism in the United States," published in *The American Jews Annual for 5648 A. M.* (New York, 1988), p. 72.

45. Jean Paul Sartre, *Anti-Semite and Jew* (New York: Schocken Books, 1948); Georges Friedmann, *The End of the Jewish People?* (New York: Doubleday, 1967); Meyer, *Jewish Identity*, 33.

46. Meyer, *Jewish Identity*, 33.

47. Rachel Wischnitzer-Bernstein, "The Problem of

Synagogue Architecture," *Commentary* (March 1947): 239–41.

48. Will Herberg, "The Postwar Revival of the Synagogue," *Commentary* (April 1950): 316.

49. Carol Herselle. Krinsky, *Synagogues of Europe* (Cambridge, MA: The MIT Press, 1985), 99.

50. Karp, "Overview," 12.

51. Karp, "Overview," 20.

52. Benny Kraut, "Ethnic-Religious Ambiguities in an Immigrant Synagogue: The Case of New Hope Congregation," in *The American Synagogue: A Sanctuary Transformed*, ed. Jack Wertheimer (Cambridge: Cambridge University Press, 1987), 231.

53. Kraut, "Ethnic-Religious Ambiguities in an Immigrant Synagogue"; Abraham Karp, "Overview," 3.

54. Theodor Herzl, *Old New Land* [*Altneuland*], trans. Lotta Levensohn (Leipzig, Germany: Hermann Seemann Nachfolger, 1902; Princeton: Markus Wiener, 1997).

55. It should be noted that Ahad Ha'am did not include other cultures beyond western Europe. Hillel Halkin, "What Ahad Ha'am Saw and Herzl Missed – and Vice Versa," *Mosaic Magazine*, accessed March 2018,

https://mosaicmagazine.com/essay/2016/10/what-ahad-haam-saw-and-herzl-missed-and-vice-versa; Jacques Kornberg, ed., *At the Crossroads: Essays on Ahad Ha-Am* (Albany: State University of New York Press, 1983).

56. Simon Dubnow, *Nationalism and History*, ed. Koppel Pinson (Philadelphia: Jewish Publication Society, 1958).

57. Meyer, *Jewish Identity*, 8, 59–83.

58. Arnold M. Eisen, *The Chosen People in America: A Study in Jewish Religious Ideology* (Bloomington: Indiana University Press, 1983), 37.

59. Eisen, *The Chosen People in America*, 37.

60. Meyer, *Jewish Identity*, 61.

61. Eisen, *The Chosen People in America*, 3.

62. Rosenfeld, *Building after Auschwitz*, 7.

63. Eisen, *The Chosen People in America*, 4.

64. Eisen, *The Chosen People in America*, 5.

65. *Rosenfeld, Building after Auschwitz*, 8, 68.

66. *Rosenfeld, Building after Auschwitz*, 8.

67. Hanoch Achiman, "The Synagogues' Sections," in *Mikdah Me-at* (The Little Sanctuary), eds. Y. Ilan, A. Shtal, and Z. Shtiner (Jerusalem: The Ministry of Education and Culture, 1976), 57 (in Hebrew).

68. Karp, "Overview," 13.

69. Anat Geva, *Frank Lloyd Wright's Sacred Architecture: Faith, Form and Building Technology* (London: Routledge, 2012), 13.

70. Buggeln, *The Suburban Church*; Price, *Temples for a Modern God*; Gordon, *Jews in Suburbia*.

71. It is estimated that between the 1950s and 1960s, eleven million new homes were built in the suburbs. Mark Gelernter, *A History of Buildings in Their Cultural American and Technological Context Architecture* (Hanover and London: University Press of New England, 1999), 270.

72. Gelernter, *A History of Buildings*; Buggeln, *The Suburban Church*, xxi; Raphael Marc, *The Synagogue in America: A Short History* (New York: New York University Press, 2011), 122.

73. Lila Corwin Berman, *Metropolitan Jews* (Chicago: University of Chicago Press, 2015), 162.

74. Will Herberg, *Protestant-Catholic-Jew: An Essay in American Religious Sociology* (Chicago: University of Chicago Press, 1983), 56; Herberg, "The Postwar Revival of the Synagogue," 315–25.

75. Walter C. Leedy Jr., *Eric Mendelsohn's Park Synagogue* (Kent, OH: The Kent State University Press, 2012), 32.

76. June Manning Thomas, *Redevelopment and Race: Planning a Finer City in Postwar Detroit* (Detroit: Wayne State University Press, 1997), 7.

77. Thomas, *Redevelopment and Race*, 7; Berman, *Metropolitan Jews,* 47.

78. Katie Nodjimbadem, "The Racial Segregation of American Cities Was Anything but Accidental," *Smithsonian Magazine*, accessed May 30, 2019, https://www.smithsonianmag.com/history/how-federal-government-intentionally-racially-segregated-american-cities-180963494/.

79. Thomas, *Redevelopment and Race*, 9.

80. Hirsh, *Making the Second Ghetto*; Thomas, *Redevelopment and Race*, 9; Marc, *The Synagogue in America,* 122.

81. Gordon, *Jews in Suburbia*, 168.

82. Gordon, *Jews in Suburbia*, 171.

83. Price, *Temples for a Modern God*, 58.

84. Leedy Jr., *Eric Mendelsohn's Park Synagogue*.

85. "The American Dream" was coined by historian James Truslow Adams in 1931.

86. The statistics of the growing percentage of the nonwhite population in various cities across the nation appears in Gordon's *Jews in Suburbia*.

87. Thomas, *Redevelopment and Race*, 7.

88. Gordon, *Jews in Suburbia*, 12.

89. Gordon, *Jews in Suburbia*, 16.

90. Gordon, *Jews in Suburbia*; Buggeln, *The Suburban Church*.

91. Reported by Karp in his "Overview," 24.

92. Karp, "Overview," 27.

93. Buggeln, *The Suburban Church*, xxvi.

94. Karp, "Overview," 24.

95. For a diagram of the synagogue's functions and their relationship, see Paul Thiry, Richard M. Bennett, and Henry L. Kamphoefner, *Church & Temples* (New

York: Reinhold Publishing Corporation, 1953), 18J, fig. 19J.

96. Gordon, *Jews in Suburbia*, 85.

97. Gordon, *Jews in Suburbia*, 127.

98. Gordon, *Jews in Suburbia*, 89.

99. Price, *Temples for a Modern God*, 15; Buggeln, *The Suburban Church*, xv.

100. Karp, "Overview," 26, quoting Rabbi Eugene Borowitz.

101. Philip Johnson and Henry-Russell Hitchcock, eds., *Modern Architecture: The International Exhibition* (New York: Museum of Modern Art, February 10–March 23, 1932).

102. It should be noted that though Wright appeared in the catalogue, he withdrew his projects from the exhibition. Gili Merin, "AD Classics: Modern Architecture International Exhibition / Philip Johnson and Henry-Russell Hitchcock," *ArchDaily*, published August 2, 2013, and accessed September 15, 2020, https://www.archdaily.com/409918/ad-classics-modern-architecture-international-exhibition-philip-johnson-and-henry-russell-hitchcock.

103. Merin, "AD Classics."

104. Robert Benson, "Douglas Haskell and the Criticism of International Modernism," in *Modern Architecture in America: Visions and Revisions*, eds. Wilson Richard Guy and Sidney K. Robinson (Ames: Iowa State University Press, 1991), 167.

105. Benson, "Douglas Haskell and the Criticism of International Modernism."

106. Johnson and Hitchcock, *Modern Architecture*; Henry-Russell Hitchcock, *Architecture: Romanticism and Reintegration* (New York: Payson & Clarke Ltd., 1929).

107. Louis H. Sullivan, "The Tall Office Building Artistically Considered," *Lippincott's Magazine*, March 1896.

108. H. A. Meek, *The Synagogue* (London: Phaidon Press, 1995), 210.

109. For example, Marian Moffett, Michael Fazio, and Lawrence Wodehouse, *Building across Time: An Introduction to World Architecture* (Boston: McGraw Hill, 2004); Gelernter, *A History of Buildings*; Jan Gympel, *The Story of Architecture from Antiquity to the Present* (Koln, Germany: Konemann, 1996), 96–105.

110. For example, Kenneth Frampton, *A Genealogy of Modern Architecture*, ed. Ashley Simone (Zurich, Switzerland: Lars Muller Publishers, 2015); Michael J. Lewis, *American Art and Architecture* (London: Thames & Hudson, 2006), 254–83; William J. Curtis, *Modern Architecture since 1900*, 3rd ed. (Upper Saddle River, NJ: Prentice-Hall, 1999); Kenneth Frampton, *Modern Architecture: A Critical History* (New York: Thames and Hudos, 1980); Vincent Scully Jr., *Modern Architecture: The Architecture of Democracy* (New York: George Braziller, 1977).

111. Just to name a few, Dale Allen Gyure, *Minoru Yamasaki: Humanist Architecture for a Modernist World* (New Haven, CT: Yale University Press, 2017); Victoria M. Young, *Saint John's Abbey Church: Marcel Breuer and the Creation of a Modern Sacred Space* (Minneapolis: University of Minnesota Press, 2014); Joseph M. Siry, *Beth Sholom Synagogue: Frank Lloyd Wright and Modern Religious Architecture* (Chicago: University of Chicago Press, 2011).

112. Avram Kampf, *Contemporary Synagogue Art* (New York: Union of American Hebrew Congregations, 1966), 27.

113. "Modern Movement," Oxford University Press, accessed December 2021, https://www.encyclopedia.com/education/dictionaries-thesauruses-pictures-and-press-releases/modern-movement.

114. Douglas Haskell, "Is It Functional," *Creative Art* 10 (May 1932): 373–78.

115. Benson, "Douglas Haskell and the Criticism of International Modernism," 165–83.

116. Benson, "Douglas Haskell and the Criticism of International Modernism," 170–71; Douglas Haskell, "What the Man About Town Will Build," *Nation* 134 (April 13, 1932): 12–16.

117. Scully Jr., *Modern Architecture*, 13; Gelernter, *A History of Buildings*, 273; Price, *Temples for a Modern God*, 16–17; Gyure, *Minoru Yamasaki*, 125.

118. Anat Geva, "Introduction: The Sacred Space," in *Modernism and American Mid-20th Century Sacred Architecture*, ed. Anat Geva (London: Routledge, 2019), 1.

119. Price, *Temples for a Modern God*, 135.

120. For an additional example, see "Part II: The Parabola, Concrete, and Modern Sacred Architecture," in Geva, *Modernism and American Mid-20th Century Sacred Architecture*, 71–152.

121. Peter Hammond, *Liturgical and Architecture* (London: Architectural Press, 1962), 13.

122. Buggeln, *The Suburban Church*, xviii.

123. Frampton, *A Genealogy of Modern Architecture*, 1.1.

124. A quote in Adrian Forty, *Concrete and Culture* (London: Reaktion Books, 2002), 169.

125. Geva, "Introduction: The Sacred Space," 3.

126. Jeremy Kargon, "Seeing, Not Knowing: Symbolism, Art, and 'Opticalism' in Mid-Century American Religious Architecture," in Geva, *Modernism and American Mid-20th Century Sacred Architecture*, 236–39; Buggeln, *The Suburban Church*, 2–3.

127. American Institute of Architects (AIA), *A Place to Worship* (1958), film, time stamp approximately 00:02:30.

128. Eric Mendelsohn, "Creating a Modern Synagogue Style."

129. Richard Meier, *Recent American Synagogue Architecture. An Exhibition Catalogue* (New York: The Jewish Museum, 1963), 24.

130. See "Part III: Denominations, Identity, and Modern Sacred Architecture," in Geva, *Modernism and American Mid-20th Century Sacred Architecture*, 153–232; Geva, *Frank Lloyd Wright's Sacred Architecture*.

131. Jeanne Halgren Kilde, *Sacred Power, Sacred Space* (Oxford: Oxford University Press, 2008), 161. Louis P. Nelson, *American Sanctuary: Understanding Sacred Spaces* (Bloomington: Indiana University Press, 2006), 3–4.

132. Gesa Elsbeth Thiessen, ed., *Theological Aesthetics: A Reader* (Grand Rapids, MI: William B. Eerdmans Publishing, 2004), 1; Richard Kieckhefer, *Theology in Stone: Church Architecture from Byzantium to Berkeley* (New York: Oxford University Press, 2004), 97–134; Nelson, *American Sanctuary*, 3–4.

133. Meier, *Recent American Synagogue Architecture*, 22.

134. Quoted by Simon Unwin, *Analysing Architecture*, 4th ed. (London: Routledge, 2014), 118.

135. Alan R. Solomon, "Preface," in Meier, *Recent American Synagogue Architecture*, 5.

136. Wischnitzer-Bernstein, "The Problem of Synagogue Architecture."

137. The architectural style of European synagogues followed mainly the dominant local style. See Carol Herselle Krinsky, *Synagogues of Europe* (Cambridge, MA: The MIT Press, 1985).

138. In the nineteenth and early twentieth centuries, the styles of the synagogues in America included "Greek Temples, the Moorish mosques, the Gothic cathedral, the Romanesque, or the Colonial American church," as well as wooden synagogues resembling Polish synagogues of the seventeenth and early eighteenth centuries. Meier, *Recent American Synagogue Architecture*, 7.

139. Meier, *Recent American Synagogue Architecture*, 8.

140. Solomon, "Preface," in Meier, *Recent American Synagogue Architecture*, 5; Meier, *Recent American Synagogue Architecture*, 10.

141. Solomon, "Preface," in Meier, *Recent American Synagogue Architecture*, 5.

142. Solomon, "Preface," in Meier, *Recent American Synagogue Architecture*, 29.

143. Solomon, "Preface," in Meier, *Recent American Synagogue Architecture*, 29.

144. Marc, *The Synagogue in America*, 170.

145. Samuel D. Gruber, *American Synagogues: A Century of Architecture and Jewish Community*, ed. Scott J. Tilden (New York: Rizzoli, 2003), 83; Halgren Kilde, *Sacred Power, Sacred Space*, 171.

Chapter 3

1. Douglas Hoffman, *Seeking the Sacred in Contemporary Religious Architecture* (Kent, OH: The Kent State University Press, 2010), xi.

2. Richard Meier, "Introduction," in *Recent American Synagogue Architecture: An Exhibition Catalogue*, ed. Richard Meier (New York: The Jewish Museum, 1963), 10.

3. A quote by Moses Ben Maimon, commonly known as Maimonides (The Rambam), in Rabbi Baruch Rabinovitch "The Place of the Synagogue in Judaism," in *I Have Housed Them*, ed. David Casuto, 2nd ed. (Jerusalem: The Ministry of Education and Culture, Department of Torah Culture, 1976), 16 (in Hebrew); Abraham Karp, "Overview: The Synagogue in America – A Historical Typology," in *The American Synagogue: A Sanctuary Transform*, ed. Jack Wertheimer (Cambridge, England: Cambridge University Press, 1987), 14; Carol H. Krinsky, *Synagogues of Europe* (Cambridge, MA: The MIT Press, 1983), 5; Walter C. Leedy Jr., *Eric Mendelsohn's Park Synagogue* (Kent, OH: The Kent State University Press, 2012), 32.

4. Gretchen T. Buggeln, "Architecture as Community Service," in *The Visual Culture of American Religions*, eds. David Morgan and Sally M. Promey (Berkeley, CA: University of California Press, 1971), 87–88.

5. Buggeln, "Architecture as Community Service."

6. For a discussion on these terminologies and the relationship between the terms *synagogue* and *temple*, see Carol Herselle Krinsky, *Synagogues of Europe: Architecture, History, Meaning* (Cambridge, MA: The MIT Press, 1985), 8–9; Ismar Schorsch, "A Synagogue Is Not a Temple," *Conservative Judaism* 43, no. 2 (Winter 1990–91): 61–70; Rabbi Solomon B. Freehof, "A Kind of Tabernacle," in *An American Synagogue for Today and Tomorrow: A Guide Book to Synagogue Design and Construction*, ed. Peter Blake (New York: Union of American Hebrew, 1954), 6–8.

7. David Einhorn, [*Olath Tamid*] *Gebetbuch* für *Israelitische Reform – Gemeinden*, 2nd ed. (Baltimore: n.p., 1862), 396–97.

8. Freehof, "A Kind of Tabernacle," 8.

9. Avram Kampf, *Contemporary Synagogue Art* (New York: Union of American Hebrew Congregations, 1966), 3; Krinsky, *Synagogues of Europe*, 8.

10. Avram Kampf, *Contemporary Synagogue Art*, 3.

11. Hanoch Achiman, "The Synagogues' Sections," in *Mikdah Me-at* (The Little Sanctuary), eds. Y. Ilan, A. Shtal, and Z. Shtiner (Jerusalem: The Ministry of Education and Culture, 1976), 57 (in Hebrew). The builders of the synagogue in Newport, Rhode Island, were all non-Jews; see Franz Landsberger, "From 70 C. E. to the Present," in Blake, *An American Synagogue for Today and Tomorrow*, 29.

12. Finis Farr, *Frank Lloyd Wright: A Biography* (Whitefish, MT: Literary Licensing, 2011).

13. Later republished in 2 Chronicles 3–5.

14. Dov Shalom Steinberg, *The Format of the First Jerusalem Temple* (Jerusalem: Vagshel, 1994; in Hebrew); Dov Shalom Steinberg, *The Format of the Second Jerusalem Temple* (Jerusalem: Vagshel, 1993; in Hebrew); Julian

Morgenstern, "The Temple and The Synagogue: To 70 C.E.," in Blake, *An American Synagogue for Today and Tomorrow*, 17.

15. John Wilkinson, *From Synagogue to Church: The Traditional Design* (London: Routledge, 2002), 23–24.

16. The book of Numbers 24:5 (the fourth book in the Torah); Morgenstern, "The Temple and the Synagogue," 11.

17. Robert L. Cohn, *The Shape of the Sacred Space: Four Biblical Studies* (Chico, CA: Scholars Press, 1981), 43.

18. Wilkinson, *From Synagogue to Church*, 31–33.

19. The Rambam (Maimonides) as quoted in Rabinovitch, "The Place of the Synagogue in Judaism," 18.

20. Cohn, *The Shape of the Sacred Space*, 1; Gavriel Rosenfeld, *Building After Auschwitz: Jewish Architecture and the Memory of the Holocaust* (New Haven, CT: Yale Press University, 2011), 51.

21. Jody Rosenblatt Naderi and Anat Geva, "*Eruv*: Transformation of an Urban Public Space to a Private Place for Spiritual Renewal," *ARRIS: Journal of the Southeast Chapter of the Society of Architectural Historians* 25 (2014): 18–29.

22. Philip Johnson, quoted in Meier, *Recent American Synagogue Architecture*, 22.

23. Philip Johnson, quoted in Meier, *Recent American Synagogue Architecture*, 22.

24. *Architectural Forum* (Editor), "Saarinen Challenges the Rectangle," *Architectural Forum* 98, no. 1 (January 1953): 127.

25. Blake, *An American Synagogue for Today and Tomorrow*, viii.

26. Ilan, "The Synagogue: Definitions and Design Concepts," 22.

27. Wilkinson, *From Synagogue to Church,* 25.

28. For example, see Steinberg, *The Format of the First Jerusalem Temple*; Steinberg, *The Format of the Second Jerusalem Temple*.

29. Steinberg, *The Format of the First Jerusalem Temple*; Steinberg, *The Format of the Second Jerusalem Temple*.

30. Ilan, "The Synagogue: Definitions and Design Concepts," 24.

31. "History of the Grand Choral Synagogue of Saint Petersburg," accessed December 2021, https://history-jewish-community-saint-petersburg.html.

32. Blake, *An American Synagogue for Today and Tomorrow*, 10.

33. Samuel Gruber, *American Synagogues: A Century of Architecture and Jewish Community* (New York: Rizzoli, 2003); Lance J. Sussman, "The Suburbanization of American Judaism as Reflected in Synagogue Building and Architecture, 1945–1975," *American Jewish History* 75, no. 1 (1985): 33; Landsberger, "From 70 C. E. to the Present," 37; Rabbi Alexander S. Kline, "The Synagogue in America," in *An American Synagogue for Today and Tomorrow*, ed. Black, 38–43.

34. Gruber, *American Synagogues*; Sussman, "The Suburbanization of American Judaism."

35. UAHC is the national synagogue organization of Reform Judaism.

36. Sussman, "The Suburbanization of American Judaism," 37.

37. Sussman, "The Suburbanization of American Judaism," 37–38.

38. Sussman, "The Suburbanization of American Judaism," 38 and footnote 16.

39. Blake, *An American Synagogue for Today and Tomorrow*, viii.

40. Kline, "The Synagogue in America," 43.

41. Kline, "The Synagogue in America," 45.

42. Anat Geva, *Frank Lloyd Wright's Sacred Architecture: Faith, Form, and Building Technology* (London: Routledge, 2011), 11–12.

43. Geva, *Frank Lloyd Wright's Sacred Architecture*, 11–12.

44. Colleen McDannell, *Material Christianity: Religion and Popular Culture in America* (New Haven, CT: Yale University Press, 1995), 7.

45. Geva, *Frank Lloyd Wright's Sacred Architecture*, 11.

46. Geva, *Frank Lloyd Wright's Sacred Architecture*, 13.

47. Geva, *Frank Lloyd Wright's Sacred Architecture*, 13–15.

48. See, for example, Frank Lloyd Wright's Unity Temple in Oak Park, Illinois, where concrete dictated the form of a cube for the sanctuary. Geva, *Frank Lloyd Wright's Sacred Architecture*.

49. For examples of the relation of building technology to form, see "Part II: The Parabola, Concrete, and Modern Sacred Architecture," in *Modernism and American Mid-20th-Century Sacred Architecture*, ed. Anat Geva (London: Routledge, 2019), 71–152.

50. See chapter 2 for the expression of the synagogue's exterior, which demonstrates the congregation's pride and confidence.

51. Louis H. Sullivan, "The Tall Office Building Artistically Considered," *Lippincott's Magazine*, March 1896.

52. Jack Wertheimer, "The American Synagogue: Recent Issues and Trends," *American Jewish Year Book* 105 (2005): 3–83.

53. Eric Mendelsohn, "Creating a Modern Synagogue Style: In the Spirit of Our Age," *Commentary* 3, no. 2 (June 1947).

54. Jay M. Price, *Temples for A Modern God: Religious Architecture in Postwar America* (New York: Oxford University Press, 2013), 176.

55. Cherles K. Gandee, "Tradition Rekindled," *Architectural Record* (June 1983): 106.

56. Geva, *Frank Lloyd Wright's Sacred Architecture*, 16–28; Mircea Eliade, *Patterns in Comparative Religion* (Lincoln: University of Nebraska Press, 1996); Yi-Fu

Tuan, "Sacred Space: Exploration on an Idea," in *Dimensions of Human Geography*, ed. Karl Butzer (Chicago: University of Chicago, Department of Geography Research Papers, 1978), 84–99; Harold W. Turner, *From Temple to Meeting House: The Phenomenology and Theology of Places of Worship* (The Hague, Netherlands, and New York: Mouton, 1979); A. T. Mann, *Sacred Architecture* (Shaftesbury, Dorset, and Rockport, MA: Element, 1993); Thomas Barrie, *Spiritual Path, Sacred Place: Myth, Ritual, and Meaning in Architecture* (Boston: Shambhala, 1996); Richard Kieckhefer, *Theology in Stone: Church Architecture from Byzantium to Berkeley* (New York: Oxford University Press, 2004); Ken Wilber, *Integral Spirituality* (Boston: Shambhala, 2006); Michael Benedikt, *God, Creativity, and Evolution: The Argument from Design(ers)* (Austin: The Center for American Architecture and Design, University of Texas at Austin, 2008).

57. Yi-Fu Tuan, "Sacred Space: Exploration on an Idea," 84; Barrie, *Spiritual Path, Sacred Place*, 4; Caroline Humphrey and Piers Vitebsky, *Sacred Architecture* (New York: Barnes & Noble Books, reprinted from Little, Brown, 1997, 2005); Geva, *Frank Lloyd Wright's Sacred Architecture*, 16–28.

58. Eric Mendelsohn, as quoted in Blake, *An American Synagogue for Today and Tomorrow*, 101.

59. For a historical development of views of the creation in Judaism from the Talmudic times to the beginning of modern era, see Blake, *An American Synagogue for Today and Tomorrow*.

60. Claude Lévi-Strauss, *Structural Anthropology* (New York: Basic Books, 1963).

61. Lee Shai Weissbach, "The Architecture of the Bimah in American Synagogues: Framing the Ritual," *American Jewish History* 91, no. 1 (March 2003): 32; Yehuda Laib Bialer, "Symbols in the Synagogue," in Ilan, Shtal, and Shtiner, *Mikdah Me-at*, 71.

62. Geva, *Frank Lloyd Wright's Sacred Architecture*.

63. Roberto Chiotti and Michael Nicholas-Schmidt, "Shared Universe, Sacred Story," *Faith & Form* 41, no. 1 (2018): 25–27.

64. Hannu Toyryla, "Theories of Creation in Judaism," published 1998 and accessed December 30, 2020, http://users.abo.fi/htoyryla/creart6.pdf.

65. Keith Critchlow, "What Is Sacred Architecture?," *Geometry in Architecture: Lindisfarne Letter* 10 (West Stickbridge, MA: Lindisfarne Association Press, 1980); Robert Lawlor, *Sacred Geometry: Philosophy and Practice* (London: Thames and Hudson, 1982); Douglas R. Hoffman, *Seeking the Sacred in Contemporary Religious Architecture* (Kent, OH: Kent State University Press, 2010), 10; Geva, *Frank Lloyd Wright's Sacred Architecture*, 19–23.

66. Geva, *Frank Lloyd Wright's Sacred Architecture*, 132.

67. Henry Plummer, "Poetic of Light," *Architecture and Urbanism* (December 1987): 8–11.

68. Louis I. Kahn, as quoted in Meier, *Recent American Synagogue Architecture*, 8.

69. Eliade, *Patterns in Comparative Religion*; Rudolf Shwartz, *The Church Incarnate: The Sacred Function of Christian Architecture* (Chicago: H. Regnery, 1958).

70. See details in chapter 4 of this book; see figure 1.4 in Geva, *Frank Lloyd Wight's Sacred Architecture*, 35.

71. Mircea Eliade, *Images and Symbols* (Princeton, NJ: Princeton University Press, 1991), 151.

72. The building's three thin concrete shells are four to seven inches thick. The front wall shell is the thickest, acting as a "reversed-curve beam."

73. Rabbi Laibl Wolf, *Practical* Kabbalah (New York: Three Rivers Press, 1999), 26.

74. *Zohar* is part of the Kabbalah.

75. This is my own interpretation. No reference(s) found.

76. Geva, *Frank Lloyd Wright's Sacred Architecture*, 17.

77. Geva, *Frank Lloyd Wright's Sacred Architecture*, 17.

78. The name *Bethel*, where the dream occurred, means "a house of God."

79. See diagrams of the tabernacle plan in Wilkinson, *From Synagogue to Church*, 26–28.

80. Cohn, *The Shape of Sacred Space*, 41, 43.

81. Cohn, *The Shape of Sacred Space*, 38–41.

82. Cohn, *The Shape of Sacred Space*, 39.

83. For a discussion and interpretation of the height of the city and the synagogue building, see Rabinovitch, "The Place of the Synagogue in Judaism," 20–24.

84. Kabbalah is a mystical Jewish theological philosophy, "an ancient wisdom that empowers us to improve our lives, discover our purpose, and achieve the lasting fulfillment we are meant to receive." The Kabbalah Centre, accessed September 3, 2018, https://kabbalah.com.

85. Geva, *Frank Lloyd Wright's Sacred Architecture*, 17.

86. Barrie, *Spiritual Path, Sacred Place*.

87. For a discussion on the various definitions of the sacred, please refer to Tuan, "Sacred Space: Exploration on an Idea," 84–85.

88. The Maharal of Prague is quoted by Joseph Shenberger, "The Synagogue's Courtyard, Its Function and Design," in Ilan, Shtal, and Shtiner, *Mikdah Me-at*, 65.

89. Shenberger, "The Synagogue's Courtyard," 63.

90. Mircea Eliade, *The Sacred and the Profane: The Nature of Religion* (New York: Harcourt, Brace and World, 1959/1987).

91. Weissbach, "The Architecture of the Bimah," 46.

92. There is no separation of men and women seating in Conservative and Reform synagogues.

93. Achiman, "The Synagogues' Sections," 59.

94. Rabbi Mordecai Kaplan cofounded the Jewish denomination of Reconstructionist Judaism (late 1920s to 1940s); Lance J. Sussman, "The Suburbanization of American Judaism as Reflected in Synagogue Building

and Architecture, 1945–1975," *American Jewish History* 75, no. 1 (1985): 36.

95. Schorsch, "A Synagogue Is Not a Temple," 64; Karp, "Overview," 20.

96. Rabinovitch, "The Place of the Synagogue in Judaism," 12.

97. Jack Wertheimer, "Preface," in *The American Synagogue: A Sanctuary Transform*, ed. Jack Wertheimer (Cambridge, England: Cambridge University Press, 1987), x.

98. Later the Jewish center became an independent entity and a building by itself.

99. Kay Kaufman Shelemay, "Music in the American Synagogue: A Case Study from Houston," in *The American Synagogue: A Sanctuary Transform*, ed. Jack Wertheimer, 395–415.

100. Krinsky, *Synagogues of Europe*, 6; Weissbach, "The Architecture of the Bimah in American Synagogues."

101. The Rambam and the scholar Jacob Finkerfeld as quoted in Rabinovitch, "The Place of the Synagogue in Judaism," 35, 45.

102. Bialer, "Symbols in the Synagogue," 73.

103. Weissbach, "The Architecture of the Bimah in American Synagogues," 29–51; Rabinovitch "The Place of the Synagogue in Judaism," 11. The axis between them in the Western hemisphere is usually oriented east to west.

104. Weissbach, "The Architecture of the Bimah," 43.

105. Krinsky, *Synagogues of Europe*, 9.

106. Rambam as quoted in Ilan, "The Synagogue: Definitions and Design Concepts," 39.

107. The arrangement of synagogues started during the Jewish emancipation period of the eighteenth century in Europe. Aharon Kashtan, "The Architecture of Synagogues," in Ilan, Shtal, and Shtiner, *Mikdah Me-at*, 14.

108. Usually, the lantern above the bimah included twelve windows to represent the twelve tribes of Israel. Nesrine Mansour and Anat Geva, "Djerbian Culture and Climate as Expressed in a Historic Landmark: The Case of El-Ghriba Synagogue in Djerba, Tunisia," in *Synagogues in the Islamic World*, ed. Mohammad Gharipour (Edinburgh, Scotland: Edinburgh University Press, 2017), 226–47.

109. See the selection criteria in this book's introduction.

110. Weissbach, "The Architecture of the Bimah," 31.

111. For a discussion and examples of conducting the service from the pulpit or bimah, see Weissbach's article "The Architecture of the Bimah."

112. Price, *Temples for a Modern God*, 71.

113. Leedy, *Eric Mendelsohn's Park Synagogue*, 47.

114. Geva, *Frank Lloyd Wright's Sacred Architecture*, 33.

115. Mollie M. Clarahan, "Inspired Illumination: Sanctuary Lighting Must Do More than Simply Chase the Shadows Away," *Your Church Magazine* 50 (September/October 2004): 42–44.

116. Amiram Harlap, *Synagogues in Israel: From the Ancient to the Modern* (Jerusalem: The Ministry of Defense Publisher and Dvir, 1984), 17 (in Hebrew); Steinberg, *The Format of the First and Second Jerusalem Temples*.

117. Henry Plummer, "Poetics of Light," *Architecture and Urbanism* (December 1987): 8–11.

118. Rabinovitch, "The Place of the Synagogue in Judaism," 46; Steinberg, *The Format of the First Jerusalem Temple*; Steinberg, *The Format of the Second Jerusalem Temple*.

119. See, for example, the ancient El Ghriba Synagogue, also known as the Djerba Synagogue, in Djerba, Tunisia.

120. For details, see chapter 5.

121. Geva, *Frank Lloyd Wright's Sacred Architecture*, 50.

122. Avram Kampf, in his seminal book *Contemporary Synagogue Art*, devoted a whole chapter to the interpretation of the second commandment (pp. 7–22).

123. Kampf, *Contemporary Synagogue Art*, 26.

124. Kampf, *Contemporary Synagogue Art*, 26.

125. Henry and Daniel Stolzman, *Synagogue Architecture in America*, 15–19; Bialer, "Symbols in the Synagogue," 70.

126. Bialer, "Symbols in the Synagogue," 70.

127. Bialer, "Symbols in the Synagogue," 70.

128. Vivian B. Mann, "If There Is No Jewish Art, What's Being Taught at the Seminary?," in *Reluctant Partners: Art and Religion in Dialogue*, ed. Ena Giuresh Heller (New York: The Gallery at the American Bible Society, 2004), 88–99.

129. "Cherubim," Bible Study Tools, accessed July 5, 2020, https://www.biblestudytools.com/dictionary/cherubim-1/.

130. Kampf, *Contemporary Synagogue Art*, 8.

131. Harlap, *Synagogues in Israel*, 25.

132. "Archaeology in Israel: Beit Alpha," Jewish Virtual Library, accessed July 5, 2020, https://www.jewishvirtual-library.org/beit-alpha.

133. William Schack, "Modern Art in Synagogue, II: Artist, Architect, and Building Committee Collaborate," *Commentary* 21 (February 1956). Modern mosaics and stone carvings can be found in small synagogues in places such as Lock Haven and Greensburg, Pennsylvania.

134. See images and interpretations in Elisheva Rabel-Nehar, "Ezekiel 37: An Additional Interpretation of the Wall Paintings in the Dura Eurpa Synagogue," in *Synagogues from Antiquity to Our Time*, eds. Yakov Eshel, Ehud Nezer, David Amit, and David Casuto (Ariel, Israel: The Academic College of Judea and Samaria, 2004), 67–75 (in Hebrew).

135. Rabel-Nehar, "Ezekiel 37," 68–74.

136. Rabel-Nehar, "Ezekiel 37," 67.

137. Kampf, *Contemporary Synagogue Art*, 17.

138. David Kaufman (1908), as quoted in Kampf, *Contemporary Synagogue Art*, 8.

139. Exodus 20:4: "You shall not make for yourself an image in the form of anything in heaven above or on the earth beneath or in the waters below."

140. Kampf, *Contemporary Synagogue Art*, 8.

141. Janay Jadine Wong, "Synagogue Art of 1950s: A New Context for Abstraction," *Art Journal* 53, no. 4 (Winter 1994): 37–43.

142. Nicholas W. Roberts, *Building Type Basics for Places of Worship* (New York: John Wiley), 8.

143. The Liturgical Arts Society's demand as described in Victoria M. Young, *Saint John's Abbey Church: Marcel Breuer and the Creation of a Modern Sacred Space* (Minneapolis: University of Minnestoa Press, 2014), xxi.

144. It is interesting to note that churches also adopted the symbol of the Ten Commandments as an artistic feature. Bialer, "Symbols in the Synagogue," 70, 78.

145. Kampf, *Contemporary Synagogue Art*, 8.

146. Schack, "Modern Art in Synagogue II," 159.

147. Kampf, *Contemporary Synagogue Art*, 52.

148. Angeli Sachs and Edward van Voolen, eds., *Jewish Identity in Contemporary Architecture* (München, Germany; New York: Prestel, 2004); Wong, "Synagogue Art of the 1950s."

149. Mordecai M. Kaplan, *Judaism as a Civilization* (Philadelphia: Reconstructionist Press, 1957), 425.

150. Kaplan, *Judaism as a Civilization*, 425.

151. Kampf, *Contemporary Synagogue Art*, 52, 54.

152. Kampf, *Contemporary Synagogue Art*, 54.

153. Kampf, *Contemporary Synagogue Art*, 41.

154. Kampf, *Contemporary Synagogue Art*, 93–94.

155. The Star of David appears on the Israeli flag.

156. Wolf, *Practical* Kabbalah, 53.

157. "Star of David: Judaism," *Encyclopedia Britannica*, accessed June 5, 2020, https://www.britannica.com/topic/Star-of-David.

158. See images of the synagogue in Kampf, *Contemporary Synagogue Art*, 33.

159. Bialer, "Symbols in the Synagogue," 87.

160. Bialer, "Symbols in the Synagogue," 87.

161. Wilkinson, *From Synagogue to Church*, 26–27.

162. Anat Geva, "Immigrants' Sacred Architecture: The Rabbi Meir Baal-Haness Synagogue in Eilat, Israel," in Gharipour, *Synagogues in the Islamic World: Architecture*, 271–92.

163. Leedy, *Eric Mendelsohn's Park Synagogue*, 43.

164. Leedy, *Eric Mendelsohn's Park Synagogue*, 43.

165. Anat Geva, "Architecture as Art and Frame for Art: Mario Botta's Church in Seriate," *Faith & Form, the Interfaith Journal on Religion* 47, no. 1 (2014): 6.

166. Robert L. Nelson, "Art and Religion: Ships Passing in the Night?," in Heller, *Reluctant Partners: Art and Religion in Dialogue*, 106–7.

167. Nelson, "Art and Religion," 107.

168. Wong, "Synagogue Art of the 1950s," 39.

169. Wong, "Synagogue Art of the 1950s," 39.

170. James Fitzsimmons, "Artists Put Faith in New Ecclesiastical Art," *Art Digest* 26 (October 15, 1951): 23.

171. Wong, "Synagogue Art of the 1950s," 39–40.

172. "Etching With Acid" published August 2016 and accessed July 2022. https://everythingstainedglass.com/glass etching#:~:text=Glass%20etching%20with%20acid%20is,resist%20remains%20shiny%20and%20untouched.

173. Robert Sowers, *The Lost Art: A Survey of 1000 Years of Stained Glass* (London: Lund Humphries, 1954).

174. Young, *Saint John's Abbey Church*, xvii.

175. Kampf, *Contemporary Synagogue Art*, 32.

176. Talbot Hamlin, *Forms and Functions of Twentieth Century Architecture* (New York: Columbia University Press, 1952), 746.

177. Hamlin, *Forms and Functions of Twentieth Century Architecture*, 746.

178. Hamlin, *Forms and Functions of Twentieth Century Architecture*, 746.

179. Kampf, *Contemporary Synagogue Art*, 256.

180. Geva, *Frank Lloyd Wright's Sacred Architecture*, 1.

Chapter 4

1. Richard Meier, ed., *Recent American Synagogue Architecture* (New York: The Jewish Museum, 1963).

2. Samuel Gruber, "Modern Synagogue Architecture," in *Jewish Religious Architecture from Biblical Israel to Modern Judaism*, ed. Steven Fine (Boston: Brill, 2020), 307–33.

3. Anat Geva, *Frank Lloyd Wright's Sacred Architecture: Faith, Form, Building Technology* (London: Routledge, 2012).

4. Kathleen James-Chakraborty, *In the Spirit of Our Age: Eric Mendelsohn's B'nai Amoona Synagogue* (St. Louis: Missouri Historical Society Press, 2000), 64.

5. Eric Mendelsohn, "Creating a Modern Synagogue Style: In the Spirit of Our Age," *Commentary* 3, no. 2 (June 1947): 541.

6. Mendelsohn, "Creating a Modern Synagogue Style"; Meier, *Recent American Synagogue Architecture*, 22–24.

7. Mendelsohn, "Creating a Modern Synagogue Style," 541.

8. Meier, "Introduction," in *Recent American Synagogue Architecture*, 7.

9. Some art historians, such as architect Rachel Wischnitzer, saw these concepts as a romanticist approach. Rachel Wischnitzer, *Synagogue Architecture in the United States: History and Interpretation* (Philadelphia: The Jewish Publication Society of America, 1955), 148, 152.

10. Eric Mendelsohn, "My Approach to Building a

Contemporary Synagogue," November 1952 (Armond E. Cohen's Papers 1925–1989, MS 4957, Box 8, Folder 28, Cleveland Jewish Archives in Western Reserve Historical Society, Cleveland, November 1952), 2.

11. Meier, "Introduction."

12. Mendelsohn, "Creating a Modern Synagogue Style," 541.

13. Angeli Sachs and Edward Van Voolen claim that both Eric Mendelsohn and Percival Goodman established the "formal, functional, and symbolic vocabularies that were sustained for decades." Angeli Sachs and Edward Van Voolen, eds., *Jewish Identity in Contemporary Architecture* (Munich: Prestel, 2004), 27.

14. Eric Mendelsohn's quote in Meier, *Recent American Synagogue Architecture*, 24.

15. Mendelsohn, "Creating a Modern Synagogue Style," 541.

16. B'nai Amoona Synagogue in University City, Missouri, no longer serves as a synagogue. It was adapted to a Center of Contemporary Arts. As such, it did not fulfill the selection criteria of this project.

17. Walter C. Leedy Jr., *Eric Mendelsohn's Park Synagogue* (Kent, OH: The Kent State University Press, 2012); Charles C. Colman (AIA Supervising Architect, Cleveland), "Some of the Construction Problems of Park Synagogue," *Ohio Architect* 8, vol. 3, no. 7, July 1950 (MS 4763, Box 1, Folder 14, Cleveland Jewish Archives in Western Reserve Historical Society, Cleveland).

18. A quote by Stephen Kaiser, the Curator of the Jewish Museum of New York in "The Architectural Concept of Park Synagogue, 1954" (Armond E. Cohen's Papers 1925–1989, MS 4957, Box 8, Folder 28, Cleveland Jewish Archives in Western Reserve Historical Society, Cleveland), 8.

19. Armond Cohen, "Eric Mendelsohn as a Man and a Friend," *The Reconstructionist* 20 (October 29, 1954).

20. Regina Stephan, ed., *Eric Mendelsohn: Architect 1887–1953* (New York: Monacelli Press., 1998), 249.

21. Armond Cohen's report on meetings with Eric Mendelsohn and on the design of the synagogue (Cleveland Jewish Archives in Western Reserve Historical Society, Cleveland), 3.

22. Armond Cohen's report.

23. Louis G. Redstone, "Modern Trends in American Synagogue Design," *Technion Year Book*, 6–7. The paper was sent by Mendelsohn in a letter to Rabbi Armond Cohen, June 30, 1948 (Armond E. Cohen's Papers 1925–1989, MS 4957, Box 2, Folder 21, Cleveland Jewish Archives in Western Reserve Historical Society, Cleveland).

24. Bruno Zevi, *Erich Mendelsohn: The Complete Works* (Bazel, Switzerland: Birkhäuser Publishers, 1999), 315.

25. See the image of B'nai Amoona Synagogue preliminary sketch (1954) in Hans R. Morgenthaler, "'It Will Be

Hard for Us to Find a Home': Projects in the United States 1941–1953," in *Eric Mendelsohn Architect 1887–1953*, ed. Stephan Regina (New York: The Monacelli Press, 1999), 243.

26. Zevi, *Erich Mendelsohn: The Complete Works*, 315.

27. Zevi, *Erich Mendelsohn*, 214–15.

28. Zevi, *Erich Mendelsohn*, 163 (plates 2, 3).

29. Zevi, *Erich Mendelsohn*, 185 (plate 353).

30. Zevi, *Erich Mendelsohn*, 310–15. In page 311, Zevi called the synagogue a community center in Cleveland, Ohio.

31. Zevi, *Erich Mendelsohn*, 313.

32. I. Thompson, a structural engineer from San Francisco, handled the design.

33. Jerusalem Temples included opaque windows to provide light but to avoid distractions from the outside.

34. Mendelsohn, "Creating a Modern Synagogue Style."

35. Zevi, *Erich Mendelsohn,* 317.

36. Mendelsohn, "Creating a Modern Synagogue Style."

37. "The Architectural Concept of the Park Synagogue," 4.

38. Leedy Jr., *Eric Mendelsohn's Park Synagogue*, 89.

39. Leedy Jr., *Eric Mendelsohn's Park Synagogue*, 91.

40. "The Architectural Concept of the Park Synagogue," 3–4.

41. The lighting design was based on indirect cold cathode ray illumination that was able to be reduced up to a quarter of the maximum light. Leedy Jr., *Eric Mendelsohn's Park Synagogue*, 82.

42. Colman, "Some of the Construction Problems of Park Synagogue."

43. From notes on a drawing (Park Synagogue archive, Cleveland).

44. The bimah is the platform from where services are conducted.

45. The Talmud is the compilation of Jewish laws and their interpretations.

46. "The Architectural Concept of the Park Synagogue," 6.

47. Mendelsohn, "My Approach to Building a Contemporary Synagogue."

48. Ben C. Bloch, "Notes on Post-War Synagogue Design," *Architectural Record* (September 1944): 104–5.

49. Bloch, "Notes on Post-War Synagogue Design."

50. Colman, "Some of the Construction Problems of Park Synagogue."

51. Redstone, "Modern Trends in American Synagogue Design," 5.

52. Leedy Jr., *Eric Mendelsohn's Park Synagogue*, 65.

53. Due to budget issues, the school was completed after the synagogue was built.

54. It should be noted that the circular windows appeared first in Mendelsohn's B'nai Amoona Synagogue.

55. This goal was geared toward B'nai Amoona

Synagogue. James-Chakraborty, *In the Spirit of Our Age*, 64. I argue that it can be applied to Mendelsohn's Park Synagogue as well.

56. A letter from Mendelsohn to Stephen S. Kayser, curator, Jewish Museum, New York, May 24, 1950 (Armond E. Cohen's Papers 1925–1989, MS 4957, Box 2, Folder 23, Cleveland Jewish Archives in Western Reserve Historical Society, Cleveland).

57. James-Chakraborty, *In the Spirit of Our Age*, 59.

58. A letter from Cohen to Mendelsohn, April 23, 1953 (Armond E. Cohen's Papers, MS 4957, Box 2, Folder 24, Cleveland Jewish Archives in Western Reserve Historical Society, Cleveland).

59. Park Synagogue East design received the 2007 *Faith & Form* Honor Award. "Park Synagogue East," Centerbrook, accessed December 2020, https://centerbrook.com/project/park_synagogue_east.

60. "Park Synagogue East"; James-Chakraborty, *In the Spirit of Our Age*, 58.

61. Geva, *Frank Lloyd Wright's Sacred Architecture*, 40.

62. The National Historic Places Register Reference Number is 07000430_NHL.

63. Geva, *Frank Lloyd Wright's Sacred Architecture*, 260–61.

64. Geva, *Frank Lloyd Wright's Sacred Architecture*, 93–94.

65. Geva, *Frank Lloyd Wright's Sacred Architecture*, 268–69.

66. "Beth Sholom Congregation, Elkins Park, Pennsylvania," Atlas Obscura, accessed May 12, 2020, https://www.atlasobscura.com/places/beth-sholom-congregation.

67. A glass corridor connecting the synagogue with the other parts of the complex was added in 1967.

68. Geva, *Frank Lloyd Wright's Sacred Architecture*, 124–25.

69. Joseph M. Siry, *Beth Sholom Synagogue* (Chicago: University of Chicago Press, 2011).

70. Geva, *Frank Lloyd Wright's Sacred Architecture*.

71. Geva, *Frank Lloyd Wright's Sacred Architecture*, 13–49.

72. Bruce Brooks Pfeiffer, *Frank Lloyd Wright: Letters to Clients* (Fresno: Press at California State University, 1986), 312.

73. Lauren Walser, "Beth Sholom Synagogue: Frank Lloyd Wright's Only Synagogue," National Trust for Historic Preservation, published March, 16, 2016, accessed May 12, 2020, https://savingplaces.org/stories/beth-sholom-synagogue-frank-lloyd-wright-only-synagogue#.Xrytr8pOmhA.

74. Geva, *Frank Lloyd Wright's Sacred Architecture*, 64, figure 2.3.1.

75. Robert L. Cohn, *The Shape of the Sacred Space: Four Biblical Studies* (Chico, CA: Scholars Press, 1981), 43.

76. Frank Lloyd Wright as quoted in Meier, *Recent American Synagogue Architecture*, 25.

77. Bruce Brooks Pfeiffer, *Masterworks from the Frank Lloyd Wright Archives*, ed. David Larkin (New York: Harry N. Abrams, 1990).

78. Frank Lloyd Wright, "In the Cause of Architecture III–IX: The Meaning of Materials," *Architectural Record* (April 1928–December 1928); all reprinted in Bruce Brooks Pfeiffer, ed., *Frank Lloyd Wright Collected Writings, Vol. 1* (New York: Rizzoli International Publications, 1992), 269–309.

79. Terry Patterson, *Frank Lloyd Wright and The Meaning of Materials* (New York: Van Nostrand Reinhold, 1994), 169.

80. Patterson, *Frank Lloyd Wright and The Meaning of Materials*, 169.

81. Wright quoted in Julia M. Klein, "The Rabbi and Frank Lloyd Wright," *Wall Street Journal*, December 22, 2009.

82. Geva, *Frank Lloyd Wright's Sacred Architecture*, 70.

83. Mortimer J. Cohen, *Beth Sholom Synagogue: A Description and Interpretation* (Elkins Park, PA: Beth Sholom Synagogue, 1959).

84. See Wright's sketch, figure 1.14, p. 35, in Geva, *Frank Lloyd Wright's Sacred Architecture*.

85. See the collaboration between Rabbi Cohen and Wright in Patricia T. Davis, *Together They Built a Mountain* (Lititz, PA: Sutter House, 1974); and in Joseph M. Siry, *Beth Sholom Synagogue*, chapter 8.

86. Mortimer J. Cohen's quote from "Wright's Temple to be Dedicated," *New York Times*, September 13, 1959, 16.

87. Oligivanna Lloyd Wright, *The Shining Brow: Frank Lloyd Wright* (New York: Horizon Press, 1960), 192.

88. Stolzman, *Synagogue Architecture in America,* 57.

89. Klein, "The Rabbi and Frank Lloyd Wright."

90. Peter Blake, ed., *An American Synagogue for Today and Tomorrow: A Guide Book to Synagogue Design and Construction* (New York: Union of American Hebrew, 1954), xiii.

91. With the exception of these conversations, there is no written evidence for this claim.

92. There is no written evidence for this claim, aside from these conversations.

93. Carl I. Wax, Bernard Bernstein, and Gerald Belz, *200 Hundred Years of American Synagogue Architecture* (New York: American Jewish Historical Society & The Rose Art Museum, 1976).

94. Geva, *Frank Lloyd Wright's Sacred Architecture*.

95. Klein, "The Rabbi and Frank Lloyd Wright."

96. Vincent Scully, *Frank Lloyd Wright* (New York: George Braziller, 1996), 111, figure 126.

97. Wright as quoted in Meier, *Recent American Synagogue Architecture*, 25.

98. Wright as quoted in Meier, *Recent American Synagogue Architecture*, 25.

99. Geva, *Frank Lloyd Wright's Sacred Architecture*, 69.

100. Geva, *Frank Lloyd Wright's Sacred Architecture*, 125.

101. Geva, *Frank Lloyd Wright's Sacred Architecture*, 220.

102. Geva, *Frank Lloyd Wright's Sacred Architecture*, 208.

103. Samuel D. Gruber, *American Synagogues: A Century of Architecture and Jewish Community* (New York: Rizzolo, 2003), 140; Gruber, "Modern Synagogue Architecture," 312; Siry, *Beth Sholom Synagogue*, 538–39.

104. Rabbi Dr. Benjamin Elton, "Cathedral Synagogues Still Have a Future," *The Jewish Chronicle*, published June 24, 2018, and accessed June 29, 2020, https://www.thejc.com/judaism/features/cathedral-synagogues-still-have-a-future-1.465950.

105. Elton, "Cathedral Synagogues Still Have a Future."

106. Gruber, *American Synagogues*, 140.

107. Gruber, *American Synagogues*, 140.

108. Geoffrey Scott, *The Architecture of Humanism* (New York: W. W. Morton, 1914; reprinted, 1947; reprinted, 1969); Rudolf Wittkower, *Architecture Principles in the Age of Humanism* (London: Warburg Institute, University of London, 1949).

109. Dale Allen Gyure, *Minoru Yamasaki: Humanist Architecture for a Modern World* (New Haven, CT: Yale University Press, 2017), 123.

110. Minoru Yamasaki, "A Humanist Architecture," *Architect and Building News* (November 1960), 665–66; Gyure, *Minoru Yamasaki*, 125–26 (Minoru Yamasaki's quote is on p. 126).

111. Minoru Yamasaki, "A Humanist Architecture," 665–66; Gyure, *Minoru Yamasaki*, 125–26.

112. Michael H. Ebner, *Creating Chicago's North Shore: A Suburban History* (Chicago: University of Chicago Press, 1988), 226, 237; "History of North Shore Congregation Israel," North Shore Congregation Israel, accessed May 30, 2020, https://www.nsci.org/history.

113. Glencoe, Illinois, is located twenty-four miles north of Chicago.

114. Ebner, *Creating Chicago's North Shore*.

115. "Our Resident Architect," in *The Architecture of Light* (Glencoe, IL: North Shore Congregation Israel, 1960, brochure).

116. Henry Goldstein, "The Architect and the Congregation," February 1959 (North Shore Congregation Israel's archive, Glencoe, IL).

117. Goldstein, "The Architect and the Congregation."

118. Goldstein, "The Architect and the Congregation."

119. A quote on the back cover of *The Architecture of Light* brochure.

120. Minoru Yamasaki, "Statements by Architects on the Architecture of the Synagogue," in Meier, *Recent American Synagogue Architecture*, 25.

121. Minoru Yamasaki as quoted in the article "Our Answer: The Architecture of Light" in *The Architecture of Light* brochure.

122. Rabbi Dr. Edgar E. Siskin of North Shore Congregation Israel in *The Architecture of Light* brochure.

123. Gyure, *Minoru Yamasaki*, 153.

124. A quote by Halpring in Gyure, *Minoru Yamasaki*, 154.

125. Gyure, *Minoru Yamasaki*, 154.

126. The original school was built as one floor; a lower floor was constructed later in 2003 by Minoru Yamasaki Associates (see details in chapter 6).

127. Gyure, *Minoru Yamasaki*, 151.

128. Yamasaki, "Statements by Architects on the Architecture of the Synagogue," 25.

129. Gyure, *Minoru Yamasaki*, 157, endnote 43.

130. "Our New Synagogue: The Seed of an Idea" in *The Architecture of Light* brochure.

131. "Our New Synagogue," 142.

132. Marilyn J. Chiat, *The Spiritual Traveler: Chicago and Illinois* (Mahwah, NJ: Hidden Spring, 2004), 186.

133. Chiat, *The Spiritual Traveler*, 186; "Our New Synagogue: The Seed of an Idea," 15.

134. "A Synagogue by Yamasaki," *Architectural Record* 9 (September 1965): 192.

135. From "Temple Tour Notes" (North Shore Congregation Israel Synagogue archive, Glencoe, IL).

136. "A Synagogue by Yamasaki," 191–96.

137. See critiques by various scholars in Gyure, *Minoru Yamasaki*, 156.

138. Geva, *Frank Lloyd Wright's Sacred Architecture*, 109–21.

139. The organ was designed by Cassavant Frerrs Ltd. of Canada, "Temple Tour Notes."

140. From "Our New Synagogue: The Seed of an Idea."

141. From "Our New Synagogue: The Seed of an Idea."

142. "Expressionist architecture was an architectural movement that developed in Europe during the first decades of the 20th century in parallel with the expressionist visual and performing arts that especially developed and dominated in Germany." "Expressionist Architecture / Neo-Expressionism," Buffalo as an Architectural Museum, accessed December 2021, https://buffaloah.com/a/archsty/expr/expr.html.

143. Zevi, *Erich Mendelsohn: The Complete Works*; Stephan *Eric Mendelsohn: Architect 1887–1953*.

144. Rabbi Dr. Edgar E. Sisking in the *Annual Report*, North Shore Congregation Israel, Glencoe, IL (June 1963).

145. Redstone, "Modern Trends in American Synagogue Design," 9.

146. Mendelsohn, "In the Spirit of Our Age," 541.

147. Eric Mendelsohn as quoted in Meier, *Recent American Synagogue* Architecture, 24.

Chapter 5

1. See chapter 4 for details on the three trends.

2. Susan G. Solomon, *Louis I. Kahn's Jewish Architecture: Mikveh Israel and the Midcentury American Synagogue* (Waltham, MA: Brandeis University Press, 2009), 6–7.

3. Anat Geva, ed., *Modernism and American Mid-20th Century Sacred Architecture* (London: Routledge, 2019); Anat Geva, *Frank Lloyd Wright's Sacred Architecture: Faith, Form and Building Technology* (London: Routledge, 2012).

4. Philip Johnson was awarded the American Institute of Architects Gold Medal in 1978 and the Pritzker Architecture Prize in 1979.

5. "Philip Johnson: Understanding the Philosophy of Philip Johnson," *Architectural Review*, accessed December 2021, https://www.re-thinkingthefuture.com/rtf-fresh-perspectives/a2042-understanding-the-philosophy-of-philip-johnson/.

6. See "Philip Johnson: Understanding the Philosophy of Philip Johnson" for images of these projects.

7. Franz Schulze, *Philip Johnson: Life and Work* (New York: Alfred A. Knopf, 1994).

8. Kazys Varnelis, "We Cannot Know History: Philip Johnson's Political and Cynical Survival," *Journal of Architectural Education* 49, no. 2 (1995): 92–104.

9. Schulze, *Philip Johnson*.

10. Anat Geva, "An Architect Asks for Forgiveness: Philip Johnson's Port Chester Synagogue," Architecture, Culture, Spirituality Forum 2014, accessed September 15, 2020, http://www.acsforum.org/symposium2014/papers/GEVA.pdf.

11. Ian Volner, *Philip Johnson: A Visual Biography* (London and New York: Phaidon Press, 2020).

12. Volner, *Philip Johnson*, 129.

13. Edgar Kaufmann Jr. (1910–89), an architect, art historian, and author.

14. It should be noted that he never apologized directly to the KTI congregation. Schulze, *Philip Johnson*, 238.

15. Congregation KTI, "Our History," accessed September 20, 2020, https://www.congkti.org/about-us/our-history.

16. Congregation KTI, "Our History."

17. Congregation Kneses Tifereth Israel, *A Century of Jewish Commitment 1887–1987* (Port Chester, NY: Congregation KTI Synagogue Archive), 16.

18. For example, Samuel Gruber, *American Synagogues: A Century of Architecture and Jewish Community* (New York: Rizzoli), 110.

19. Lindsay Cook, "Religious Freedom and Architectural Ambition at Vassar College, 1945–1954," in Geva, *Modernism and American Mid-20th Century Sacred Architecture*, 43–45.

20. Cook, "Religious Freedom and Architectural Ambition," 43, figure 2.8.

21. Frank D. Welch, *Philip Johnson and Texas* (Austin: University of Texas Press, 2000), 57.

22. Henry-Russell Hitchcock, "Introduction," in *Philip Johnson: Architecture 1949–1965*, ed. Henry-Russell Hitchcock (New York: Holt, Rinehart and Winston, 1966), 10.

23. Cook, "Religious Freedom and Architectural Ambition at Vassar College," 45.

24. Congregation Kneses Tifereth Israel, *A Century of Jewish Commitment*, 16; John Jacobus Jr., *Philip Johnson* (New York: George Braziller), 34.

25. William Schack, "Modern Art in the Synagogue, II: Artist, Architect, and Building Committee Collaborate," *Commentary* (February 1956).

26. Gruber, *American Synagogues*, 110–11.

27. Avram Kampf, *Contemporary Synagogue Art* (New York: Union of American Hebrew Congregations, 1966), 37.

28. Peter Blake, *Philip Johnson* (Basel/Berlin/Boston: Birkhauser Verlag, 1996), 65.

29. Blake, *Philip Johnson*.

30. Vincent Scully, "Philip Johnson: Art and Irony," in *Philip Johnson: The Constancy of Change*, ed. Emmanuel Petit (New Haven, CT: Yale University Press, 2009), 18–37.

31. Gruber, *American Synagogues*, 112.

32. Scully, "Philip Johnson: Art and Irony," 29.

33. "Brick House: Overview," accessed October 2020, https://theglasshouse.org/eplore/brick-house/.

34. A letter from Philip Johnson to Ms. Marjorie Tunick, one of the congregates (May 21, 1986), Congregation KTI Synagogue Archive, Port Chester, NY.

35. A letter from Philip Johnson to Ms. Marjorie Tunick.

36. Richard Meier, ed., *Recent American Synagogue Architecture* (New York: The Jewish Museum, 1963), 8.

37. Meier, *Recent American Synagogue Architecture*.

38. A quote by Robert Walker in Phil Reisman, "Synagogue's Design Blends Beauty, Apology," *The Journal News*, January 30, 2005.

39. Interesting note: Leonardo da Vinci already stated this concept four hundred years before.

40. Gruber, *American Synagogues*, 115.

41. Congregation Kneses Tifereth Israel, *A Century of Jewish Commitment*, 21.

42. Congregation Kneses Tifereth Israel, *A Century of Jewish Commitment*, 21.

43. Robert L. Nelson, "Art and Religion: Ships Passing in the Night?," in *Reluctant Partners: Art and Religion in Dialogue*, ed. Ena Giuresh Heller (New York: The Gallery at the American Bible Society, 2004), 106–7.

44. Janay Jadine Wong, "Synagogue Art of the 1950s:

NOTES TO PAGES 96–102

A New Concept for Abstraction," *Art Journal* (Winter 1994): 37.

45. Wong, "Synagogue Art of the 1950s," 40.

46. Kampf, *Contemporary Synagogue Art*, 193.

47. Kampf, *Contemporary Synagogue Art*, 193.

48. His first commission of an eternal light object was by Percival Goodman for Temple Beth El in Springfield, Massachusetts, in 1951.

49. Kampf, *Contemporary Synagogue Art*, 37–43.

50. Congregation Kneses Tifereth Israel, *A Century of Jewish Commitment*, 17.

51. A letter from Ibram Lassaw to Ms. Marjorie Tunick, one of the congregates (July 2, 1986) (Congregation KTI Synagogue Archive, Port Chester, NY).

52. KTI Congregation, Project committee meeting: minutes (June 23, 1953; Congregation KTI Synagogue Archive, Port Chester, NY).

53. Jananne Abel, "Congregation KTI Gets a Facelift," *News*, September 22, 2006.

54. Fred A. Bernstein, "A Redesign Brings a Congregation Closer Together," *New York Times*, February 18, 2007.

55. Bernstein, "A Redesign Brings a Congregation Closer Together."

56. It is interesting to note that current architects and designers called on the MOMA to remove the name of the late Philip Johnson from all titles and public spaces due to his "widely documented white supremacist [and anti-Semitic] views and activities." Matt Hickman, "Architects and Designers Call on the MoMA to Remove Philip Johnson's Name," *The Architect's Newspaper*, published December 2, 2020, and accessed December 2020, https://www.archpaper.com/2020/12/architects-and-designers-call-on-the-moma-to-remove-philip-johnson-name/.

57. Gruber, *American Synagogues*, 93; Kimberly J. Elman, "The Quest for Community: Percival Goodman and the Design of the Modern American Synagogue," in *Percival Goodman: Architect, Planner, Teacher, Painter*, eds. Kimberly J. Elman and Angela Giral (New York: Miriam and Ira D. Wallach Art Gallery, Columbia University in the City of New York, 2001), 57.

58. Percival Goodman and Paul Goodman, "Modern Artist as Synagogue Builder," *Commentary* (January 1949): 51–55.

59. See chapter 3 for more on the abstract expressionist movement.

60. Janay Jadine Wong, "Synagogue Art of the 1950s: A New Context of Abstraction," *Art Journal* (Winter 1994): 43.

61. Alexander Kline, "Art and Synagogue," *National Jewish Monthly* (January 1956): 6.

62. Percival Goodman, "A Jewish Style," article draft (September 9, 1963), 3.

63. Goodman, "A Jewish Style," 4.

64. Percival Goodman and Paul Goodman, "Tradition from Function," *Commentary* (June 1947): 542–44.

65. Gyorgy Kepes, *Language of Vision* (Chicago: Paul Theobald and Company, 1961).

66. Lionel Reiss, "Art for the Synagogue," *Reconstructionist* 17 (October 1951): 27–29.

67. Belluschi et al., "Views of Art and Architecture: A Conversation," *Dædalus* 89, no. 1 (Winter 1960): 62–73.

68. Walter Gropius in Belluschi et al., "Views of Art and Architecture," 72.

69. Irena Rice Pereira in Belluschi et al., "Views of Art and Architecture," 69.

70. Belluschi et al., "Views of Art and Architecture," 41.

71. Chapter 3 of this book details the collaboration between architects and artists and notes Talbot Hamlin's principles of collaboration between architects and artists. See also Talbot Hamlin, *Forms and Functions of Twentieth Century Architecture* (New York: Columbia University Press, 1952), 746.

72. Elman, "The Quest for Community," 55.

73. Rachel Wischnitzer-Bernstein, "The Problem of Synagogue Architecture: Creating a Style Expressive of America," *Commentary* (March 1947): 233–41.

74. Rabbi Martin Freedman, "A Client's Perspective," in Elman and Giral, *Percival Goodman*, 108.

75. Congregation B'nai Israel, "Our History," accessed November 2020, https://cbi-nj.org/about-us/our-history/.

76. A congregation brochure from April 23, 1965.

77. Kristallnacht, also called the "Night of Broken Glass," was a pogrom conducted by the Nazis. History, "Kristallnacht," History.com, accessed August 2020, https://www.history.com/topics/holocaust/kristallnacht; Congregation B'nai Israel, "Our History."

78. Dore Ashton, "Reverend Comments," *Art Digest* 26 (October 15, 1951): 15.

79. A quote by Percival Goodman in Michael Z. Wise, "Forward: America's Most Prolific Synagogue Architect after Hitler," published March 9, 2001, and accessed August 2020, http://michaelzwise.com/americas-most-prolific-synagogue-architect/.

80. Karen Rosenberg, "Audacious Expressions on the Walls of the Temple," *New York Times*, April 8, 2010.

81. Rosenberg, "Audacious Expressions on the Walls of the Temple," 58; Goodman and Goodman, "Modern Artist as Synagogue Builder."

82. Rosenberg, "Audacious Expressions on the Walls of the Temple," 58; Goodman and Goodman, "Modern Artist as Synagogue Builder."

83. The 2011 major renovation and expansion included an early childhood center, a religious school, expanded social hall, catering kitchen, intimate chapel, library, and multipurpose room. Congregation B'nai Israel, "Our History."

84. Ashton, "Reverend Comments," 15.

85. The abstract sculpture of the burning bush on the building's façade, by sculptor Herbert Ferber, was removed for cleaning, repair, and restoration in 2010.

86. Kampf, *Contemporary Synagogue Art*, 79.

87. Kampf, *Contemporary Synagogue Art*, 79.

88. Wong, "Synagogue Art of the 1950," 38.

89. Kampf, *Contemporary Synagogue Art*, 78.

90. Robert Motherwell's mural was restored in 2010.

91. Kampf, *Contemporary Synagogue Art*, 81.

92. Adolph Gottlieb's Ark curtain was given as a gift to the Jewish Museum in New York City when maintenance was no longer feasible. The synagogue now uses a replica of the original.

93. Maurice Berger et al., *Masterworks of the Jewish Museum* (New York: The Jewish Museum, 2004), 150–51.

94. Congregation Shaarei Zedek History. Accessed February 2023. https://www.shaareyzedek.org/wp-content/uploads/2019/09/Congregation-Shaarey-Zedek%E2%80%99s-History-2.pdf

95. For the location of the synagogue, see https://www.google.com/maps/@42.4880334,-83.2758091,16.42z.

96. Henry Stolzman and Daniel Stolzman, *Synagogue Architecture in America: Faith, Spirit & Identity* (Mulgrave, Victoria, Australia: Images Publishing 2004), 190.

97. Constance Hope Associates, "White Diamond-Shaped Terne-Roofed Sanctuary Provides Dominant Focal Point of New Michigan Synagogue," *News*, box 7, folder 11, Avery Library's Drawings & Archives, Columbia University Libraries, New York).

98. "Frame Tentlike Synagogue Roof," *Engineering News-Record* (December 13, 1962).

99. Many manufacturers promoted their building technology by advertising the synagogue's innovations (e.g., Acier Stahl Steel).

100. Constance Hope Associates, "White Diamond-Shaped Terne-Roofed Sanctuary," 2.

101. Constance Hope Associates, "White Diamond-Shaped Terne-Roofed Sanctuary," 2.

102. "Marble Ark Focal Point Synagogue," *Stone Magazine* (August 1964; Albert Kahn Associated Architects & Engineering Archive, Detroit).

103. It should be noted that Goodman also used this pattern of triangular concrete trusses in Ohev Shalom Synagogue in Baltimore, Maryland.

104. Constance Hope Associates, "White Diamond-Shaped Terne-Roofed Sanctuary," 3.

105. Constance Hope Associates, "White Diamond-Shaped Terne-Roofed Sanctuary," 3.

106. Acier Stahl Steel, "Steel Synagogue," no. 4 (1963), an article by the steel company (Albert Kahn Associated Architects & Engineering Archive, Detroit).

107. Follansbee terne coated metal roofing is no longer in fabrication.

108. Elman, "The Quest for Community," 53–61.

109. Percival Goodman, "The New Synagogue," *Brooklyn Jewish Center Review* 35, no. 8 (October 1953): 4.

110. Solomon, *Louis I. Kahn Jewish Architecture*, 31–55.

111. Solomon, *Louis I. Kahn Jewish Architecture*, 31.

112. Editors of *Encyclopedia Britannica*, "Pietro Belluschi: Italian-American Architect," *Encyclopedia Britannica*, accessed October 2020, https://www.britannica.com/biography/Pietro-Belluschi.

113. Pietro Belluschi, "The Meaning of Regionalism, in Architecture," *Architectural Record* 118, no. 6 (December 1955): 132.

114. Pietro Belluschi, "An Architect's Challenge," *Architectural Forum* 91 (December 1949): 72.

115. Belluschi, "An Architect's Challenge," 72.

116. Pietro Belluschi, "Architects and Artists: Interpreting Man's Spiritual Dreams," *Faith & Form* (Spring/Summer 1979): 8–9.

117. Edward Gunts, "For Belluschi, Designing Churches Was an Act of Worship," *Baltimore Sun*, February 27, 1994.

118. Gunts, "For Belluschi, Designing Churches Was an Act of Worship."

119. Belluschi et al., "Views of Art and Architecture: A Conversation," 64.

120. Meredith L. Clausen, *Spiritual Space: The Religious Architecture of Pietro Belluschi* (Seattle: University of Washington Press, 1992); Gruber, *American Synagogues*, 122.

121. Jason John Paul Haskins, "Wukasch's Lutheran Architecture in Texas," in Geva, *Modernism and American Mid-20th Century Sacred Architecture*, 195–96.

122. The building was demolished in 2014. Steven A. Rosenberg, "Saying Goodbye to an Era That Could Not Be Saved," *Boston Globe*, published January 2, 2014, and accessed November 2020, https://www.bostonglobe.com/metro/regionals/north/2014/01/02/saying-goodbye-era-that-could-not-saved/5oujxrMuprX4cAcGOLx7XN/story.html.

123. Pietro Belluschi in Meier, *Recent American Synagogue*, 19.

124. Clausen, *Spiritual Space,* 29.

125. Clausen, *Spiritual Space,* 29.

126. See the image of Portsmouth Abbey Church, Rhode Island, in Clausen, *Spiritual Space,* 81–85.

127. Clausen, *Spiritual Space,* 108–11; Gruber, *American Synagogues*, 122–27; Meier, *Recent American Synagogue,* 26–27.

128. See image in Clausen, *Spiritual Space,* 90; Architectural Record, "Building Type Study No. 272: Pietro Belluschi, Synagogue for Temple Adath Israel," *Architectural Record* 126, no. 1 (July 1959): 154–59.

129. "Congregation B'nai Jeshurun/First Jewish Synagogue," Newark Religion: Old Newark, accessed October 2020, http://newarkreligion.com/jewish/bnaijeshurun.php.

130. Congregation B'Nai Jeshurun, "Our History."

131. Congregation B'Nai Jeshurun, "Our History."

132. The definition of *Halacha* by *Merriam-Webster Dictionary*: "the body of Jewish law supplementing the scriptural law and forming especially the legal part of the Talmud." Accessed November 2020, https://www.merriam-webster.com/dictionary/halacha.

133. ReformJudaism.org, "What Is Reform Judaism?," accessed November 2020,
https://reformjudaism.org/what-reform-judaism.

134. Annual Meeting of the congregation from October 30, 1960 (Congregation B'nai Jeshurun Archives, Short Hills, NJ).

135. Marcel Breuer Digital Archive, "Temple B'nai Jeshurun," Syracuse University Libraries, accessed October 2020, https://breuer.syr.edu/project.php?id=515; Robert McCarter, *Breuer* (London: Phaidon Press, 2016).

136. Marcel Breuer Digital Archive, "Temple B'nai Jeshurun"; McCarter, *Breuer*.

137. Special meeting of the Board of Trustees, August 28, 1963 (Congregation B'nai Jeshurun Archives, Short Hills, NJ).

138. The Board meeting from February 18, 1964 (Congregation B'nai Jeshurun Archives, Short Hills, NJ).

139. Congregation B'Nai Jeshurun, "B'Nai Jeshurun Facilities," accessed November 2020, https://www.tbj.org/facilities.

140. Congregation B'Nai Jeshurun, "B'Nai Jeshurun Facilities."

141. The House of Glass, "Glass Terminology & Facts," accessed November 2020, https://www.thehouseofglassinc.com/dictionary.htm.

142. Kampf, *Contemporary Synagogue Art*, 41.

143. See images of the interior of Belluschi's St. Mary Cathedral in San Francisco, California, 1963–70, in Clausen, *Spiritual Space*, 127; and in Gabriele Neri, "The Structural Modeling and Design of St. Mary's Cathedral, San Francisco, 1963–71," in Geva, *Modernism and American Mid-20th Century Sacred Architecture*, 95.

144. The image of the seraphim can be seen in Frank Lloyd Wright's Beth Sholom Synagogue Ark (see figure 4.45).

145. Clausen, *Spiritual Space*, 29.

146. Gunts, "For Belluschi, Designing Churches Was an Act of Worship."

147. Tohid Fardpour, "Analysis of Iranian Traditional Architecture through the Lens of Kenneth Frampton's 'Critical Regionalism,'" *American Journal of Engineering and Applied Sciences* 6, no. 2 (2013): 205–10.

148. Rabbi Floyd S. Fierman, the dedication of the building 1962. Accessed February 2023. https://www.templemountsinai.com/History/Our-Building

149. During the 1970s–80s, another movement developed out of regionalism – critical regionalism, which became an intellectual construct to counter "modernist and post modernist's lack of identity and disregard of context." Kenneth Frampton, "Towards a Critical Regionalism: Six Points for an Architecture of Resistance," in *The Anti-Aesthetic: Essays on Postmodern Culture*, ed. Hal Foster (New York: New Press, 2002), 16–29; Kenneth Frampton, "Critical Regionalism: Modern Architecture and Cultural Identity," *Modern Architecture: A Critical History*, ed. Kenneth Frampton (London: Thames and Hudson, Limited, 2007), 314–27.

150. Sinem Kultur, "503 Role of Culture in Sustainable Architecture," Proceedings of the Second International Conference, Mukogawa Women's University (July 14–16, 2012), accessed November 2020, https://www.semanticscholar.org/paper/503-role-of-culture-in-sustainable-architecture-Kultur/92fce9e282f6b9cfc528ceba7f1c1e03590c5250#paper-header.

151. "Sustainability (World Commission on Environment and Development Definition)," accessed December 2021, https://link.springer.com/referenceworkentry/10.1007%2F978-3-642-28036-8_531.

152. World and US Green Building Councils, accessed December 2021, https://www.worldgbc.org and https://www.usgbc.org.

153. Online Archive of California, "Finding Aid of the Sidney Eisenshtat Papers 4000," Helen Topping Architecture and Fine Arts Library, University of Southern California Libraries, accessed March and November 2020, https://oac.cdlib.org/findaid/ark:/13030/kt5870386n/entire_text/.

154. Los Angeles Conservancy, "Sidney Eisenshtat," accessed November 2020, https://www.laconservancy.org/architects/sidney-eisenshtat.

155. Sidney Eisenshtat Papers, Helen Topping Architecture and Fine Arts Library, University of Southern California Libraries, accessed February 2020, https://oac.cdlib.org/findaid/ark:/13030/kt5870386n/entire_text/.

156. "*Tikkun olam* has been reinterpreted since the 1950s to mean that humans have the responsibility for the perfection and maintenance of the world." Lawrence Troster, "*Tikkun Olam* and Environmental Restoration: A Jewish Eco-Theology of Redemption," *Eco-Judaism Jewish Education News*, published fall 2008 and accessed November 2020, https://www.bjpa.org/content/upload/bjpa/tikk/Tikkun%20Olam%20and%20Environmental%20Restoration.pdf.

157. SoCal Landmarks. Accessed February 2023. https://socallandmarks.com/index.php/2022/08/01/sinai-temple/?utm_source=rss&utm_medium=rss&utm_campaign=sinai-temple."

158. Southwest Jewish Archives, "Temple Mount Sinai," University of Arizona, accessed February 2020, http://swja.arizona.edu/content/temple-mount-sinai.

159. Temple Mount Sinai, "Who We Are," accessed February 2020, http://www.templemountsinai.com/Who-We-Are.

160. Temple Mount Sinai, "Who We Are."

161. Jewish Federation of Greater El Paso, "History Overflow," accessed February 2020, https://jewishelpaso.org/history-overflow.

162. Rabbi Floyd S. Fierman, "Dedication of the Synagogue" (1962), Aemple Mount Sinai, accessed November 2020, https://www.templemountsinai.com/history/our-building.

163. The phrase "And I will lift up mine eyes unto the mountains" (Psalms 121:1) is posted on the main elevation of the synagogue.

164. Fierman, "Dedication of the Synagogue."

165. Jaanen Rojas, "El Paso Follows National Trend of Decrease in Religious Affiliation," *Borderzine*, published May 11, 2016, and accessed November 2020, https://borderzine.com/2016/05/el-paso-follows-national-trend-of-decrease-in-religious-affiliation/.

166. Frampton, "Critical Regionalism."

167. Thermal mass effect is based on a thick wall that protects the space from heat during the day, while transmitting the heat from the exterior to the interior during the night when the weather is cooler. This is a sustainable measure for hot-arid regions like deserts.

168. A *mezuzah* is a small box placed on the right doorpost of Jewish homes and institutions. It contains a parchment scroll with verses from the Bible to bless the building.

169. Fierman, "Dedication of the Synagogue."

170. Fierman, "Dedication of the Synagogue."

171. Duval Glass Company from New York executed the stained-glass panels in Mount Sinai Temple's chapel.

172. Mount Sinai Temple's chapel and Eisenshtat's designs of the Ark, eternal light, and lectern were executed by Ted Egri from Taos, New Mexico.

173. Fierman, "Dedication of the Synagogue."

174. Goodman, "The Essence of Designing a Synagogue."

Chapter 6

1. Thomas C. Jester, ed., *Twentieth-Century Building Materials: History and Conservation* (Los Angeles: The Getty Conservation Institute, 2004); Theodore H. M. Prudon, "Lee Nelson Award Winner 2008: Preservation of Modern Architecture," *APT Bulletin: The Journal of Preservation Technology* 40, no. 2 (2009): 45–48.

2. Adrian Forty, *Concrete and Culture: A Material History* (London: Reaktion Books, 2012).

3. Catherine Croft, Susan Macdonald, and Gail Ostergren, eds., *Concrete: Case Studies in Conservation Practice* (Los Angeles: The Getty Conservation Institute, 2019).

4. Docomomo International, accessed December 2020, http://www.docomomo.com; Docomomo US, accessed December 2020, https://www.docomomo-us.org/.

5. The Association of Preservation Technology International (APTI), "Modern Heritage Technical Committee," accessed December 2020, https://www.apti.org/modern-heritage.

6. The Getty Conservation Institute, "Conserving Modern Architecture Movement," accessed December 2020, http://www.getty.edu/conservation/our_projects/field_projects/cmai/cmai_related_mats.html.

7. ICOMOS, Twentieth Century Heritage International Scientific Committee, "Madrid – New Delhi Document 2017," accessed December 2020, http://www.icomos-isc20c.org/madrid-document/.

8. National Park Service, US Department of the Interior, "Standards for the Treatment of Historic Properties (The Ten Points of the Secretary of the Interior's Standards for Rehabilitation)," accessed December 2020, http://www.nps.gov/tps/standards/rehabilitation.htm.

9. Prudon, "Lee Nelson Award Winner 2008," 47.

10. Prudon, "Lee Nelson Award Winner 2008," 48.

11. It should be noted that modern American churches faced similar changes and challenges.

12. Christopher J. Miller, "Beth Sholom Accessibility Project," *Memorandum* (April 4, 2011). (Courtesy of John Milner Architects Inc.)

13. Miller, "Beth Sholom Accessibility Project."

14. Miller, "Beth Sholom Accessibility Project."

15. Lee Shai Weissbach, "The Architecture of the *Bimah* in American Synagogues: Framing the Ritual," *American Jewish History* 91, no. 1 (March 2003): 36.

16. Edward Jamilly, "The Architecture of the Contemporary Synagogue," in *Jewish Art: An Illustrated History*, ed. Cecil Roth, rev. ed. Bezalel Narkiss (Greenwich, CT: New York Graphic Society), 280–81.

17. Jamilly, "The Architecture of the Contemporary Synagogue," 37.

18. Samuel Gruber, *American Synagogues: A Century of Architecture and Jewish Community* (New York: Rizzoli, 2003), 128–33.

19. Weissbach, "The Architecture of the Bimah," 29–51.

20. Levin/Brown Architects won the 2003 honor award by the Interfaith Forum of Religion, Art, and Architecture (IFRAA) and *Faith & Form* journal for designing the Ark at Temple Oheb Shalom, Baltimore, Maryland.

21. Levin/Brown Architects, "Projects: Religious Architecture," accessed December 2020, https://www.levinbrown.com/projects/temple-oheb-shalom/.

22. Weissbach, "The Architecture of the *Bimah*," 43.

23. The article "Joyful Noise Unto the Lord" in *Sound Ideas* (May 1964; Albert Kahn Associated Architects & Engineering archive, Detroit) mentions Bolt, Beranek, & Newman as the acoustical consultants.

24. Shonan Noronha, "The Sound of Praise," *Sound & Communications*, Archives, House of Worship, published April 2007 and accessed December 2020, https://www.soundandcommunications.com/sound-praise/.

25. Noronha, "The Sound of Praise."

26. Noronha, "The Sound of Praise."

27. Gruber, *American Synagogues*, 183.

28. Gruber, *American Synagogues*, 182.

29. Cherles K. Gandee, "Tradition Rekindled," *Architectural Record* (June 1983): 106.

30. The spiritual assessment of Temple Mount Sinai was based on William C. Helm II (founder/owner of In*Situ architectural firm), "Numinous Space; Exploring the Spiritual Dimension of Architecture" (Master's thesis, Graduate School of New York State University, Department of Architecture, 2006).

Chapter 7

1. Vitruvius, *The Ten Books of Architecture*, trans. Morris Hicky Morgan (New York: Dover Publications Inc, 1960).

2. Gretchen T. Buggeln, "Architecture as Community Service," in *The Visual Culture of American Religions*, eds. David Morgan and Sally M. Promey (Berkeley: University of California Press, 1971), 88.

3. The expression derives from an earlier German proverb, *Der liebe Gott steckt im detail*, which translates as "God is in the details."

4. Robert A. Emmons and Raymond F. Paloutzian, "The Psychology of Religion," *Annual Review of Psychology* 54, no. 1 (2003): 377–402.

5. Nesrine Mansour, "Virtually Sacred: Effect of Light on The Spiritual Experience in Virtual Sacred Architecture" (PhD dissertation, Texas A&M University, College Station, TX, 2019).

6. See chapter 3 in Peter Blake, *An American Synagogue for Today and Tomorrow* (New York: Union of American Hebrew, 1954), viii.

References

Achiman, Hanoch. 1976. "The Synagogues' Sections." In *Mikdah Me-at* (The Little Sanctuary), edited by Y. Ilan, A. Shtal, and Z. Shtiner, 57 (in Hebrew). Jerusalem: The Ministry of Education and Culture.

Architectural Forum (Editor). 1953. "Saarinen Challenges the Rectangle." *Architectural Forum* 98, no. 1 (January): 127.

Architectural Record (Editor). 1959. "Building Type Study No. 272: Pietro Belluschi, Synagogue for Temple Adath Israel." *Architectural Record* 126, no. 1 (July): 154–59.

Architectural Record (Editor). 1965. "A Synagogue by Yamasaki." *Architectural Record* 9 (September): 192.

Ashton, Dore. 1951. "Reverend Comments." *Art Digest* 26 (October 15): 15.

Barrie, Thomas. 1996. *Spiritual Path, Sacred Place: Myth, Ritual, and Meaning in Architecture*. Boston: Shambhala.

Belluschi, Pietro. 1949. "An Architect's Challenge." *Architectural Forum* 91 (December): 72.

———. 1955. "The Meaning of Regionalism, in Architecture." *Architectural Record* 118, no. 6 (December): 132.

———. 1979. "Architects and Artists: Interpreting Man's Spiritual Dreams." *Faith & Form* (Spring/Summer): 8–9.

Belluschi, Pietro, Harry Bertoia, Reg. Butler, Eduardo Chillida, Jimmy Ernst, Walter Gropius, Le Corbusier et al. 1960. "Views on Art and Architecture: A Conversation." *Daedalus* 89, no. 1 (Winter): 62–73.

Benedikt, Michael. 2008. *God, Creativity, and Evolution: The Argument from Design(ers)*. Austin: The Center for American Architecture and Design, University of Texas at Austin.

Benson, Robert. 1991. "Douglas Haskell and the Criticism of International Modernism." In *Modern Architecture in America: Visions and Revisions*, edited by Wilson Richard Guy and Sidney K. Robinson, 165–83. Ames: Iowa State University Press.

Berger, Maurice, Joan Rosenbaum, Vivian Mann, and Norman Kleeblatt. 2004. *Masterworks of the Jewish Museum*. New York: The Jewish Museum.

Berman, Lila Corwin. 2015. *Metropolitan Jews*. Chicago: University of Chicago Press.

Bialer, Yehuda Laib. 1976. "Symbols in the Synagogue." In *Mikdah Me-at* (The Little Sanctuary), edited by. Y. Ilan, A. Shtal, and Z. Shtiner, 68–97 (in Hebrew). Jerusalem: The Ministry of Education and Culture.

Blake, Peter, ed. 1954. *An American Synagogue for Today and Tomorrow: A Guide Book to Synagogue Design and Construction*. New York: Union of American Hebrew.

Blake, Peter. 1996. *Philip Johnson*. Basel/Berlin/Boston: Birkhauser Verlag.

Bloch, Ben C. 1944. "Notes on Post-war Synagogue Design." *Architectural Record* (September): 104–6.

Buggeln, Gretchen T. 1971. "Architecture as Community Service." In *The Visual Culture of American Religions*, edited by David Morgan and Sally M. Promey, 87–88. Berkeley: University of California Press.

———. 2015. *The Suburban Church: Modernism and Community Postwar America*. Minneapolis: University of Minnesota Press.

Chiat, Marilyn J. 2004. *The Spiritual Traveler: Chicago and Illinois*. Mahwah, NJ: Hidden Spring.

Ching, Francis D. K. 2007. *Architecture, Form, Space, & Order*. 3rd ed. New York: John Wiley & Sons.

Chiotti, Roberto, and Michael Nicholas-Schmidt. 2018. "Shared Universe, Sacred Story." *Faith & Form* 41, no. 1: 25–27.

Clausen, Meredith L. 1992. *Spiritual Space: The Religious Architecture of Pietro Belluschi*. Seattle: University of Washington Press.

Cohen, Armond. 1954. "Eric Mendelsohn as a Man and a Friend." *The Reconstructionist* 20 (October 29): 10.

Cohn, Robert L. 1981. *The Shape of the Sacred Space: Four Biblical Studies*. Chico, CA: Scholars Press.

Colman, Charles C. 1950. "Some of the Construction Problems of Park Synagogue." *Ohio Architect* 8, no. 7 (July).

Cook, Lindsay. 2019. "Religious Freedom and Architectural Ambition at Vassar College, 1945–1954." In *Modernism and American Mid-20th Century Sacred Architecture,* edited by Anat Geva, 43–45. London: Routledge.

Croft, Catherine, Susan Macdonald, and Gail Ostergren, eds. 2019. *Concrete: Case Studies in Conservation Practice.* Los Angeles: The Getty Conservation Institute.

Curtis, William J. 1999. *Modern Architecture since 1900.* 3rd ed. Upper Saddle River, NJ: Prentice-Hall.

Davis, Patricia T. 1974. *Together They Built a Mountain.* Lititz, PA: Sutter House.

De Sola Pool, David. 1942. "Judaism and the Synagogue." In *The American Jew,* edited by Oscar I. Janowsky, 54. New York: Harper and Brothers.

Dubnow, Simon. 1958. *Nationalism and History.* Edited by Koppel Pinson. Philadelphia: Jewish Publication Society.

Ebner, Michael H. 1988. *Creating Chicago's North Shore: A Suburban History.* Chicago: University of Chicago Press.

Einhorn, David. 1862. [*Olath Tamid*] *Gebetbuch* für *Israelitische Reform—Gemeinden.* 2nd ed. Baltimore.

Eisen, Arnold. 1983. *The Chosen People in America: A Study in Jewish Religious Ideology.* Bloomington: Indiana University Press.

Eliade, Mircea. 1959/1987. *The Sacred and the Profane: The Nature of Religion.* New York: Harcourt, Brace and World.

———. 1991. *Images and Symbols.* Princeton, NJ: Princeton University Press.

———. 1996. *Patterns in Comparative Religion.* Lincoln: University of Nebraska Press.

Elman, Kimberly J. 2001. "The Quest for Community: Percival Goodman and the Design of the Modern American Synagogue." In *Percival Goodman: Architect, Planner, Teacher, Painter*, edited by Kimberly J. Elman and Angela Giral, 53–61. New York: Miriam and Ira D. Wallach Art Gallery, Columbia University.

Emmons, Robert A., and Raymond F. Paloutzian. 2003. "The Psychology of Religion." *Annual Review of Psychology* 54, no. 1: 377–402.

Fardpour, Tohid. 2013. "Analysis of Iranian Traditional Architecture through the Lens of Kenneth Frampton's 'Critical Regionalism.'" *American Journal of Engineering and Applied Sciences* 6, no. 2: 205–10.

Farr, Finis. 2011. *Frank Lloyd Wright: A Biography.* Whitefish, MT: Literary Licensing.

Fitzsimmons, James. 1951. "Artists Put Faith in New Ecclesiastical Art." *Art Digest* 26 (October 15): 23.

Forty, Adrian. 2012. *Concrete and Culture: A Material History.* London: Reaktion Books.

Frampton, Kenneth. 1980. *Modern Architecture: A Critical History.* New York: Thames and Hudos.

———. 2002. "Towards a Critical Regionalism: Six Points for an Architecture of Resistance." In *The Anti-Aesthetic: Essays on Postmodern Culture*, edited by Hal Foster, 16–29. New York: New Press.

———. 2007. "Critical Regionalism: Modern Architecture and Cultural Identity." In *Modern Architecture: A Critical History*, edited by Kenneth Frampton, 314–27. London: Thames and Hudson.

———. 2015. *A Genealogy of Modern Architecture.* Edited by Ashley Simone. Zurich, Switzerland: Lars Muller Publishers.

Freedman, Martin. 2001. "A Client's Perspective." In *Percival Goodman: Architect, Planner, Teacher, Painter*, edited by Kimberly J. Elman and Angela Giral, 107–25. New York: Miriam and Ira D. Wallach Art Gallery, Columbia University.

Freehof, Solomon B. 1954. "A Kind of Tabernacle." In *An American Synagogue for Today and Tomorrow: A Guide Book to Synagogue Design and Construction*, edited by Peter Blake, 6–8. New York: Union of American Hebrew.

Friedmann, Georges. 1967. *The End of the Jewish People?* New York: Doubleday.

Gandee, Charles K. 1983. "Tradition Rekindled." *Architectural Record* (June): 106.

Gelernter, Mark. 1999. *A History of Buildings in Their Cultural American and Technological Context Architecture.* Hanover and London: University Press of New England.

Geva, Anat. 2012. *Frank Lloyd Wright's Sacred Architecture: Faith, Form and Building Technology.* London: Routledge.

———. 2014. "Architecture as Art and Frame for Art: Mario Botta's Church in Seriate." *Faith & Form, the Interfaith Journal on Religion* 47, no. 1: 6.

———. 2017. "Immigrants' Sacred Architecture: The Rabbi Meir Baal-Haness Synagogue in Eilat, Israel." In *Synagogues in The Islamic World: Architecture, Design, and Identity*, edited by Mohammad Gharipour, 271–92. Edinburgh, Scotland: Edinburgh University Press.

———. 2019. *Modernism and American Mid-20th Century Sacred Architecture.* London: Routledge.

Goodman, Percival. "The New Synagogue." *Brooklyn Jewish Center Review* 35, no. 8 (October 1953): 4.

Goodman, Percival, and Paul Goodman. 1947. "Tradition from Function." *Commentary* (June): 542–44.

———. 1949. "Modern Artist as Synagogue Builder." *Commentary* (January): 51–55.

Gruber, Samuel. 2003. *American Synagogues: A Century of Architecture and Jewish Community.* New York: Rizzoli.

———. 2004. "Jewish Identity and Modern Synagogue Architecture." In *Jewish Identity in Contemporary Architecture*, edited by Angeli Sachs and Edward Van Voolen, 21–31. Munich: Prestel.

———. 2020. "Modern Synagogue Architecture." In *Jewish Religious Architecture from Biblical Israel to Modern Judaism*, edited by Steven Fine, 307–33. Boston: Brill.

Grubiak, Margaret. 2007. "Educating the Moral Scientist: The Chapels at I.I.T. and M.I.T." *ARRIS: Journal of the Southeast Chapter of the Society of Architectural Historians* 18: 1–14.

Gympel, Jan. 1996. *The Story of Architecture from Antiquity to the Present*. Koln, Germany: Konemann.

Gyure, Dale Allen. 2017. *Minoru Yamasaki: Humanist Architecture for a Modern World*. New Haven, CT: Yale University Press.

Hamlin, Talbot. 1952. *Forms and Functions of Twentieth Century Architecture*. New York: Columbia University Press.

Hammond, Peter. 1962. *Liturgical and Architecture*. London: Architectural Press.

Handlin, Oscar. 1961. "Immigration in American Life: A Reappraisal." In *Immigration and American History: Essays in Honor of Theodore C. Blegen*, edited by Henry Steele Commager, 8–25. Minneapolis: University of Minnesota Press.

Harlap, Amiram. 1984. *Synagogues in Israel: From the Ancient to the Modern*. Israel: The Ministry of Defense Publisher and Dvir.

Haskell, Douglas. 1932. "Is It Functional?," *Creative Art* 10 (May): 373–78.

———. 1932. "What the Man about Town Will Build," *Nation* 134 (April 13): 12–16.

Haskins, Jason John Paul. 2019. "Wukasch's Lutheran Architecture in Texas." In *Modernism and American Mid-20th Century Sacred Architecture*, edited by Anat Geva, 194–213. London: Routledge.

Herberg, Will. 1950. "The Postwar Revival of the Synagogue." *Commentary* 9 (April).

———. 1955. *Protestant-Catholic-Jew*. New York: Doubleday & Co.

———. 1983. *Protestant-Catholic-Jew: An Essay in American Religious Sociology*. Chicago: University of Chicago Press.

Herzl, Theodor. 1902/1997. *Old New Land* [*Altneuland*]. Translated by Lotta Levensohn. Leipzig, Germany: Hermann Seemann Nachfolger, 1902; Princeton, NJ: Markus Wiener, 1997.

Hirschman, Charles. 2004. "The Role of Religion in the Origins and Adaptation of Immigrant Groups in the United States." *International Migration Review* 38, no. 3, Conceptual and Methodological Developments in the Study of International Migration (September): 1206–33.

Hirsh, Arnold. 1983. *Making the Second Ghetto: Race and Housing in Chicago, 1940–1960*. Cambridge: Cambridge University Press.

Hitchcock, Henry-Russell. 1929. *Architecture: Romanticism and Reintegration*. New York: Payson & Clarke.

———. 1966. *Philip Johnson: Architecture 1949–1965*. New York: Holt, Rinehart and Winston.

Hoffman, Douglas R. 2010. *Seeking the Sacred in Contemporary Religious Architecture*. Kent, Ohio: Kent State University Press.

Humphrey, Caroline, and Piers Vitebsky. 1997/2005. *Sacred Architecture*. New York: Barnes & Noble Books, reprinted from Little, Brown.

Jacobus, John, Jr. *Philip Johnson*. New York: George Braziller.

James-Chakraborty, Kathleen. 2000. *In the Spirit of Our Age: Eric Mendelsohn's B'nai Amoona Synagogue*. St. Louis: Missouri Historical Society Press.

Jamilly, Edward. 1971. "The Architecture of the Contemporary Synagogue." In *Jewish Art: An Illustrated History*, edited by Cecil Roth, revised by Bezalel Narkiss, 280–81. Greenwich, CT: New York Graphic Society.

Jester, Thomas C., ed. 2014. *Twentieth-Century Building Materials*. Los Angeles: Getty Conservation Institute.

Johnson, Philip, and Henry-Russell Hitchcock, eds. 1932. *Modern Architecture: The International Exhibition, February 10–March 23, 1932*. New York: Museum of Modern Art.

Kampf, Avram. 1966. *Contemporary Synagogue Art*. New York: Union of American Hebrew Congregations.

Kaplan, Mordecai M. 1957. *Judaism as a Civilization*. Philadelphia: Reconstructionist Press.

Kargon, Jeremy. 2019. "Seeing, Not Knowing: Symbolism, Art, and 'Opticalism' in Mid-Century American Religious Architecture." In *Modernism and American Mid-20th Century Sacred Architecture*, edited by Anat Geva, 235–54. London: Routledge.

Karp, Abraham J. 1976. "Ideology and Identity in Jewish Group Survival in America." *American Jewish Historical Quarterly* 65, no. 4 (June): 310–34.

———. 1987. "Overview: The Synagogue in America—a Historical Typology." In *The American Synagogue: A Sanctuary Transform*, edited by Jack Wertheimer, 14. Cambridge: Cambridge University Press.

———. 1998. *Jewish Continuity in America: Creative Survival in a Free Society*. Tuscaloosa: University of Alabama Press.

Kater, Michael H. 2019. *Culture in Nazi Germany*. New Haven, CT: Yale University Press.

Kepes, Gyorgy. 1961. *Language of Vision*. Chicago: Paul Theobald and Company.

Kieckhefer, Richard. 2004. *Theology in Stone: Church Architecture from Byzantium to Berkeley*. New York: Oxford University Press.

Kilde, Jeanne Halgren. 2008. *Sacred Power, Sacred Space.* Oxford: Oxford University Press.

Kline, Alexander. 1954. "The Synagogue in America." In *An American Synagogue for Today and Tomorrow: A Guide Book to Synagogue Design and Construction,* edited by Peter Blake, 38–43. New York: Union of American Hebrew.

Kornberg, Jacques, ed. 1983. *At the Crossroads: Essays on Ahad Ha-Am.* Albany: State University of New York Press.

Kraut, Benny. 1987. "Ethnic-Religious Ambiguities in an Immigrant Synagogue: The Case of New Hope Congregation." In *The American Synagogue: A Sanctuary Transformed,* edited by Jack Wertheimer, 231–73. Cambridge: Cambridge University Press.

Krinsky, Carol Herselle. 1985. *Synagogues of Europe.* Cambridge, MA: The MIT Press.

Landsberger, Franz. 1954. "From 70 C.E. to the Present." In *An American Synagogue for Today and Tomorrow: A Guide Book to Synagogue Design and Construction,* edited by Peter Blake, 29. New York: Union of American Hebrew.

Leedy, Walter C, Jr. 2012. *Eric Mendelsohn's Park Synagogue: Architecture and Community.* Edited by Sara Jane Pearman. Kent, OH: Kent State University Press.

Lewis, Michael J. 2006. *American Art and Architecture.* London: Thames & Hudson.

Mann, A. T. 1993. *Sacred Architecture.* Shaftesbury, Dorset, and Rockport, MA: Element.

Mann, Vivan B. 2004. "If There Is No Jewish Art, What's Being Taught at the Seminary?" In *Reluctant Partners: Art and Religion in Dialogue,* edited by Ena Giuresh Heller, 88–99. New York: The Gallery at the American Bible Society.

Mansour, Nesrine. 2019. "Virtually Sacred: Effect of Light on the Spiritual Experience in Virtual Sacred Architecture." PhD diss., Texas A&M University.

Mansour, Nesrine, and Anat Geva. 2017. "Djerbian Culture and Climate as Expressed in a Historic Landmark: The Case of El-Ghriba Synagogue in Djerba, Tunisia." In *Synagogues in The Islamic World,* edited by Mohammad Gharipour, 226–47. Edinburgh, Scotland: Edinburgh University Press.

McCarter, Robert. 2016. *Breuer.* London: Phaidon Press.

McDannell, Colleen. 1995. *Material Christianity: Religion and Popular Culture in America.* New Haven, CT: Yale University Press.

Meek, H. A. 1995. *The Synagogue.* London: Phaidon Press.

Meier, Richard. 1963. *Recent American Synagogue Architecture.* Exhibition catalog. New York: The Jewish Museum.

Mendelsohn, Eric. 1947. "Creating a Modern Synagogue Style: In the Spirit of Our Age." *Commentary* 3, no. 6 (June).

Meyer, Michael. 1990. *Jewish Identity in the Modern World.* Seattle: University of Washington Press.

Moffett, Marian, Michael Fazio, and Lawrence Wodehouse. 2004. *Building across Time: An Introduction to World Architecture.* Boston: McGraw Hill.

Morgan, David, and Sally M. Promey, eds. 1971. *The Visual Culture of American Religions.* Berkeley: University of California Press.

Morgenstern, Julian. 1954. "The Temple and the Synagogue: To 70 C.E." In *An American Synagogue for Today and Tomorrow: A Guide Book to Synagogue Design and Construction,* edited by Peter Blake, 10–27. New York: Union of American Hebrew.

Morgenthaler, Hans R. 1999. "'It Will Be Hard for Us to Find a Home': Projects in the United States 1941–1953." In *Eric Mendelsohn: Architect, 1887–1953,* edited by Stephan Regina, 242–61. New York: The Monacelli Press.

Naderi, Jody Rosenblatt, and Anat Geva. 2014. "*Eruv*: Transformation of an Urban Public Space to a Private Place for Spiritual Renewal." *ARRIS: Journal of the Southeast Chapter of the Society of Architectural Historians* 25: 18–29.

Nelson, Louis P. 2006. *American Sanctuary: Understanding Sacred Spaces.* Bloomington: Indiana University Press.

Nelson, Robert L. 2014."Art and Religion: Ships Passing in the Night?" In *Reluctant Partners: Art and Religion in Dialogue,* edited by Ena Giuresh Heller, 106–7. New York: The Gallery at the American Bible Society.

Neri, Gabriele. 2019. "The Structural Modeling and Design of St. Mary's Cathedral, San Francisco, 1963–71." In *Modernism and American Mid-20th Century Sacred Architecture,* edited by Anat Geva, 93–112. London: Routledge.

Patterson, Terry. 1994. *Frank Lloyd Wright and The Meaning of Materials.* New York: Van Nostrand Reinhold.

Pfeiffer, Bruce Brooks. 1986. *Frank Lloyd Wright: Letters to Clients.* Fresno: Press at California State University.

———. 1990. *Masterworks from the Frank Lloyd Wright Archives.* Edited by David Larkin. New York: Harry N. Abrams.

———, ed. 1992. *Frank Lloyd Wright Collected Writings, Vol. 1.* New York: Rizzoli International Publications.

Plummer, Henry. 1987. "Poetic of Light." *Architecture and Urbanism* (December): 8–11.

Price, Jay M. 2013. *Temples for a Modern God: Religious Architecture in Postwar America.* New York: Oxford University Press.

Prudon, Theodore H. M., ed. 2008. *Preservation of Modern Architecture.* Hoboken, NJ: John Wiley & Sons.

———. 2009. "Lee Nelson Award Winner 2008: Preservation of Modern Architecture." *APT Bulletin: The Journal of Preservation Technology* 40, no. 2: 45–48.

Rabel-Nehar, Elisheva. 2004. "Ezekiel 37: An Additional Interpretation of the Walls Paintings in the Dura Europa Synagogue." In *Synagogues from Antiquity to Our Time*, edited by Yakov Eshel, Ehud Nezer, David Amit, and David Casuto, 67–75 (in Hebrew). Ariel, Israel: The Academic College of Judea and Samaria.

Rabinovitch, Baruch. 1976. "The Place of the Synagogue in Judaism." In *I Have Housed Them*, edited by David Casuto, 9–13 (in Hebrew). Jerusalem: The Ministry of Education and Culture, Department of Torah Culture.

Raphael, Marc. 2011. *The Synagogue in America: A Short History*. New York: New York University Press.

Reiss, Lionel. 1951. "Art for the Synagogue." *Reconstructionist* 17 (October): 27–29.

Roberts, Nicholas W. 2004. *Building Type Basics for Places of Worship*. New York: John Wiley.

Rosenfeld, Gavriel. 2011. *Building after Auschwitz: Jewish Architecture and the Memory of the Holocaust*. New Haven, CT: Yale University Press.

Sachs, Angeli, and Edward Van Voolen, eds. 2004. *Jewish Identity in Contemporary Architecture*. Munich: Prestel.

Sartre, Jean Paul. 1948. *Anti-Semite and Jew*. New York: Schocken Books.

Schack, William. 1956. "Modern Art in Synagogue, II: Artist, Architect, and Building Committee Collaborate." *Commentary* 21 (February).

Schorsch, Ismar. 1990–91. "A Synagogue Is Not a Temple." *Conservative Judaism* 43, no. 2 (Winter): 61–70.

Schulze, Franz. 1994. *Philip Johnson: Life and Work*. New York: Alfred A. Knopf.

Scott, Geoffrey. 1969. *The Architecture of Humanism*. New York: W. W. Morton, 1914; reprinted, 1947; reprinted, 1969.

Scully, Vincent. 1977. *Modern Architecture: The Architecture of Democracy*. New York: George Braziller.

———. 1996. *Frank Lloyd Wright*. New York: George Braziller.

———. 2009. "Philip Johnson: Art and Irony." In *Philip Johnson: The Constancy of Change*, edited by Emmanuel Petit, 18–37. New Haven, CT: Yale University Press.

Shelemay, Kay Kaufman. 1987. "Music in the American Synagogue: A Case Study from Houston." In *The American Synagogue: A Sanctuary Transform*, edited by Jack Wertheimer, 395–415. Cambridge: Cambridge University Press.

Shenberger, Joseph. 1976. "The Synagogue's Courtyard, Its Function and Design." In *Mikdah Me-at* (The Little Sanctuary), edited by Y. Ilan, A. Shtal, and Z. Shtiner, 65. Jerusalem: The Ministry of Education and Culture.

Shwartz, Rudolf. 1958. *The Church Incarnate: The Sacred Function of Christian Architecture*. Chicago: H. Regnery.

Siry, Joseph. 2011. *Beth Sholom Synagogue: Frank Lloyd Wright and Modern Religious Architecture*. Chicago: The University of Chicago Press.

Solomon, Susan G. 2009. *Louis I. Kahn's Jewish Architecture: Mikveh Israel and the Midcentury American Synagogue*. Waltham, MA: Brandeis University Press.

Sowers, Robert. 1954. *The Lost Art: A Survey of 1000 Years of Stained Glass*. London: Lund Humphries.

Steinberg, Dov Shalom. 1993. *The Format of the Second Jerusalem Temple*. Jerusalem: Vagshel (in Hebrew).

———. 1994. *The Format of the First Jerusalem Temple*. Jerusalem: Vagshel (in Hebrew).

Stephan, Regina, ed. 1998. *Eric Mendelsohn: Architect, 1887–1953*. New York: Monacelli Press.

Stolzman, Henry, and Daniel Stolzman. 2004. *Synagogue Architecture in America: Faith, Spirit and Identity*. Mulgrave, Victoria, Australia: The Images Publishing Group.

Sussman, Lance J. 1985. "The Suburbanization of American Judaism as Reflected in Synagogue Building and Architecture, 1945–1975." *American Jewish History* 75, no. 1: 31.

Tajfel, Henri, ed. 1978. *Differentiation Between Social Groups: Studies in the Social Psychology of Intergroup Relations*. London: Academic Press.

———. 1978. "Social Categorization, Social Identity, and Social Comparison." In *Differentiation between Social Groups: Studies in the Social Psychology of Intergroup Relations*, edited by Henri Tajfel, 63. London: Academic Press.

———. 1982. "Social Psychology of Intergroup Relations." *Annual Review of Psychology* 33: 1–39.

Tajfel, Henri, and John C. Turner. 1979. "An Integrative Theory of Intergroup Conflict." In *The Social Psychology of Intergroup Relations*, edited by William G. Austin and Stephen Worchel, 38–48. Monterey, CA: Brooks Cole.

———. 1986. "The Social Identity Theory of Intergroup Behavior." In *Psychology of Intergroup Relations*, edited by Stephen Worchel and William G. Austin, 7–24. Chicago: Nelson-Hall.

Taylor, Charles. 2007. *A Secular Age*. Cambridge, MA: Belknap Press of Harvard University Press.

Thiessen, Gesa Elsbeth, ed. 2004. *Theological Aesthetics: A Reader*. Grand Rapids, MI: William B. Eerdmans Publishing.

Thiry, Paul, Richard M. Bennett, and Henry L Kamphoefner. 1953. *Church and Temples*. New York: Reinhold Publishing.

Thomas, June Manning. 1997. *Redevelopment and Race: Planning a Finer City in Postwar Detroit*. Detroit: Wayne State University Press.

Tuan, Yi-Fu. 1978. "Sacred Space: Exploration on an Idea." In *Dimensions of Human Geography*, edited by Karl Butzer, 84–99. Chicago: University of Chicago, Department of Geography Research Paper.

Turner, Harold W. 1979. *From Temple to Meeting House:*

The Phenomenology and Theology of Places of Worship.
The Hague, Netherlands/New York: Mouton.

Unwin, Simon. 2014. *Analysing Architecture.* 4th ed.
London: Routledge.

Vitruvius. 1960. *The Ten Books of Architecture.* Translated by Morris Hicky Morgan. New York: Dover
Publications.

Volner, Ian. 2020. *Philip Johnson: A Visual Biography.*
London, New York: Phaidon Press.

Wax, Carl I., Bernard Bernstein, and Gerald Belz. 1976.
*Two Hundred Years of American Synagogue Architec-
ture.* Waltham, MA: Rose Art Museum,

Weininger, Otto. 1920. *Geschlecht und Charakter.* Vienna,
Austria: W. Braumuller.

Weissbach, Lee Shai. "The Architecture of the Bimah in
American Synagogues: Framing the Ritual." *American
Jewish History* 91, no. 1 (March): 32.

Welch, Frank D. 2000. *Philip Johnson and Texas.* Austin:
University of Texas Press.

Wertheimer, Jack. 2003. *The American Synagogue: A Sanctuary Transformed.* Cambridge: Cambridge University
Press, 1987.

———. 2005. "The American Synagogue: Recent Issues
and Trends." *American Jewish Year Book* 105: 3–83.

Wilber, Ken. 2006. *Integral Spirituality.* Boston:
Shambhala.

Wilkinson, John. 2002. *From Synagogue to Church: The
Traditional Design.* London: Routledge.

Wilson Guy, Richard, and Sidney K. Robinson, eds. 1991.
Modern Architecture in America: Visions and Revisions.
Ames: Iowa State University Press.

Wischnitzer-Bernstein, Rachel. 1947. "The Problem of
Synagogue Architecture: Creating a Style Expressive of
America." *Commentary* (March): 233–41.

———. 1955. *Synagogue Architecture in the United States:
History and Interpretation.* Philadelphia: The Jewish
Publication Society of America.

Wittkower, Rudolf. 1949. *Architecture Principles in the Age
of Humanism.* London: Warburg Institute, University
of London.

Wolf, Laibl. 1999. *Practical Kabbalah.* New York: Three
Rivers Press.

Wong, Janay Jadine. 1994. "Synagogue Art of 1950s: A
New Context for Abstraction." *Art Journal* 53, no. 4
(Winter): 37–43.

Wright, Frank Lloyd. 1928. "In the Cause of Architecture
III–IX: The Meaning of Materials." *Architectural
Record* (April–December): 350–56.

Wright, Oligivanna Lloyd. 1960. *The Shining Brow: Frank
Lloyd Wright.* New York: Horizon Press.

Young, Victoria. 2014. *Saint John's Abbey Church: Marcel
Breuer and the Creation of a Modern Sacred Space.*
Minneapolis: University of Minnesota Press.

Zevi, Bruno. 1999. *Erich Mendelsohn: The Complete
Works.* Bazel, Switzerland: Birkhäuser Publishers.

Index